Me, You, Us

SOCIAL–EMOTIONAL LEARNING IN PRESCHOOL

Related HighScope Press Preschool Resources

Essentials of Active Learning in Preschool: Getting to Know the High/Scope Curriculum

Educating Young Children: Active Learning Practices for Preschool and Child Care Programs, Third Edition

You Can't Come to My Birthday Party! Conflict Resolution With Young Children

Supporting Children in Resolving Conflicts (Video and DVD)

These and other HighScope publications are available from
HighScope® Press
A division of the HighScope Educational Research Foundation
600 North River Street, Ypsilanti, MI 48198-2898
ORDERS: (800)40-PRESS; fax (800)442-4FAX
e-mail: *press@highscope.org*
or visit our online store at highscope.org

Me, You, Us

SOCIAL-EMOTIONAL LEARNING IN PRESCHOOL

Ann S. Epstein

Foreword by Lilian G. Katz

HIGHSCOPE PRESS®

Ypsilanti, Michigan

Washington, DC

Published by

HighScope® Press
A division of the
HighScope Educational Research Foundation
600 North River Street
Ypsilanti, Michigan 48198-2898
734/485-2000, FAX 734/485-0704
press@highscope.org

National Association for the Education of Young Children
1313 L Street NW, Suite 500
Washington, DC 20005-4101
Toll free 1-800-424-2460
www.naeyc.org

Orders: (800) 40-PRESS; FAX: (800) 442-4FAX; highscope.org

Editor: Jennifer Burd

Cover design, text design, production: Wagner Design Associates, LLC

Photography: Bob Foran, front cover (upper left and center) and pp. 4, 7, 15, 17, 21, 27, 48, 59, 71, 86, 113, 115, 117, 137, 139, back cover (upper); Gregory Fox, front cover (upper right) and pp. 10, 29, 31, 37, 39, 41, 49, 53, 62, 73, 78, 83, 87, 93, 95, 103, 126, 132, 147, 150, 156, 158, 160, 168, back cover (lower); Patricia Evans, pp. 105 and 107; HighScope staff, p. 165.

ISBN: 978-1-57379-425-1

Library of Congress Cataloging-in-Publication Data
Epstein, Ann S.
  Me, you, us : social-emotional learning in preschool / Ann S. Epstein.
      p. cm.
  Includes bibliographical references.
  ISBN 978-1-57379-425-1 (soft cover : alk. paper)
  1. Affective education. 2. Social skills--Study and teaching (Early childhood) 3. Early childhood education.
I. Title.
  LB1072.E67 2009
  370.15'34--dc22

                              2008042658

Printed in the United States of America

10 9 8 7 6 5 4 3 2 1

Contents

123181

CONTENTS

Foreword

The field of early childhood education has a long tradition of concern for the social and emotional development of young children. The comprehensive classical work of Susan Isaacs — one of the early specialists in the field — titled "Social Development in Young Children" that addressed these topics was first published in 1937.[1] In more recent times it has become clear that unless a child achieves at least a minimal level of social competence by about the age of six, he or she is likely to be at risk for many social difficulties for the rest of his or her life (Parker & Asher, 1987).[2] Currently, research reports appear almost daily indicating that early social relationships predict academic achievement as well as school completion and dropout rates (see Ladd et al., 2008).[3]

This book is a welcome, comprehensive overview of all facets of this important aspect of development. With its highly readable form and structure, it will be helpful to students as well as practitioners whose work involves them in the development of young children.

The book is divided into three main sections that address emotional learning, social learning, and related concerns beyond the classroom such as cultural and community matters. Several sidebars offered throughout are especially helpful in linking the discussions of the various components of social and emotional development to promising teaching practices.

Altogether the sixteen chapters cover the full range of issues of concern to early childhood educators. In addition, a chapter describing various ways that parents can support social development at home provides good recommendations for teachers to share with them. There is also an important chapter with useful suggestions about how to reach out to the communities around the educational setting.

The opening chapter offers a clear definition of social-emotional development and its many complex components. Epstein takes this opportunity to remind us that contemporary emphasis on academic instruction as it relates to school readiness frequently neglects the important contribution of social-emotional competences to successful adaptation to school. Indeed, the case is well made here that social-emotional development affects all other areas of development.

The second chapter begins with an insightful overview of child development as it relates to teaching practice. It is accomplished by using rich, practical examples of children's interactions that clearly explicate the connections between all aspects of development in ways that all readers will be able to grasp.

Each of the subsequent chapters begins with a clear definition of the topic under discussion and includes vivid and rich illustrations of the behaviors being addressed. The recommended teaching strategies are placed in practical contexts that make the suggested practices readily understandable and adoptable.

Another welcome feature of the book is the convincing presentation of the valuable role of play in social and emotional development. It is clear that some play is more beneficial than other play. The teacher's role and contribution to increasing the potential benefits of spontaneous play is explored fully. Furthermore, all discussions are well-supported by recent, relevant research. Among many examples is the clear discussion of the concept of self-efficacy and its emphasis on the dynamic nature of development and the adult's role in getting the dynamics off to a good start.

[1] Isaacs, S. (1937). *Social development in young children*. New York: Harcourt Brace.

[2] Parker, J., & Asher, S. (1987). Peer relations and later personal adjustment: Are low-accepted children at risk? *Psychological Bulletin, 102*(3), 357–389.

[3] Ladd, G. W., Herald-Brown, S. L., Reiser, M. (2008). Does chronic classroom peer rejection predict the development of children's classroom participation during the grade school years? *Child Development, 79*(4), 1001–1015.

Epstein's emphasis on the importance of adults' being sincere with young children is especially appreciated. I am so often amazed at the extent of phony talk I hear when visiting early childhood programs. For example, I often hear teachers say to young children who have just violated a rule of some kind, "We don't do that in this school" when we just *did* do that! Perhaps these kinds of phrases are a part of the nursery and primary school culture of earlier times, but they should be discarded. Yes, in most cases, the children do know what the teacher really means. But my guess is that after a year or two of adults' expressing themselves in such phony phrases and also offering frequent empty flattery like "Awesome," "Super," and so forth, children have to dismiss teachers as "not for real" or not genuine people.

Speaking to children in these insincere ways may be one of the inevitable effects of working with young children daily over long periods of time. Perhaps such automated phrases are a temptation in all the helping professions. But awareness of this strong temptation to use such clichés is one of the many topics that staff can discuss together during the staff gatherings that Epstein recommends as opportunities for reflecting on our interactions with children and how we can best serve them as role models.

In the many examples offered throughout the book, it is again clear that most of the important aspects of social and emotional development cannot be learned very well in the early years from instruction, indoctrination, or preaching. But appropriate opportunities to engage children in discussion and conflict resolution activities in their real contexts as they arise can lay the groundwork for what we all hope will be the start of a growing capacity to participate in and contribute to a democratic society. This book provides many suggestions for practices that can help us with this important part of our mission.

— *Lilian G. Katz, PhD, University of Illinois, Urbana-Champaign, Illinois*

Acknowledgments

The early childhood tradition to which I belong has always viewed human development as comprehensive — an interplay of cognitive, affective, creative, and physical components. Yet in recent years, the spotlight has shone intensely on young children's academic skills while the focus on their social and emotional learning has dimmed. There was ample incentive to write about reading and mathematics, or assessment and accountability, to the neglect of these other areas of development. Fortunately, respected professionals from many fields including education, pediatrics, and psychology, have begun to voice dismay at this serious oversight. Their concerns are shared by parents, as well as corporate and civic leaders, all worried about the compassion, tolerance, and ethics of those who will comprise the societies of the future.

Thus, while still writing about a child's wonder for words, numbers, maps, and moonbeams, I am grateful to simultaneously have had the time to focus again on social and emotional development. Writing *Me, You, Us* allowed me to revisit and update what early childhood has to say about the uniquely human characteristics that define who we are, how we view others, and the ways we interact in pursuit of individual and common goals. Most important, working on this book helped me pull together our knowledge about how we, as adults, can use our understanding of early growth to help young children become the kinds of adults we value and aspire to be ourselves.

Many people encouraged me to undertake this book and provided valuable input, review, and support throughout the process. Their help gave me the resources, technical skills, and emotional fuel to persist in the face of competing demands and the challenges of not only mastering this topic but also inspiring teachers to risk venturing into unfamiliar territory. They are my "us."

First, I want to thank my early childhood colleagues for the unique perspective they each brought to reviewing the manuscript. The entire early childhood staff at HighScope was enthusiastic about the Foundation's publishing a comprehensive book on this subject and offered many observations and anecdotes from their personal experiences as teachers and trainers. In particular, I appreciated Beth Marshall's comprehensive knowledge of early development and supportive teaching practices in this area. Grounded by her work with children and adults, Beth was able to simultaneously simplify ideas to ensure comprehension and specify nuances to differentiate well-intentioned from well-executed implementation. Polly Neill brought particular expertise to all the chapters that touched on issues related to community and diversity. While many early childhood educators shy away from confronting what can be difficult issues, Polly's ability to empathize with all perspectives — and adopt non-threatening interaction strategies with children, staff, and parents — enriched the sensitivity and "diversity" with which those topics were addressed in this volume. Julie Hoelscher reviewed the manuscript through the lens of her years of experience working with young children and teachers in many different educational settings. She was able to validate the authenticity of the anecdotal examples and assess the feasibility of integrating the social-emotional teaching strategies with the other domains of early learning in the classroom.

In addition to the above HighScope staff, two Foundation field consultants with expertise in child development and professional development contributed their ideas to the manuscript. Trish Murphy inquired thoughtfully about lessons from current research and was not afraid to examine both sides of those issues about which the field continues to debate. Her balanced perspective helped to broaden the range of questions as well as answers provided in the book. Catherine Calamari, who mentors teachers to implement high-quality programs in the classroom, looked most closely at the teaching strategies for scaffolding social-emotional learning. Because of her extensive work with staff, she was able to find the intersection between what was desirable and what was feasible. It was reassuring to know that there need not be a gap between the two.

No book comes to life without the care and nurture of the editorial and production staff. HighScope Publications Director Nancy Brickman was tenacious in pursuing a publication on social-emotional development and was an enthusiastic supporter of the wide-ranging approach to the topic taken in this book. Jennifer Burd, who edited the manuscript, consistently raised thoughtful queries that led me to clarify, expand, and illustrate the book's central ideas. Together with her suggestions for formatting the text, Jennifer's contributions ensure that *Me, You, Us* will be comprehensible and useful to its readers. My thanks and appreciation also go to Laura Herold, whose design not only further enhances the user-friendliness of the publication but also adds to its aesthetic appeal. Artistry evokes an "emotional" response, so I hope the book's outward appearance contributes to the internalization and implementation of its ideas. Photographs also work toward a publication's attractiveness and use, and toward that end

I thank the discerning eye and technical expertise of Bob Foran, Gregory Fox, and Patricia Evans. A further thanks for shepherding the book from discussion to dissemination goes to HighScope Marketing and Communications Director Kathy Woodard, who asked thoughtful questions about the book's potential audiences and applications. Her involvement from the outset helped to shape the content, format, and outreach of the final publication.

Finally, my sincere thanks are extended to Lilian Katz for her encouraging and insightful foreword. She has provided years of wise and dedicated leadership to the field. No matter how erratically the pendulum swings, Lilian steadfastly advocates for including social-emotional learning in the early education curriculum. She continues to be a respected public spokesperson for all the researchers, educators, parents, and children whose voices fill this book.

As the support of my colleagues sustained me in writing *Me, You, Us,* I hope this book in turn fortifies its readers. Applying the evidence gained from research, and the wisdom accumulated through practice, together let us proceed to help young children become the confident and caring people who fulfill themselves and are valued members of their families and communities.

— *Ann S. Epstein, PhD*

Part One

INTRODUCTION

Part
One

The Importance of Social–Emotional Learning

It is not easy to be a child in an early childhood pro-gram. Imagine experiencing it for the first time. You come into a strange building full of other children and adults who are strangers, full of enticing toys that are not your own…There are many things to learn about — but in order to learn you have to wade in and try things. Learning is hard work, and it involves taking risks … of being laughed at, of being wrong, of being ignored or rejected. Yet this desire for mastery is what leads to social and intellectual competence. It is almost impossible for children to have the courage to start on this journey without a foundation of emotional security. (Hyson, 2004, p. 49)

Early childhood educators seem to periodically rediscover the importance of social-emotional learning (SEL; also variously referred to in the field, and throughout this book, as social-emotional development, social-emotional competence, or even just social competence, with the emotional component implied). Although it began as the field's primary focus, and has never disappeared from view, teachers today confront special challenges preparing preschoolers to face a complex and rapidly changing world. Media images present young children with often contradictory expectations for individual behavior and social norms. Pressure to perform academically at ever-younger ages adds stress at the very time when the experiences that could help children develop coping skills are cut from the curriculum. All of these factors make atten-tion to social-emotional teaching and learning particularly relevant today.

What This Book Offers the Thoughtful Educator

In this book, we look at the importance of social-emo-tional skills to the development of the whole child. We define the many different aspects of the social-emotional skills and knowledge young children need, look at them in the context of child development research and theory, and consider teaching strategies — illustrated by anec-dotes and examples — that can be used directly in the classroom. We also consider how educators can foster children's positive social-emotional development by ex-amining their own attitudes and behaviors, by partnering with parents, and by reaching out to others in the local community. Through a comprehensive approach, this book helps the thoughtful educator chart a path for plac-ing social-emotional learning on an equal footing with academic subjects.

How This Book Is Organized

Part 1 (Chapters 1 and 2) will help you review the research and thinking in the field and your own ideas about social-emotional development. The rest of Chapter 1 defines and explains the importance of social-emotional learning, while Chapter 2 describes how it develops in children and summarizes the teaching practices that promote it. Following these introductory chapters, Parts 2 and 3 focus, respectively, on emotional learning and social learning. Although they often overlap, looking at them separately can help teachers think about the instructional practices that best advance knowledge and skills in each domain.

Emotional learning (Part 2; Chapters 3–6) addresses developing a positive self-identity, feeling empathy, developing feelings of competence, and recognizing and labeling emotions. Social learning (Part 3; Chapters 7–13) covers developing a sense of community, engaging in co-operative play, valuing diversity, developing a framework for moral behavior, engaging in conflict resolution, creating and following rules, and creating and participating in a democracy. Each of these chapters provides specific strategies for helping children develop knowledge and skills in that area, with examples and anecdotes to build a bridge between theory and classroom practice.

Part 4 (Chapters 14–16), goes beyond the classroom and looks both inward and outward. It examines how we as teachers can become better role models, support children's social-emotional learning at home, and advocate for its inclusion in the community. For those wishing more information on social-emotional development re-search, a comprehensive reference list is provided at the end of the book.

Preparing young children to live in our changing world demands that we be aware of social-emotional development in all its complexity. This book is intended to provide readers with the knowledge and skills to undertake that vital and worthy task.

Social-emotional learning is key to feelings of self-efficacy and to successful interactions with adults and peers.

What Is Social–Emotional Learning?

Emotional learning is the knowledge and skills needed to recognize and self-regulate feelings. **Social learning** comprises the principles and strategies for interacting successfully with others. Dealing with one's emotional state is often a prerequisite to socializing effectively with others, but these dimensions often overlap. Conflict resolution,

for example, involves both emotional self-regulation and social problem-solving skills. Because of their interdependence, the joint term **social-emotional learning** (or **development** or **competence**) best captures this vital area of human growth. Thus, in the following anecdote, Zeke is able to keep his emotions from escalating as he comes up with a solution to a social problem in response to a prompt from the teacher.

> *At work time in the house area, Zeke and Mariah want the same pan lid. Their teacher asks how they can solve the problem. Zeke says he can make a lid. He gets a piece of paper, traces around the pot, and cuts it out with scissors.*

The Collaborative for the Advancement of Social and Emotional Learning (CASEL), founded in 1994 and currently based in the Department of Psychology at the University of Illinois at Chicago (UIC), is widely recognized as a leader in advancing the science and evidenced-based practice of social-emotional learning. CASEL defines social-emotional competence as "the ability to understand, manage, and express the social and emotional aspects of one's life in ways that enable the successful management of life's tasks such as learning, forming relationships, solving everyday problems, and adapting to the complex demands of growth and development" (Elias, Zins, Weissberg, Frey, Greenberg, Kessler, et al., 1997, p. 2).

Similarly, noted early childhood researchers Lilian Katz and Diane McClellan say, "Socially competent young children are those who engage in satisfying interactions and activities with adults and peers and through such interactions further improve their own competence" (1997, p. 1). Head Start defines social competence broadly as comprising the knowledge and abilities young children need to succeed in school and life. More specifically, social-emotional development is the sixth domain in the Head Start Child Outcomes Framework (Head Start Bureau, 2007) and comprises the following elements: self-concept, self-control, cooperation, social relationships, and knowledge of family and communities. Finally, in the National Association for the Education of Young Children (NAEYC) Accreditation Standards (2007), the curriculum standard for social-emotional development (2B) includes interacting positively with others (adults and peers); recognizing and naming feelings; regulating one's emotions, behavior, and attention; developing a sense of competence and positive attitudes toward learning; resolving conflicts; and developing empathy.

The Components of Social-Emotional Learning

Across the child development and educational literature then, with only minor variations, researchers and practitioners agree that social-emotional learning (or development or competence) includes four components (Epstein, 2007, p. 69):

Emotional self-regulation and self-awareness. This aspect of social-emotional development is defined as responding to experiences with an appropriate range of immediate or delayed emotions. In preschool, it is characterized by a growing ability to focus and organize actions; greater forethought and less impulsivity; and enhanced awareness of and ability to follow rules, rituals, and common procedures. Language development and the ability to hold mental images (representations) in mind enable young children to defer gratification, anticipate the eventual satisfaction of their needs, and be flexible in creating alternative goals and solutions to problems. In the following anecdote, for example, Sklar is able to moderate his emotions by devising an alternate play scenario.

> *At work time in the block area, Sklar wants Carrie to be his dog, and so does Lily. The teacher asks how they can solve the problem. Sklar says, "I can be a dog too, and Lily can be the owner for both dogs." Lily agrees to this idea and cuts long pieces of string for Sklar and Carrie to hold on to as leashes.*

A related aspect that is developing over the preschool years is self-awareness, the understanding that one exists as an individual separate from others, with private thoughts and feelings. Seeing oneself as independent and self-motivated is essential to the ability to control one's own behavior, rather than feeling or being at the mercy of forces outside oneself.

Social knowledge and understanding. This component is defined as knowledge of social norms and customs. Acquiring this knowledge in the early years is called "socialization" or becoming a member of the "community." The emphasis on the classroom as a community, and the teacher's role in establishing a supportive group environment, is central in early childhood practice (as is establishing ties with families and the community beyond the school, topics this book covers in Chapters 15 and 16, respectively). To become a participating member of the group, children must be able to give up some individuality for the greater good, making the transition from the "me" of toddlerhood to the "us" of preschool. This shift is also the underpinning of civic competence (Jantz & Seefldt, 1999), or understanding the role of the individual in a functioning society, which is the goal of social studies education. (For more on the relationship of social competence to social studies, see Chapter 2, "An Overview of Child Development and Teaching Practices.") In the following anecdotes, we see children demonstrating an understanding of how their behavior can make things better for one or more other people in the group:

> *At work time in the block area, while playing puppies, Fernanda announces she is making soup. She says, "It's for my friend next door."*

> *While getting ready for outside time, Max helps Kayla put on her tennis shoes. "Now we can all go outside quicker," he tells the teacher.*

Social skills. This third component comprises the range of strategies for interacting with others. Cognitive development, especially perspective-taking and empathy, assists the development of social skills. Emerging classification skills — understanding similarities and differences and concepts such as "some" versus "all" — give preschoolers an awareness of how they are "like" and "not like" others.

> *At work time in the house area, Bret looks at Kimi and says, "How did you get so tall? What did you eat?"*

Teachers play a role in helping young children respect differences they encounter in gender, race and ethnicity, religion, language(s) or dialect spoken, ability/disability, ideas and beliefs, and other characteristics.

and using the rolling pin as a steering wheel. He invites other children to ride the bus, and Timmy, Leila, and Theron sit down. Christian announces, "We're gonna catch speeders," and Leila says, "There's a fast one over there!"

Focus on the whole child. Two landmark reports from the National Research Council (NRC) also highlight the importance of early social-emotional development. *Eager to Learn* insists "it is the *whole* child that must be developed" (NRC, 2000a, p. 8) while *Neurons to Neighborhoods* recommends that "resources on a par with those focused on literacy and numerical skills should be devoted to translating the knowledge base on young children's emotional, regulatory, and social development into effective strategies for fostering … curiosity, the ability to cooperate, and the enhanced motivation associated with feeling competent and loved" (NRC, 2000b, p. 5).

Likewise, the National Education Goals Panel (NEGP; Kagan, Moore, & Bredekamp, 1995) includes social-emotional development as one of five school readiness dimensions, noting that emotional support and secure relationships engender self-confidence, enable children to function as members of a group, and give meaning to school experience. "Approaches to learning," a related dimension, includes the personal traits labeled curiosity, creativity, confidence, independence, initiative, and persistence.[1] Although these traits are not easy to define and measure, NEGP said they nevertheless shape children's educational experiences across all content areas. In the following anecdote, for example, Jabiari not only explores science, he also discovers himself to be a capable and confident learner who can apply his new-found knowledge in independent actions:

> *At small-group time, after planting his seeds in a cup with his teacher's help, Jabiari says, "I want to do another one by myself." With his teacher standing by, Jabiari tells her what he is doing, step-by-step. The next week, when the teacher*

gives each child seeds for the outdoor flower garden, Jabiari says, "I already know what to do." He digs a hole, put in his seeds, and covers them up. "That's how it works," he says.

Concerns about balancing the acquisition of academic and social skills are also echoed in policy reports from other professional groups, such as the Society for Research in Child Development (Raver, Izard, & Kopp, 2002), the American Psychological Association (APA Task Force on Psychology in Early Education and Care, 2003), and the Kauffman Foundation's Early Education Exchange (2002). Achieving this balance is particularly critical with children whose home environments place them at risk for later behavioral and academic problems.

For example, there is evidence that aggressive young children have trouble adjusting to school, are more likely to commit delinquent acts, and become liabilities rather than assets to society (Fight Crime, Invest in Kids, 2000). Longitudinal research confirms that appropriate early intervention can help set at-risk children on a path toward better social adjustment throughout their school years and well into adulthood (Reynolds, Temple, Robertson, and Mann, 2001; Schweinhart, Montie, Xiang, Barnett, Belfield, and Nores, 2005; and Yoskikawa, 1995).

> *Most "at-risk" kids, even if they must overcome poor child care, grow up to be contributing adults. But many fall short of making the contribution they could have made if they had been in better child care as babies and toddlers. And new research confirms that failing to ensure at-risk children access to quality child care can actually multiply the danger that they will grow up with problem behaviors that can lead to later crime and violence against America's families* (**Fight Crime, Invest in Kids, 2000, p. 7**).

What Are the Implications of Renewed Interest in Social-Emotional Learning?

Public awareness. Renewed professional interest in social-emotional development has also resulted in its increased coverage in the popular press. This has proved to be a mixed blessing. For one thing, not everyone uses

---

[1] The other three NEGP school readiness dimensions are physical well-being and motor development, language development, and cognition and general knowledge.

the term in the same way. And how we define it reflects why we think it is important and our goals for including it in the early childhood curriculum. At one extreme is the idea that if we just let children play and encourage them to share, emotional wellness and social niceties will emerge naturally with minimal adult intervention. At the other end of the spectrum is the view that values must be explicitly taught and inculcated, although this inevitably leads to debates about whose values best represent societal norms. So the focus on social-emotional development puts a burden on the field — a fair one — to be clear about what the term means.

Increased demand for accountability. Another reality to contend with is that the demand for accountability will not go away. It will merely expand to include this area in addition to traditional academic domains. Such scrutiny may not be welcomed, but it, too, is justified. Early childhood is not (or should not be) against accountability, but only opposed to assessments that do not validly reflect the true nature of how young children learn. Therefore, we must be clear about the kinds of observable behaviors that indicate whether social-emotional development is proceeding along healthy lines versus when children would benefit from early and appropriate intervention. Developing valid assessments in this domain also means we must exercise extreme caution in defining the range of "normal" behavior, so as not to (mis)label young children and exacerbate problems, or even create problems where none existed before.

Rethinking early development. Finally, if we accept that social-emotional learning should be an essential part of the curriculum, we must identify and train ourselves to implement the teaching strategies that promote it. This process may in turn require us to rethink long-held ideas about early development. First and foremost, we must recognize that social-emotional learning is a content area on a par with literacy, mathematics, and other disciplines. As such, there is a body of knowledge and skills young children can and should learn with appropriate adult guidance and scaffolding. Second, we need to reexamine our ideas about the range of young children's abilities in this domain. Current research and pilot programs, for example,

challenge old assumptions about young children's capacity for empathy, solving conflicts, developing a sense of morality, and carrying out basic principles of democracy.

We used to assume, for example, that preschoolers were too egocentric to show empathy, that is, they were cognitively incapable of "decentering" from their own perspective to see things from the viewpoint of someone else. Then research (e.g., Dixon & Moore, 1990; Legerstee, 2005; Warneken & Tomasello, 2006) revealed that even infants and toddlers are attuned to the distress cries of other babies, while preschoolers, without being asked, often demonstrate a responsiveness to the needs of their peers and take steps to alleviate their distress:

> *At greeting circle, when Andrew looks sad after his mother leaves, Jessica walks over to give him a hug and says, "Don't worry. Your mommy's gonna come back."*

> *At work time in the art area, Casey sees that his friend Xavier is upset and says, "Come play with me at the water table. It will help make you happy."*

In sum, the renewed interest in young children's social and emotional development is timely, but it needs to keep up with the times. As enlightened practitioners, we should be open to an expanded awareness of early development and the changing contexts in which young children are called upon to exercise their knowledge and skills in this multidimensional domain.

The rest of this chapter explores further why social-emotional development is a vital component of early learning. A summary of the research on how this development proceeds and how adults support the young child's acquisition of social-emotional abilities is the focus of Chapter 2, which concludes Part I of this book.

Why Is Social-Emotional Development Important in the Preschool Years?

Social-emotional learning and overall development. The definitions of social-emotional learning provided earlier in this chapter make the case that this domain of development affects all other areas of behavior. Rima Shore, in her book *What Kids Need: Today's Best Ideas for Nurturing, Teaching, and Protecting Young Children* (2002), says that scientific and practical lessons, including those from brain research, teach us that social and cognitive skills are linked. Many of the abilities involved in learning reading, mathematics, and other subjects are elements of social and emotional development, namely listening, task persistence, and flexible problem solving. The best way to help young children grow into curious, confident, and able learners is to provide them with warm, emotionally secure, and positive social experiences. Conversely, restricted social environments and early emotional trauma can place children at risk for a wide variety of short- and long-term developmental delays — cognitive, perceptual-motor, and social.

Preschoolers demonstrate a range of emotional and social skills that can be fostered and extended through scaffolding by adults.

Head Start promotes an equally strong and comprehensive view in its statement that "it is time to discard debates about social-emotional versus cognitive development and which comes first or is more important. Clearly, children develop in both areas over the same period, and learning and development in one influences learning and

development in the other" (Head Start Bureau, 2007). The Head Start Child Outcomes Framework further explains that social-emotional development is vital for three interrelated reasons:

1. Positive social-emotional development provides a base for lifelong learning.

2. Social skills and emotional self-regulation are integrally related to later academic success in school.

3. Prevention of future social and behavioral difficulties is more effective than later remediation.

Social-emotional learning as a valuable end in itself. Dr. Daniel Goleman, who was a science writer for *The New York Times* (and a cofounder of CASEL) when he wrote his ground-breaking book *Emotional Intelligence* (1995), argues in the book that skills such as self-awareness, self-discipline, persistence, and empathy could be of greater consequence in life than those measured by IQ and achievement tests. He says children and society are at risk if schools exclusively teach academics at the expense of these other abilities. In his later book, *Social Intelligence: The New Science of Human Relationships* (2006), Goleman makes the case that interpersonal relationships can actually shape our brains and affect cells throughout our bodies, with significant effects on study, work, and physical and mental health. He also argues that rapport and empathy can be taught from preschool through adulthood.

Since its introduction, the concept of emotional intelligence has gained in popularity and impact, particularly among educators. On his Web site, Goleman (undated) notes that when his 1995 book *Emotional Intelligence* was first published, there were only a handful of programs on social-emotional learning (SEL), but that ten years later, "tens of thousands of schools worldwide offer children SEL" and many states set competency standards for social-emotional learning just as they do for math and language. A typical standard might state, for example, that young children should be able to recognize and label their emotions and how they lead them to act.

Decades of research, synthesized in CASEL meta-analyses of over 200 scientifically valid studies (Weissberg & O'Brien, 2004; Viadero, 2007), show that students in

SEL programs do better academically, have higher attendance, and have more positive attitudes than nonprogram students. Schools that offer such programs are also safer than those that do not. Goleman posits that the effects on the brain of positive social and emotional experiences can actually improve attention and working memory, which are key factors in learning. In this hypothesis, neuroplasticity, the shaping of the brain by repeated experience, may explain why SEL provides such significant benefits to program participants.

Social-emotional learning and school readiness. In the edited volume *School Readiness and the Transition to Kindergarten in the Era of Accountability* (Pianta, Cox, & Snow, 2007), social-emotional development features prominently in the section on what it means to be ready for school. Ruby Takanishi and Fasaha Traylor, President and Senior Program Officer, respectively, of the Foundation for Child Development, argue in the book's foreword that "the integration of cognitive and learning motivational skills in aligned educational programs for young children from ages 3 to 8 holds great promise to narrow (not close) the achievement gap" (p. xvii).

In support of their argument, note the complex interplay of cognitive skills (using representational props, demonstrating an awareness of number and measurement concepts) and social interaction (listening to and conversing with an adult) in this seemingly simple exchange between a child and his teacher:

> *At work time in the block area, Leon dresses in a firefighter coat and hat. He says that there is a fire and points to the toy area. When Benedette (the teacher) asks him what he can do to stop the fire, Leon says he needs a hose. He pulls out a tape measure and says, "I have to open it 'til a big number shows because the hose needs to be really long." He directs the hose at the fire and makes "swishing" noises. "There," he says, looking satisfied. "Now it's out and we can go back to the firehouse."*

Summarizing the research on cognitive-social integration and school readiness, Snow (2007) identifies several thought-provoking connections. For example, although

the direction of the relationship is not yet clear, behavioral problems and reading difficulties appear linked. Work-related skills (a subclass of social skills including paying attention to directions, participating in groups, and focusing on classroom tasks) are positively related to later academic achievement. Children with poor work-related skills have higher rates of special education, while having stronger work-related skills can buffer against socioeconomic risk factors in early learning. Finally, research shows a young child's social relationships with other children and teachers can smooth the transition to kindergarten. A child's ability to form friendships leads to peer acceptance in the classroom, which in turn supports school engagement and emerging academic achievement. At the same time, the more children establish close and conflict-free relationships with teachers, the more they "acquire the skills taught in school, maximizing the impact of instruction and deriving the most benefit from school" (Snow, 2007, p. 208).

In Conclusion

In *The Emotional Development of Young Children: Building an Emotion-centered Curriculum,* Hyson (2004) argues that if we expect children to enter school "ready to learn," they must have the underlying security and emotional foundations for that learning. Most school reform movements focus on academic instruction without paying corresponding attention to the personal and interpersonal factors that contribute to school readiness and lifelong success and satisfaction. Reviewing two decades of research on early learning, and the role of adults in supporting social-emotional competence, Hyson concludes that this domain must be an essential component of the early childhood curriculum. Social-emotional development, she says, "is too important to be left to chance" (p. 9).

five-year-olds are also increasingly social. Their network of adults and peers widens, they develop preferences and form friendships, and they associate with new communities at home and at school.

How Other Areas of Learning Affect Social-Emotional Development

Given its importance, it is no surprise that early social-emotional learning is affected by many parallel strands of development. Two emerging capacities of particular significance are the ability to hold mental images in mind and language development.

Mental representation. As young children develop the capacity to form mental representations, they are less tied to the present and can delay gratification. For example, preschoolers know that when cleanup is finished it will be time for snack, so their hunger pangs become manageable. Or they understand it will be their turn to use the swing when the sand reaches the bottom of the timer; picturing this imminent event helps them wait a short time. The ability to mentally represent objects, people, and actions thus allows young children to gain control over their feelings and actions. (For more on the development of representation, see Hohmann, Weikart, & Epstein, 2008, especially pp. 488–490.)

Being able to imagine the future or predict if/then events also enables preschoolers to anticipate consequences. They know, for example, that grabbing a toy from a playmate can result in an adverse response, and they may therefore choose an alternative means of getting access to the object. Although preschoolers still operate in concrete ways, their growing representational abilities make them less vulnerable to instincts and impulses and more capable of controlling their behavior and making choices. Consider Lili "anticipating" how she would feel angry "if" something happened and taking steps to prevent it:

> *At work time in the toy area, Lili builds a tower with unit blocks and tells the following to Sue, her teacher:*
>
> **Lili:** *I'm worried they might knock it down.*
>
> **Sue:** *You're worried that your tower might get knocked down by the other children.*

> **Lili:** *I'll be angry.*
>
> **Sue:** *Is there something you can do so that doesn't happen?*
>
> **Lili:** *I can put a work-in-progress sign on it and then they'll know to be more careful.*

Communication. The ability to understand what others are saying and to express one's thoughts and desires in return is also a vital component of early social and emotional learning. Many frustrations of infancy and toddlerhood are resolved when adults can engage in simple dialogue with children to find out what they need or want. Language gives young children more control over achieving their objectives, whether it is getting fed ("Want banana"), receiving comfort ("When will mommy be back?"), or securing help to accomplish a task ("Hold the corner while I staple it"). Words are also tools that expand a toddler's ability to express positive affiliations ("Me grandma book") and preferences ("Apple good").

By preschool, children use language to collaborate in constructive play ("I'll bring the blocks to build our tower") and sociodramatic play ("Let's be kitties"), as well as to solve social problems ("You always get to be the baby! I know — there can be two babies!"). They understand simple rules and routines, enabling them to function as community members at home and in the classroom.

Perhaps nowhere do the social benefits of representational and communication skills come together more clearly than in the constructive play and role play of preschool children. In this exchange with her teacher, a girl builds a mountain and in simple, poetic words and gestures, tells her teacher about climbing to the top:

> *At work time in the toy area, Gretchen connects squares of magnetiles in a line. Then she links triangle magnetiles together and says, "I made a mountain. You go out on the grass (she walks her fingers across the squares), climb up and over (she traces up the slope of the mountain), and there's the city.*

The central role language plays in social-emotional development should also alert educators to the importance of helping English language learners (ELLs) and those with communicative disabilities find alternative ways of comprehending others and expressing themselves. Relationships are the primary avenue for young children's learning. Attending to their social needs can help set them on a path of successful academic progress, too.

The Importance of Play in Social-Emotional Learning

As described in the previous chapter, play is an intrinsic part of early social-emotional learning. Scientists who study play in animals and children conclude it is a central part of neurological growth and development. Behavioral neurologist Sergio Pellis (2006) suggests play is essential to the "pruning" process that trims away excess neural connections and strengthens necessary ones in early brain development. Affective neuroscientist Jaak Panksepp (1998) found evidence that a "play drive" is hard-wired into the thalamus, the part of the brain that receives sensory information and relays it to the more "thinking" regions of the cortex.

Play is one of the most varied forms of human behavior, says evolutionary biologist Marc Bekoff (2007). It builds socially and cognitively flexible brains by calling on a wide range of functions. In fact, social play even has its own vocabulary (Henig, 2008). Dogs adopt a "play posture," chimps put on a "play face," and goats frisk in a "play gait" to communicate that their actions; while bearing some commonality to aggression, all are in fun and not to be seen as threatening. In children, the equivalent behavior is the child's smile, an open expression that indicates there is no anger involved even in the rough and

Sociodramatic play helps build social-emotional competence as well as language skills.

tumble or challenging gestures that often characterize the play of very young children. Thus play, although it may appear purposeless, lets even nonverbal animals and preverbal children establish social relationships through physical language.

The importance of sociodramatic play. Pretend play, in which children use language as well as gesture to invent identities, actions, and situations, begins at about 18 months of age. It takes on a parallel function (playing *alongside* others) in the second year, and becomes social (playing *with* others) around age three.

> *At work time in the house area, Christian, Jacob, and Lute are playing firefighters. Jacob uses the phones and calls Christian to help put out the fire. Lute follows with his "chemicals."*

> *At work time in the house area, Ellie and Gabrielle are playing kitties and say that the arch is their "kitty hotel." They lay on the pillows, meowing and crawling around.*

Studies show that children play for longer periods of time and with greater complexity as they get older, but even younger children engage in more complex play when interacting with older peers and adults (Brownell, 1990). By age six, however, sociodramatic play often declines (Cole & LaVoie, 1985). One reason is that children's imagination is more internalized by then. They can entertain "What if" thoughts in their mind without needing to act them out. Children may also be responding to pressures to play in more productive ways during the elementary grades. So, for example, they may practice writing skills as they "play school," or they may use measuring skills to build a space station.

Professor and teacher-educator Doris Fromberg says, "There is a consensus that sociodramatic play influences social competence. In general, social and moral development take place as young children interact with others. The social negotiations of pretend play are a particularly potent and influential realm of experience" (1999, p. 35). Research shows that social behavior is more mature and reciprocal in pretend play than in nonpretend activities. Drawing on affective, social, and cognitive aspects of do not learn social competence through direct instruction — lessons, lectures, magic circles, workbook exercises, or suggestive and sometimes exhortatory approaches … [especially] when they are attempted with the class as a whole" (p. 20). The authors instead advise "individualized guidance" because it maximizes the child's participation in constructing new knowledge and allows teachers to be warm and supportive during the interaction.

On the other hand, there are some social lessons that can be learned in a group setting, provided they are not presented as didactic lectures. For example, young children can learn how to solve problems collaboratively and contribute to classroom policies through group strategies such as class meetings (Vance & Weaver, 2002). And whether adults are working with individuals or with a group to scaffold learning, researchers and early childhood practitioners recognize the value of explicit adult intervention in such areas as conflict resolution and violence prevention (Levin, 2003). "Explicit" means teachers are immediate and intentional in addressing a problem; but here, too, they invite children's participation rather than deliver a one-way lesson or lecture.

Choosing appropriate teaching practices. Strategies to promote social-emotional development may be divided into two sets of related practices. The first are conducive to fostering overall healthy behavior in this domain, and the second, to helping children learn specific knowledge and skills. Depending on their intentions, teachers can use either or a combination of the two types of strategies.

Recommendations in the first category address classroom practices as a whole and come from the preschool literature in general plus work explicitly focused on dealing with challenging behavior. Researchers and practitioners in this field recognize that classroom routines and expectations that allow young children to function securely and confidently can help prevent behavioral difficulties in the first place. The second set of teaching strategies, which offers advice on working with young children at both the individual and group levels, comes more directly from the social-emotional learning (SEL) literature and includes concrete ideas to help preschoolers enter into and negotiate the interpersonal world.

Both sets of practices are summarized below, and then applied specifically to each domain of social-emotional learning in Chapters 3–13, with a summary list of classroom strategies at the end of each chapter. In addition, Chapters 14–16 discuss issues that extend beyond the immediate classroom; namely, examining ourselves as role models, helping parents extend social-emotional learning at home, and connecting to the community within and outside the agency.

Classroom Practices to Promote Overall Social-Emotional Learning

The Center for Evidence-Based Practice on Young Children with Challenging Behavior (Dunlap, Conroy, Kern, DuPaul, VanBrakle, et al., 2003) synthesized the research literature to identify program strategies that prevent problems by promoting healthy and adaptive "normal" social-emotional development. While cautioning that methodological limitations mean results need further confirmation, they concluded that prosocial behavior was more likely to occur when young children (a) are actively engaged with materials, activities, peers, and/or adults; (b) understand the expectations for their behavior including knowing what to do, when to do it, and how to do it; and (c) have effective and appropriate communication strategies.

In a chapter on classroom practices (Hemmeter & Ostrosky, 2003), the Center identified three strategies proven to be successful in bringing about these classroom conditions at the preschool level: Arrange and group classrooms for social play, implement predictable schedules and routines, and plan transitions. These are each described below, along with a fourth overall strategy derived from the literature on play: create opportunities for sociodramatic play.

Arrange and equip classrooms for social play. Children demonstrated higher levels of social interaction in a smaller as compared to a larger space when they used "social toys" (amenable to use by several children) versus "isolate" toys (more conducive to solitary play), and when they were involved in socially designed learning centers (that accommodated several children) versus isolated areas (meant for singles). In classrooms employing these principles, children were more engaged in play, communicated more, and had fewer disagreements. Other research (Epstein, 1993) shows that when children have access to plentiful and diverse materials they can retrieve and put away on their own, they are also more likely to play productively and have fewer conflicts. The following anecdote illustrates how duplicate materials available in a program's woodworking area can lead to increased social interaction and cooperative play between children.

> *At work time in the woodworking area, Shannon (a teacher) tells Ashley that she needs to wear goggles. Jerzy (who is wearing goggles) stops what he is doing, goes to the shelf, gets another pair of goggles, and hands them to Ashley. After she puts them on, she asks him, "Do you want me to hold your board so you can pound in the (golf) tees?" Ashley and Jerzy take turns helping one another create designs in the foam boards with colored golf tees.*

Implement predictable schedules and routines. Predictable schedules and consistent routines are fundamental in supporting children's social-emotional development and preventing challenging behaviors. Children demonstrated higher levels of play and social interaction during longer play periods (sustained engagement) when staff were organized and used "zone" staffing patterns (each staff member having primary responsibility for monitoring a given area) and when there was flexibility in terms of when children changed activities.

Plan transitions. Challenging behaviors frequently occur during transition times (shifting from one activity to another). Investigations found higher levels of engagement when children were given choices about when and how they transitioned. In addition, children demonstrated fewer disruptive behaviors and shifted more quickly when the transition was preceded by a more passive activity, such as story time.

Center researchers (Joseph & Strain, 2003) then looked at specific programs for evidence of effectiveness. Reviewing documented curricula (i.e., with written manuals for dissemination), they found those that promoted positive social skills and reduced risk factors and problem behaviors shared the following characteristics:

- The curriculum models were comprehensive, relating social-emotional development to all other domains.

- The programs were multiweek or ongoing, not short-term or theme-based interventions.

- Programs emphasized choice and problem-solving skills, including verbal interaction among children.

- Adults modeled appropriate behavior but did not give children a didactic set of rules to follow.

- Children were encouraged to reflect on and take responsibility for their own actions.

- Esteem for oneself and for others was emphasized.

- There was intensive teacher training in how to implement the curriculum.

- There were parent workshops or other family-based training to support implementation at home.

Create opportunities for sociodramatic play. Finally, as noted earlier in this chapter, opportunities for sociodramatic play contribute significantly to the overall development of social-emotional knowledge and skills. In a review of the research on play, Fromberg (1999) cites these classroom strategies for encouraging sociodramatic play in young children:

- Provide props and other materials conducive to sociodramatic play. These include dress-up clothes, construction toys, art materials, and real items found in household, work, and community settings.

- Model sociodramatic play consistent with children's developmental levels. For toddlers, this involves "acting like …" a person or object in their everyday lives. For preschoolers, appropriate modeling also includes acting out familiar activities, but also pretend play based on storybooks and imaginary scenes.

- Encourage interage play to increase attention and complexity among younger children and to promote perspective-taking among older children.

- Plan sociodramatic play with children. The more they talk about what they will do (including where it will happen, what they will need to carry it out, who they will play with, what problems they might encounter,

Promoting Social-Emotional Development

For both emotional and social learning to occur, the central role of adults is to create a warm and caring environment. Teachers can also explicitly transmit specific skills and knowledge. Use the following classroom practices to promote overall social-emotional development and abilities in specific domains.

Classroom Practices to Promote Overall Social-Emotional Development

- Arrange and equip classrooms for social play.

- Implement predictable schedules and routines.

- Plan transitions.

- Create opportunities for socio-dramatic play.

Classroom Practices to Promote Specific Social-Emotional Knowledge and Skills

- Model through "teaching by example."

- Coach children by breaking behavior into sequenced steps.

- Provide opportunities for practice.

ignorant or willful by not reading or doing arithmetic! Young children simply do not know any better — yet. But through the variety of general and specific strategies described above, preschoolers can acquire the social knowledge and skills that promote individual and collective well-being. As their mastery of the social-emotional domain increases, young children's confidence in themselves, and positive interactions with others, become effective resources for learning in all other domains.

Part Two

EMOTIONAL DEVELOPMENT

Developing a Positive Self-Identity

At the open house, Astrid asks a teacher if she can make labels for the different colors of foam. Her teacher replies, "Yes, I'd like to see how you do that." Astrid maneuvers her wheelchair to a set of low shelves and gets paper, markers, scissors, and tape. Setting them on her chair tray, she colors areas of her paper blue, yellow, and red and then cuts a rectangle of each. Holding them against the containers, she observes, "They're a little too big. I will cut them down." She makes the labels smaller and tapes them on the containers. "I am helpful," she says, and wheels her chair back to the shelves to put the unused materials away.

Definition

Self-identity refers to how we see and feel about ourselves as people. Identity is who we are, as opposed to what we can do (the latter is covered in Chapter 5, "Developing a Sense of Competence"). Children's sense of identity emerges as they become aware of their own characteristics and develops further as their attributes and the value attached to them is reflected back to them by others. In the opening anecdote, for example, Astrid sees herself as a person who is "helpful." When her teacher expresses interest in seeing how she would make labels for the containers of foam, she validates the image Astrid has of herself as a helpful person.

Healthy development of one's individual identity depends on establishing trusting and secure relationships, especially early in life. Research shows that a sense of self first appears as infants realize they and those caring for them are not extensions of one another but are separate beings. Identity formation continues in the preschool years and

proceeds positively when children learn to respect their personal characteristics, or attributes, including their name, gender, physical appearance, (dis)abilities, family composition, race, ethnicity, language(s), religious affiliation (if any), and the place (neighborhood, city, state, nation) where they live. Although a child's developmental level makes for some consistency of identity formation across attributes, there are also intriguing — and challenging — differences in how children come to see themselves and others on these defining dimensions.

For example, because children are concrete, they may focus on one particular aspect of gender identity and ignore another that contradicts it (insisting a boy baby with "curls" must be a girl). Their need to sort and classify can also make them somewhat rigid; for example, insisting that only children who are "as tall as the door knob" are old enough (age) to go to kindergarten. Thus, the development of identity, described below, involves not only understanding about the categories that define us, but learning how to apply them with the appropriate balance of consistency and flexibility.

A Sense of Identity

Self-identity refers to how we see and feel about ourselves as people. Identity is who we are, as opposed to what we can do.

Development

Developing an identity is a complex process because we are each defined by many attributes, as discussed above. Young children have to learn the names of these attributes, the dimensions or categories on which they vary, and how they are viewed by their family members, their peers, and society as a whole. It is no wonder that identity formation extends well into adolescence and beyond. Even as adults, we may find ourselves rethinking "who we are" and "how we feel about ourselves." In that sense, developing a self-identity is a process that never stops.

There are, however, certain aspects of the self that are fixed or unchanging. Research has examined young children's awareness of such relatively stable attributes as race, social class, culture, gender, and disability. How children come to understand these characteristics in themselves and others is based on many perceptual, cognitive, and experiential, or social, factors. Although further research is needed, some clear developmental patterns have emerged about how young children conceptualize and deal with differences in identity and how they feel about their own place within a category or along a continuum. These are summarized below. (See Ramsey, 2006, for a comprehensive review of the research on early identity formation.)

Identity Development

How children come to understand identity attributes such as race, social class, culture, gender, and ability/disability is based on many perceptual, cognitive, and experiential, or social, factors. Children's developing classification skills play into this understanding, including the ability to make multiple classifications and see overlap between categories.

Race. Racial awareness and self-identity begins in toddlerhood and is well-developed by preschool. Children know their own race and the race(s) of those around them. Even mixed-race children have begun to identify themselves in one category or another. By preschool, when asked who they want to play with, white children show stronger same-race preferences than minority children. This prowhite bias affects intraracial attitudes as well; that is, African-American children prefer other African-Americans who have lighter skin (Clark & Clark, 1947). At the same time, however, all children, including minorities, prefer to play with same-race peers (Ramsey, 1991). These preferences and play patterns solidify with age. Helping minority children to develop a positive self-identity is thus a challenge for families and educators since an awareness of the desirability of "the other" emerges so early.

Finishing her self-portrait during small-group time and drawing in oil pastels from her photo, Kelly blends the skin color with shades of brown to make it "look more real." She holds the paper with one hand as she rubs the color with the other. "Now it looks like me," she beams. "I will take it home to show my mom."

Social class. Most preschoolers have little awareness of the concepts underlying economic or class disparities (Harrah & Friedman, 1990). Although they may understand the meaning of the term "boss" or attach "prices" (however unrealistic) to items when they play store or restaurant, their knowledge is limited when it comes to defining characteristics such as earned income or inherited wealth, job status, or level of education. Children begin to acquire this knowledge in mid- to late-elementary school, but not until age 14 do they start to develop a comprehensive understanding of the dynamics that underlie social class.

For younger children, there can be an initial awareness of concrete signs of wealth in terms of clothing, homes, and material possessions (toys and to a growing degree, electronics), but even this realization does not appear until about age 6 (Dittmar & Van Duuren, 1993). Dominant social values are absorbed earlier, however. Even preschoolers assume rich people are happier and more likeable than poor people. They believe it is unfair for some people to have more money than others and favor rich people sharing their wealth with those less well off. Not until the later elementary grades, when they have absorbed cultural norms, do children profess that poor people "get what they deserve" and that income should therefore not be redistributed. Whether this position is maintained or amended over time is then a function of various personal experiences and social and political influences (Ramsey, 1991; Furnham & Stacey, 1991).

Research on the effects of living in a consumer culture is just beginning, but preliminary results show it leads to a focus on *having* rather than *enjoying* possessions, and may breed unhappiness by highlighting desires that are often not fulfilled (Kline, 1993). And although past studies indicated that young children did not categorize themselves as "rich" or "poor," perhaps because they were surrounded by others of comparable status, media exposure may hasten this self-awareness and open the door to a negative self-identity. Even preschoolers may begin to classify themselves as "have nots" when surrounded by screen images of children who have so much more.

Developing a self-identity is a complex process in which young children begin to understand their personal attributes and how these are viewed by other people and the society at large.

Culture. Most young children do not have a concept of "culture," such as national origin or particular traditions. Yet when confronted with its practical manifestations, such as speech or dress, they respond appropriately (Orellana, 1994). Bilingual children, for example, know when to switch languages. Moreover, preschoolers notice language differences and often associate them with people who wear other styles of clothing or live in unfamiliar dwellings, although they do not necessarily understand

the sources and connections among such distinctions (Hirschfield & Gelman, 1997).

When they do observe cultural differences, preschoolers' concrete thinking may lead them to exaggerate the salience of these differences. Young children have difficulty grasping the fact that people can be different in some ways but alike in others. Their classification skills push them to choose "different" or "same," not some of each. Preschoolers cannot handle ambiguity or "gray areas" of identity. No amount of direct teaching can alter this framework until the children have the cognitive capacity to classify along multiple dimensions. (For a discussion of how young children's classification skills can also affect their understanding of diversity, see Chapter 9, "Valuing Diversity.")

> **Anthony:** *I think I'm from Irish and something else.*
>
> **Teacher:** *How do you know you're Irish?*
>
> **Anthony:** *Because I have freckles like my mommy.*
>
> **Teacher:** *What about the something else?*
>
> **Anthony:** (Thinks a minute) *Just from Irish.* (Pauses) *But not my daddy.*

Identifying oneself or others as belonging to a particular cultural group begins to emerge at 6–10 years, but tends to be concrete and literal; for example, "I'm Mexican-American because I eat Mexican-American food" or "I'm Muslim because my family celebrates Ramadan." However, children in this older age group are capable of entertaining the idea that people can be both the same and different, and so are more amenable to appreciating cultural differences without judging them. By age 10–14, children are more aware of the underlying social differences in race and ethnicity and may become less trusting of other groups. Not until mid-adolescence does ethnic identity and loyalty begin to solidify. (For more on this developmental sequence, see Quintana, 1998.) At the same time, depending on social influences, children may develop a sense of social (in)justice and the capacity for greater understanding and tolerance. Because outside forces play such a significant role in shaping attitudes, even preschoolers with their limited understanding of culture may benefit from everyday, positive exposure to differences (see also Chapter 9).

Gender. Preschoolers have already learned *gender stereotypes,* and these affect their behavior, educational and career aspirations, interactions with other children, learning motivation and style, self-identity, and self-esteem (Bigler, 1997). Although they see gender as a relatively stable personal attribute, they do not always realize it is a constant, regardless of stylistic and behavioral variations. For example, a child may know she is a girl but say she wants to be a "daddy" when she grows up so she can cut the grass with the riding lawnmower.

In their need to establish clear-cut guidelines for classification, young children may therefore be quite inflexible about sex-role stereotypes. (So, for example, the girl who wants to become a daddy has clear expectations about what women and men can and cannot do.) These gender stereotypes continue to increase in the preschool years (again because of children's inability to make multiple classifications), peak in the elementary years, and then decline thereafter, although they are ultimately affected by personal and social forces. Moreover, gender stereotypes, like racial ones, tend to be self-perpetuating, especially in younger children. Observations that contradict their beliefs are denied or explained away, rather than being allowed to alter the belief system itself (Liben & Bigler, 2002).

Gender segregation (the preference for same-sex peers) begins even before preschool and becomes entrenched during the early childhood years (Bigler, 1995). Same-sex preferences for playmates grow stronger with age, and children who choose cross-gender playmates or engage in nonstereotypical play are often ridiculed or rejected by their peers. By elementary school, boy-girl friendships established earlier often dissolve under such pressure, and children associate almost exclusively with same-sex peers.

Parents and teachers may inadvertently reinforce gender stereotypes and segregation; for example, through the types of toys and clothes they purchase and in assigning tasks, acknowledging behavior, and expecting differential abilities. Because of the rigidity of gender stereotypes in the early years, however, even intentional efforts by adults to overcome young children's beliefs and actions do not often meet with success. For example, children assigned to cross-gender groups still gravitate toward same-sex peers

when given a choice (MacNaughton, 2000). Despite such setbacks, educators agree that early, consistent, and positive nonstereotyped experiences do, in the long run, affect self-identity and attitudes toward others. For preschoolers to feel good about the fact that they have been born as girls or boys, gender sameness — that is, equality of the sexes — should be emphasized and gender differences acknowledged without valuing one set of traits over another.

Abilities and disabilities. Research into children's awareness and understanding of disabilities, which began about two decades ago, shows that it varies with the type of disability (Diamond & Innes, 2001). For preschoolers, not surprisingly, the more evident the problem — such as orthopedic and sensory disabilities — the greater their awareness. Their explanations for disabilities also reflect their concrete level of thinking. Preschoolers focus on the equipment ("He can't see because he wears special glasses"); the person's age or immaturity ("She hasn't learned how to walk yet"); or illness, injury, and trauma ("She had a really bad earache, so now she can't hear").

Children's attitudes toward people with disabilities make a shift in the early years (Diamond & Hestenes, 1996). Preschoolers are more likely to see them as potential friends. Elementary students, who compare their skills to those of others, are more likely to place limits on associating with less-able children, although they are more likely to see themselves as "caregiver friends." At all ages, children tend to reject those with emotional or cognitive impairments, including language delays, perhaps because they do not understand them. Children generalize from mental disabilities to an overall negativity of character. They see impulsivity, for example, as "bad" behavior from a "bad" person. Likewise, they are less accepting of those they see as responsible for their disability (e.g., poor impulse control, obesity) than those whose disabilities they see as beyond their control (e.g., blindness).

Despite such early misconceptions and biases, program evaluations show that all children benefit from attending integrated classrooms (Diamond, Hestenes, Carpenter, & Innes, 1997; Favazza & Odom, 1997). In such classrooms, "able" children become more sensitive and accepting. As their classification skills increase, they are also capable of seeing that those with disabilities possess strengths as well as limitations and can relate to those with disabilities on dimensions of sameness as well as difference. Children with disabilities develop a more accepting and less limiting self-identity. They, too, perceive their sameness, not just their differences, and think of themselves as people for whom a disability is just one of many defining characteristics.

Teaching Strategies

Adults can help children develop a positive sense of who they are by supporting their transition from home to school, providing labels for the many characteristics that make up their identity, and establishing a classroom atmosphere in which all children feel valued and respected. Children's self-identities can flourish when teachers use the strategies listed below to create a secure and welcoming environment.

Help children make the transition from home to school. Preschool children's sense of identity is still closely bound up with being "attached" to their primary caregivers. In their minds, who they are is defined by who they are with. So, being left on their own for several hours at school — especially before they are comfortable with their new caregivers — can raise alarms. To help young children make the transition from home to school (or from one child care setting to another), support them through separations until they are confident they can handle them on their own. Acknowledge and accept their feelings about being apart from family members and their worries about whether a parent will return later to take them home. Encourage family members to stay as long as they are able while children settle in, and allow children to (re)enter classroom activities at their own pace. Help parents support children's feelings at these times. (See Chapter 6, "Recognizing and Labeling Emotions," for relevant strategies.)

Also, be alert to signs of children's separation anxiety throughout the day. Though concerns about being by themselves typically emerge at drop-off times, other events during the day may trigger an episode of anxiety. For example, pretending to go to the doctor may remind a child of feeling alone during a scary medical procedure. Even putting on his or her coat at the end of the day

may awaken a child's worries that a parent will not come, especially if there have been any past incidents of parents being late or mixing up whose turn it is to pick up the child. Family stresses, such as the birth of a sibling, a parent's illness, or even the visit of a grandparent, can result in a child's worrying about being lost in the confusion or excitement. Reassure children that they are valued members of their families and the classroom and that who they are and their well-being are important to all the adults who care for them. Children may benefit from having a family picture they can carry around with them or a class book with photographs from every child's family that they can curl up with in the book area.

When teachers help parents understand the parts and functions of the daily routine, parents can in turn help their children make the transition between home and school.

Focus primarily on children throughout the day. Your positive attention is the single most important factor in letting children know they are valued. Spend most of your time attending to children and what they are doing, rather than arranging materials, cleaning up, or interacting with other adults. Interact with children in calm and respectful tones. Do not shout, shame, or use harsh words and actions. Finally, address comments directly to children; don't talk "about" children in front of them, as though they were not there.

At small-group time, while drawing with chalk, Jacob says, "It's cool. Mine is really cool because I have green. It turned black." His teacher, Eva, asks Jacob to show her how he made the green turn black, and he demonstrates on another corner of his paper. When it is time to clean up and Jacob is reluctant to stop, Eva asks how he could continue to work on his drawing. "I can take it home," says Jacob, "and do it more at the table." At the end of the day, when his father comes to get him, Eva says to Jacob, "Remember that you wanted to take your picture home to keep working on it. It's in your cubby." As he heads out the door, Jacob tells his father all about how he rubbed the chalk on the paper and made the colors change.

Address diversity and differences positively.
As they investigate the world, preschoolers are curious about the differences they observe and are not shy about asking questions. Answer them forthrightly in a normal, conversational voice. Supply identity labels and use them in respectful ways. Talking with children about differences in gender, skin color, religious observances, family composition, and so on can be affirming and instructive as long as the tone is accepting and factual, not judgmental. Talk about differences between people in the same way you converse about the attributes of objects or events that interest children. (For more on addressing diversity though classroom materials, daily activities, and adult-child interactions, see Chapter 9.)

"Inaya's hair is dark brown and curly, and Aggie's is blonde and straight. But you're both wearing flowered headbands today."

A group of preschoolers is drawing pictures of their families during small-group time. Les says, "It's just me and my mom, so I only need a little paper." Magda tells the others at the table, "I need two pieces of paper 'cause I have two families, one with my mom and one with my dad." Their teacher comments, "Each family is different. Some are small and some are big. Some live in one place and some in more than one place." Susannah adds, "They come in different colors, too!"

Provide nonstereotyped materials, activities, and role models. Because the media, and possibly people and settings outside of school, may bombard children with stereotypes, it is especially important to provide them with alternative images. Read picture books showing women as nontraditional professionals and men doing housework and nurturing children. Provide clothes and props for children of both sexes to role-play different occupations, and encourage children to work with all types of equipment (carpentry tools, cooking utensils). Look for books and magazine photos that show elderly people and those with disabilities involved in a variety of activities that young and able-bodied people do. Talk about the accommodations that disabled people may need to make for some activities, but how they still carry out and enjoy them.

At work time in the house area, Christian says, "I'm the maker. I make some pancakes and some food." He pretends to make and serve pancakes to his teacher.

At work time in the construction area, Gayla uses a screwdriver to take apart an old alarm clock. "These are the gears," she tells Milton, her teacher. "Show me how they work," he says. Gayla makes circular motions in opposite directions with the forefingers of both hands. "They go around like this," she explains, "and catch each other. My uncle Joe [a jeweler] lets me help him fix 'em."

Encourage family members to become involved in the program. A child's first source of identity is the family, so making family members part of the program provides both continuity and validation in the formation of a child's positive self-concept. Don't limit invitations and participation to mothers. Include fathers, grandparents, and other regular caregivers, as well as siblings when appropriate.

Provide many options so family members can choose a type and level of participation that suits them. For example, family members can volunteer in the classroom (give them opportunities to interact with children, not just perform "custodial" chores); contribute materials (new and especially recycled/reusable items); attend parent meetings and workshops; write and/or receive a program newsletter; serve on advisory councils; meet with teachers formally and informally to discuss the program and their child's progress; and extend children's learning at home. (For resources and ideas on how teachers can help families support social-emotional learning at home, see Chapter 15.) Where feasible, provide transportation and child care to enable families to participate in program activities.

As this father interacts with children in the house area, we see a parent involved as a partner in a nonstereotyped role-playing scenario.

In the following anecdote, the pictures Christopher's father took provide a conversational focus that allows the class to learn more about Christopher's family and helps the children extend their language skills. This illustrates how children can learn to value their backgrounds and identities when staff encourage family involvement.

At greeting time, Christopher brought in photographs his father took at his workplace the previous afternoon. Christopher asked his teacher how to spell picnic, *wrote it on a small chalkboard, and drew a detailed picture of a bus. Christopher initiated a conversation about the picnic:*

Christopher: *I went to a picnic with my dad and I saw a Miami Dade new bus.*

Teacher: *Your dad is a bus driver for Miami Dade. How is the new bus different from the bus he drives?*

Christopher: *It's sparkly and clean. The old one is white.*

Jonathan: *Which one is the new one? The white one or the sparkly one?*

Christopher: *The new one is sparkly. It's only for the bus drivers to take a break. It has a bathroom and a living room with a couch. It has a place for shade.*

Jonathan: *What is shade?*

Christopher: *A place to rest outside.*

Gabriel: *Is it a long couch?*

Christopher: *No a little bit short. Like this big. (He demonstrates with his hands.) My dad just sits on it 'cause when he lies down, his feet hang over the end. He says I'm gonna be big like him!*

Establish ties with the community. Programs often network with social services agencies to make referrals for family crises and long-term problems. However, to promote children's positive identity formation, programs should also establish relationships with community members who can contribute time and caring directly to the children. Individuals and groups, including artists, tradespeople, business owners, tribal leaders, elders, and senior citizens can serve as mentors and role models, thereby supporting children's interests and emerging sense of self. See if such community members can host visits at their workplaces and interact with children in the classroom. Talk to them ahead of time about the things likely to interest the children and how to make these exchanges hands-on and interactive for preschoolers. The more diverse these community connections, the better it communicates to children that people of all backgrounds are valued and welcomed in the program. (For ideas on community outreach to support children's social-emotional development, see Chapter 16.)

In Conclusion

To develop emotional competence, children must feel good about themselves and believe they will be seen positively by others. The first step on the road to healthy emotional development is knowing and valuing who we are as people. Teachers, together with families and community members, play a vital role in the formation of children's earliest self-perceptions. By helping preschoolers discover who they are and accepting them in all their diversity, early childhood educators can establish the fertile soil in which positive self-identity blooms.

Developing a Positive-Identity: Teaching Strategies

Help children make the transition from home to school.

- Support children during separations until they are confident they can handle them on their own.

- Acknowledge and accept children's feelings about being apart from family members.

- Encourage family members to stay as long as they are able while children settle in. Help parents support children's feelings at these times.

- Allow children to enter or reenter classroom activities at their own pace.

- Be alert to signs of separation anxiety throughout the day; reassure children that they are valued members of their families and the classroom and that who they are and their well-being are important to all the adults who care for them.

- Suggest to parents that children may benefit from having a family picture to carry around with them.

Focus primarily on children throughout the day.

- Spend most of your time attending to children and what they are doing, rather than doing classroom chores or interacting with other adults.

- Interact with children in calm and respectful tones.

- Address your comments directly to children rather than talking "about" children as if they were not there.

Address diversity and differences positively.

- Answer children's questions forthrightly about the differences they observe, using a normal, conversational voice.

- Supply identity labels, and use them in respectful ways.

- Talk with children about differences in gender, skin color, religious observances, family composition, and so forth in a tone that is accepting and factual, not judgmental.

- Talk about differences between people in the same way you converse about the attributes of objects or events that interest children.

Provide nonstereotyped materials, activities, and role models.

- Read picture books showing women as nontraditional professionals and men doing housework and nurturing children; provide clothes or props for children of both sexes to role-play different occupations, and encourage children to work with all types of equipment.

- Look for book and magazine photos that show elderly people and those with disabilities involved in a variety of activities that young and able-bodied people do; talk about the accommodations that disabled people may need to make for some activities but how they still carry out and enjoy them.

Teaching Strategies *(cont.)*

Encourage family members to become involved in the program.

- Don't limit invitations and participation to mothers — include fathers, grandparents, and other regular caregivers, as well as siblings when appropriate.

- Provide many options so family members can choose a type and level of participation that suits them. Where feasible, provide transportation and child care to enable families to participate in program activities.

Establish ties with the community.

- Establish relationships with community members who can contribute time and caring directly to children; for example, artists, tradespeople, business owners, tribal leaders, elders, and senior citizens.

- See if community members can host visits at their workplace or interact with children in the classroom; talk to them ahead of time about the things likely to interest children and how to make these exchanges interactive.

Feeling Empathy

Today is Connor's first day at school. At work time, Jamaica is playing with friends in the house area. She walks over to Connor, who is standing to the side of the room, and says, "You don't have any friends, so you can play with us." She takes his hand and leads him to the house area. "He can be the baby," she says, and hands him a blanket and a bottle. She pats Connor's arm and tucks the blanket around him.

> ### Empathy
>
> *Empathy* is the ability to understand others' feelings by experiencing the same emotion oneself.

Definition

Empathy is the ability to understand another person's feelings by experiencing the same emotion oneself. Empathic behavior is demonstrated through caring, compassion, and altruism. To experience and demonstrate empathy, we must be able to see situations from others' perspective, which is captured in the expression "putting yourself in their shoes." Seeing things from another perspective is an ability that applies to a wide range of cognitive as well as social situations. For example, when we give someone directions to our house or teach a child to ride a bicycle, we are thinking not only of how we use this information ourselves but also how to help another person understand and apply it, sometimes quite literally considering "where they are coming from." What differentiates empathy from other types of perspective taking is that empathy involves emotions as well as cognitive or intellectual processes.

Empathy can be expressed in either nonsocial (even antisocial) or prosocial ways (Riley, San Juan, Klinkner, & Ramminger, 2008). This full spectrum of reactions is true for adults as well as children. For example, we may witness another person's physical or mental pain and feel distress. Our response may be to turn away and even deny what we observe. If we are upset at having such negative emotions stirred up, we may even react with anger toward the person whose own trauma evoked these feelings in us. By contrast, empathizing with someone else's pain may lead us to offer comfort and/or assistance specifically aimed at alleviating the source of the other person's pain. If we help because it is the right thing to do, not because we seek a reward, our behavior is considered altruistic. Sometimes we initially act empathically because we do seek external acknowledgment, but as our sense of moral or ethical behavior matures, positive expressions of empathy become a gratifying end in themselves.

Development

Theoretical perspectives. Taking a viewpoint other than one's own, which is the basis of empathy, is a complex cognitive as well as emotional process. Piaget (1950) called this process "decentering" because it involves shifting from an egocentric view of the world to a position outside oneself. Assuming the perspective of others involves imagining or forming a mental representation of what the world looks or feels like to them, even though one is not directly undergoing that experience or perceiving that emotion oneself. Empathy therefore involves conjecture or speculation. We take both a cognitive and a social risk by making an educated guess about how someone else feels, based upon a projection of our own feelings.

Empathy Development

Empathy involves conjecture or speculation; we take both a cognitive and a social risk by making an educated guess about how someone else feels, based upon a projection of our own feelings. Research shows that children as young as 18 months display empathy through gestures and actions. Family is critical in developing the child's capacity for empathy, and parents, siblings, teachers, and peers all provide important influences on social perspective taking.

Dulce says that she will share her Halloween pumpkin bucket with Iva because Iva does not have one: "She might cry if nobody gives her candy."

For preschoolers who are just beginning to form mental representations of their own experiences, trying to picture what is going on in someone else's head requires yet another leap in their thinking. Developmental psychologists have long debated, therefore, whether young children have the capacity for empathy. Yet there is growing evidence, summarized below, that toddlers and even infants exhibit early signs of empathic behavior. Observations of children's cognitive and social problem-solving during play, and current brain research on developing neural connections, reveal that empathy or its precursors emerge very early in children's development.

What the research says. As early as the 1970s, studies challenged the notion that perspective taking did not appear until age seven, at the beginning of concrete operations (Marvin, Greenberg, & Mossler, 1976). Children as young as three are capable of *perceptual perspective taking* (making inferences about what another person

sees or hears), while four-year-olds can exhibit *conceptual perspective taking* (inferring another's internal or intangible experience such as thoughts, desires, and feelings).

During outside time, another child is upset because her mother has left. Emily says to that child, while patting her shoulder, "That's okay, your mommy will be back at outside time. When I'm sad, I make a picture for my mommy. Want to go make one for your mommy?"

Marvin et al. (1976) concluded that earlier studies used tasks that were too novel or complex to get an accurate reading of preschoolers' empathic abilities. By using simpler and more familiar situations, they could see greater evidence of social perspective taking. For example, the researchers put children aged two-and-a-half to six-and-a-half in a scenario in which one other person was informed of a secret and another was not. In this case, either the parent or the experimenter saw which "secret" toy the child played with while the other one hid his or her eyes. By age four, nearly all the children correctly identified which adult knew the secret toy and which one did not. Although this task might seem simple to an adult, for a preschool child, "it is not so direct" (p. 512). The child must *infer* from noting who did (or did not) hide his or her eyes whether or not that person knew the secret.

More recent research shows that toddlers between 18 and 22 months display empathy as measured by orienting themselves to the sound of distress, visually checking what is happening, showing emotional arousal (such as appropriate facial expressions), and engaging in prosocial activities such as helping, soothing, or sharing (Zahn-Waxler, Radke-Yarrow, Wagner, & Chapman, 1992).

When Kelsey, aged 20 months, sees another child frowning near the water table, she walks over to her and says, "What matter?"

Thus, two-year-olds not only grasp the idea that it is important to help people who are hurt, they can understand that causing hurt is bad and begin to create a rudimentary system of moral behavior (discussed in Chapter 10).

As reviewed in the *Neurons to Neighborhoods* chapter titled "Making Friends and Getting Along with Peers," babies are interested in one another from at least as early as two months of age (National Research Council, 2000b). Young infants get excited by the sight of other babies and, when given the opportunity, stare avidly at one another. In the middle of the first year of life, infants monitor the emotional expressions of significant others and change their behavior accordingly (for example, approaching a smiling caregiver or turning away from one who is frowning). These early signs of "social referencing" are a precursor of the empathy that appears less than a year later in toddlerhood. They have their roots in both genetic factors, such as the temperamental differences we are born with, and environmental factors, especially parenting (Emde, 1998).

Current thinking. These studies, spanning several decades, have sparked early childhood researchers and practitioners to change their ideas about fostering empathy in young children. We know the family is critical in developing the child's capacity for empathy; parents and siblings model empathic behavior and help children become aware of the perspectives of peers and other family members. However, as young children move into group-care settings, their interactions with teachers and peers also become an important influence on social perspective taking. By providing children with concrete experiences that enhance an awareness of the feelings of others, and encouraging children to learn a range of appropriate responses, we can build on the growing cognitive and social skills that underlie empathy.

Teaching Strategies

Adults help young children develop the capacity for empathy by showing empathy themselves. (See Chapter 14, "Preparing Ourselves to Be Role Models," for a discussion of how our own behavior serves as a model for children.) Preschoolers, eager to emulate grown-ups, imitate the caring behaviors they see in their parents and teachers. Since the roots of empathy lie in recognizing how our own emotions are shared by others, helping preschoolers become aware of their feelings also sets the stage for empathic behavior. Additionally, adopting another viewpoint, which is the cognitive basis of empathy, can be encouraged by perspective-taking activities that involve objects and actions as well as people. Finally, creating opportunities for

As she takes her friend's hand, the child at right shows empathy for the boy's feelings as he makes the transition from his mother's care to the classroom environment.

children to understand and help one another helps them learn empathic behaviors and feel the satisfaction of relating to others with compassion. You can use the following strategies to help foster children's growing empathic abilities.

Model caring behavior. Create an empathic classroom by responding to the needs of children who are upset or angry. You can use spoken language, facial expressions, and body language to communicate that you are aware of how others feel and that you accept responsibility for helping them deal with those feelings. Preschoolers may not be aware of what is behind your behavior, so describe what you see and the actions you are taking.

> *A teacher explains to the group of children watching, "I'm giving Taryn the fuzzy monkey to cuddle. She's sad because her grandma is leaving today."*

Individualize the type of comfort you provide, based on your observations of children and your knowledge of what will be effective for them. Some children are soothed by physical contact such as a hug or stroking. Others prefer to have a brief talk about what is bothering them, while in some cases having an adult standing nearby is all that is required. Be sensitive as well to when children just want to have their feelings recognized and instances in which they want help solving the problem at the root of their distress.

At work time in the house area, Amelia is pretending to be a cat and begins to hiss. Shannon, her teacher, asks why she is hissing. Amelia says, "Because the kitty is scared. The problem is there's lots of sounds," and she points to all the other children in the area. Shannon asks Amelia what the kitty can do so she will be less scared. Amelia answers, "Make a 'Do Not Disturb' sign and hang it on the chair." Amelia gets writing materials, writes do *and* not *and asks Shannon to help her spell* disturb. *Then Amelia tapes the sign to a chair. When the other children ask Amelia what her sign says, and she explains it to them, they talk in whispers when they come near her. Amelia, still pretending to be a kitty, doesn't hiss again.*

As children observe the interactions in the classroom, they will follow the examples set by caring adults. In the following scenario, an older toddler demonstrates the capacity for empathy that researchers now recognize:

Devon sees his teacher, Hal, give a teddy bear to Jason, who cries when his father drops him off. Hal holds Jason in his lap until he calms down and is ready to join others in play. The next day, Devon sees Susan crying after her mother leaves. He brings her a cuddly toy and pats her arm. They sit quietly together, then walk to the toy area and begin to work on puzzles.

Acknowledge and label the feelings that children have in common. Although we now recognize that preschoolers are capable of empathy, we also know they are still primarily bound up in their own emotions. We can help young children become aware that others share these feelings. To make this concrete, focus on the situation and point out that others have the same emotions under similar circumstances. Preschoolers can then understand and even anticipate the responses of their peers by recalling their own experiences. For example, a teacher might say something like "Claudia is mad because her dog chewed a hole in her new shoe. Remember how angry Tommy felt the time his brother's puppy peed on his baseball hat?"

In a social problem-solving situation, it is especially important that attempts to help children understand the feelings of others be done in a nonjudgmental way. Imagine, for example, that Joanne is working at the computer and Ian wants a turn. If the teacher says to Joanne, "How would you feel if you had to wait?" it implies Joanne is being unkind, perhaps deliberately. Suppose the teacher instead makes a factual statement such as, "Ian has been waiting a long time for a turn at the computer. You know how it feels to wait when you really want to do something." This not only acknowledges that Joanne knows what it is like to have such feelings, it also credits her capacity to choose a prosocial (empathic) response.

Children are most likely to call up feelings of empathy in response to people they depend upon, such as parents and caregivers. It is not uncommon for the child's own anxiety to trigger an empathic response:

At work time in the writing area, Aubrey asks her teacher to write on a card she is making for her daddy, "I hope you don't get a cold like Mommy and me."

At message board time, Mr. Brian (a teacher) tells the children that Miss Natalie (the other teacher) will be out sick that day. At work time, Nicholas makes Miss Natalie a get-well card. He draws the top half of a body and a heart.

Brian: *You drew her head.*

Nicholas: *And a heart.*

Brian: *What does the heart mean?*

Nicholas: *I made Miss Natalie a heart because I'm so sad and I hope she feels better.*

Children are also more likely to show compassion toward good friends (that is, those with whom they choose to play) than they are to peers with whom they have only casual contact. Preschoolers not only express concern about playmates who are ill or upset, they may also display remorse if they feel responsible for their friend's distress. In such cases, apologies (saying "I'm sorry") can be spontaneous and genuine, because they are not coerced by adults.

At work time in the art area, Shelby uses tape, scissors, paper, and muffin cups to make a card for her friend Abby, who is having surgery that day. Her teacher (pointing to each material) comments, "You used four different things to let your friend in the hospital know you're thinking about her." "I hope she will be okay," says Shelby, "because I know she wants to come back and play with me."

While carrying his paint cup and brush to the sink, Quentin drips some on Daryl's sneaker. "My new shoes!" Daryl cries, sounding upset. "I'm sorry," says Quentin. "I'll wipe it off." He wets a paper towel and wipes the paint off Daryl's shoe. "Now your mommy won't be mad you got your shoe dirty."

When children, such as those in the above anecdotes, express concern about the well-being of others, it is important for teachers to label and acknowledge their observations and actions. For example, Quentin's teacher might say, "You wiped the paint off Daryl's shoe so his mommy wouldn't be angry." This type of validation is more effective in encouraging the internalization of empathic behavior than is praising children for being thoughtful.

Sometimes children explore shared emotions and empathic responses indirectly through role play. They attribute their own and others' feelings to characters, pets, or imaginary creatures, as Amelia did when she pretended the cat was bothered by noise (see p. 38). Stories about animals can help children reflect on these feelings and spark discussion that promotes perspective-taking. Children also display great sensitivity to animals directly, as illustrated by these anecdotes:

When Mrs. Mel, who is reading with a small group, turns to the picture of Buttons McKitty being sad on a rainy day, Chelsea says, "Cats don't like to get wet." "I wonder why that is," Mrs. Mel asks the children. "It tickles their whiskers," says Brady, "and that feels bad. I don't like to be tickled either."

Malika tells her teacher, "I'm worried about Fuzzball (the class guinea pig). I think someone forgot to feed him yesterday." When the teacher asks what makes her think so, Malika answers, "He's just sleeping all morning. He's hungry, tired and hungry." Malika puts food and water

in the guinea pig's dish. "Eat up," she whispers to him, "I got it just for you." She keeps quiet watch over the cage for another 10 minutes until the animal wakes up and eats and drinks. Malika runs to her teacher and says excitedly, "Fuzzball is okay now!"

Children explore shared emotions, such as anxiety about going to the doctor, through collaborative role play.

Although encouraging and expecting children to recognize shared feelings is a valuable teaching strategy, there are times when caution applies. For example, adults should be sensitive to children experiencing stress at home (such as parental separation or divorce, domestic violence, substance abuse, illness, incarceration) that may overwhelm them with negative emotions. Even "positive events" (such as a new sibling, a grandparent's visit, or a vacation that disrupts the routine) can produce anxiety. Young children, like adults, may not be capable of showing empathy to others when their emotional resources are absorbed by coping with their own feelings.

The lesson here is that teachers should not hold unrealistic expectations. Adults should make it clear that antisocial responses to another's distress are not permitted, but children should not be forced to demonstrate prosocial behavior that simply goes through the motions or goes against the children's feelings. For example, a child who is angry at a peer may be told hitting is not allowed, but he should not be urged to give the other child a hug. Empathy should be permitted to emerge naturally as children learn to transfer feelings and shift perspective. Only then will the idea of "doing unto others as you would have others do unto you" make sense.

Create opportunities for children to act with empathy. Like other social and emotional skills, learning to feel empathy takes practice. While emotions are inevitably expressed throughout the day in a classroom full of preschoolers, teachers can also create situations in which children are explicitly encouraged to listen, respond to, and think about the feelings of others. Greeting time offers these kinds of opportunities. For example, with a drawing on the message board and/or in conversation, you can mention who is absent that day. Talking about why someone is not there (is he or she sick?), where that person may be instead (did he or she go to visit someone?), the activities the absent person will miss (today is our special field trip), and how the person will feel upon returning (will he or she be disappointed to have missed the fun?), all encourage children to think about their school day from the viewpoint of someone they know who is having a parallel but different experience.

Here is what transpired in one classroom when a child drew a message about an incident that happened to her at home the previous day:

Kelly draws a full-body figure with a sad expression and a mark on the thigh:

Kelly: *I got a cut right here (points to the mark on the message board).*

Christopher: *You're sad.*

Kelly: *I was working outside and then I got hurt.*

Jonathan: *Where did you get hurt?*

Kelly: *On my thigh.*

Sabrina: *With what?*

Kelly: *An umbrella.*

Bianca: *You were playing with the umbrella?*

Jeremy: *It was a broken one?*

Kelly: *You know the plastic part like bubbles? I was using it to pop them.*

Christopher: *You were trying to pop bubbles and the broken part on the umbrella scratched you?*

Daniel: *Then you fell down?*

Kelly: *I didn't. Just the umbrella did.*

Sabrina: *Was it in the day or in the night?*

Kelly: *It was late, but there was still sun out.*

Daniel: *Does it still hurt?*

Kelly: *No. It hurt when I went to bed, but it was okay when I got up this morning.*

Jonathan: *I'm glad it stopped hurting.*

Bianca: *Me, too!*

The children in this extended conversation are clearly interested in hearing the details of what happened to Kelly and how the umbrella cut her thigh. But they also express curiosity and concern about Kelly's emotional reaction to getting hurt and share her relief that the injury was minor and that she is now feeling okay.

Another strategy for helping preschoolers learn and practice empathy is to encourage them to help one another. For example, a child can hold a cup steady while another child pours; bend to pick up something dropped by a child in a wheelchair; or respond to another child's request for help writing his or her name. By encouraging all children to be helpful, without differentiating either the providers or the recipients by age or ability level, you can help children accept that everyone needs — and can offer — assistance. This even-handed strategy not only supports the development of empathy, it embodies and promotes tolerance as well.

Taking care of plants and animals can also help children appreciate how their actions affect the survival and well-being of others. For example, having live plants or a garden that children tend together makes the effects of their nurturance or neglect immediately apparent. A classroom pet helps children learn the responsibility of providing food, water, attention, and diversion. If keeping a live pet is not feasible, children can still practice loving and caring for the stuffed animals in the classroom. You can engage children in talking about what they imagine the animal is thinking and feeling as they incorporate it into their role-playing scenarios.

Practice perspective-taking in nonsocial situations. As noted above, being able to see things from more than one perspective is a cognitive accomplishment for young children. Developing and exercising this capacity across a wide range of settings can help preschoolers specifically apply this ability to social situations. In the following anecdote, Marcus demonstrates his understanding that, even though members of the class will travel in different vehicles, they will all arrive at the same place. In processing this information at a cognitive level (there are different ways to reach the same destination) Marcus also reassures himself that none of his friends will be left behind.

> *At work time in the art area, Marcus talks with Rachel (a teacher) about how the class will get to the apple orchard on their field trip the next day. He says that some children can ride with his father who has "a big white blue car." Others can go in Rachel's car and some in the preschool van. Rachel comments that the children can get there many different ways. "But all to the same place," says Marcus.*

There are many science and nature activities that can involve children in looking at things from different perspectives. Think of being outside and asking children what they notice about a bush when they are looking straight at it, lying on the ground looking up at it, or standing on the climber gazing down at it. What looks the same (for example, the color) and what new information do they get from each position (for example, the play of shadows, the visibility of the branch structure, whether they see the berries on top or the new growth spreading out on the sides)? Engaging in these kinds of conversations can help children realize there is more than one way to look at things.

> *Lute says, "You're farther," when looking out the opposite end of the binoculars.*
>
> *Juan says to his teacher, Sandor, "I have a mom who sleeps downstairs." They talk about the bedrooms in Juan's house and where each family member sleeps. Juan says he and his brother sleep upstairs in bunk beds and that their grandmother also sleeps upstairs, but at the other end of the hallway. "I can see the picnic table in the yard from my mom's bedroom," says Juan. Sandor asks Juan what he can see out the other windows. Juan says he can see the backyard from his grandmother's room, too, but that he can see his friend*

> *Sammy's house from his own bedroom. "And when I climb on Michael's [his brother's] bunk," he adds, "I can see all the way to the corner!"*

Viewing things from different perspectives, such as looking up from the floor to the ceiling with a flashlight, can help children learn to see things from other people's viewpoints, too.

Mathematics activities in which young children gather data can highlight differences of opinion or preferences. For example, you can ask children to name their favorite ingredient in trail mix from among four or five choices and tabulate the results using a simple chart or graph. Suppose it becomes apparent that all children like raisins and chocolate chips, only three like pretzels, just one is a fan of sesame sticks, and no one chooses almonds. Based on these findings, children can share ideas about the relative proportion of ingredients to include the next time the class has trail mix at snack. Not only are they learning important mathematical principles during this investigation but, because they are developing a plan to accommodate a range of likes and dislikes, the children are simultaneously solving a social problem with empathic understanding.

Reading presents many opportunities to explore perspective taking. Storybooks for preschoolers often depict situations in which a central character has to solve a problem. As you read the story, ask children what different characters in the book are thinking and feeling and what they might see or hear from various locations or roles. Of course, stories that present social problems can provide direct experience with understanding multiple points of view. You can ask children how they think the characters in the book feel about the situation, what their different goals or desires might be, and how they might each approach solving the problem.

> *Looking at a book of farm animals, Ben says, "These are inside the barn and those are outside. The other ones want to get inside." When his teacher asks how they could get inside, Lily pipes up, "They can't because the outside ones are wild." Ben says, "The farmer could adopt them." Lily thinks this over and decides, "Then they (pointing to the inside animals) could have brothers and sisters."*

Books are especially useful in talking about difficult feelings such as jealousy, envy, embarrassment, or shame. Topics that may be hard for children to discuss from their own perspective — because the children are too emotionally invested or threatened — may be easier to approach when considered in the light of someone else's situation.

Movement activities in which children take turns being the leader can also help preschoolers consider other perspectives. If they want classmates to imitate their actions, they have to provide verbal and/or gestural directions that someone standing in a different position — facing, behind, or next to them — can understand and follow. Teachers should encourage children to describe their movements using words, rather than just demonstrating what to do, so they will have to put themselves in the place of the person receiving instructions. For example, you might say, "I'm going to close my eyes. Now tell me how to do exactly what you are doing." As the child observes whether you are (or are not) performing the movement correctly, he or she can modify the instructions to better communicate with you. Activities like this encourage children to use position and direction terms that someone else, situated in a different location, can apply in solving a movement problem.

> *At large-group time, when it is her turn to lead, Honey goes behind the screen to give directions. She tells the group two places to pat. "First you pat your head with both hands," she says, "Then pat your knee with one hand." When the music stops, Honey runs back out to the circle. "Did they do it?" she asks her teacher. The teacher replies, "Your directions were very clear. Everyone knew exactly what to do!"*

Art is another content area that offers many opportunities for young children to gain experience with perspective taking. For example, as children build structures with three-dimensional materials, you can encourage them to view their work from many angles. Taking photographs from different perspectives helps to make these viewpoints concrete. Another, related, strategy is to encourage children to draw or paint the same thing from different angles. You might ask, "How would it look if you were standing over by the bookcase? Can you draw what you would see from there?"

Activities that promote art appreciation are also excellent venues for developing perspective-taking skills. As you look at artwork with children, ask them to consider why some artists like to paint or sculpt on a grand scale while others prefer to work small. Ask them what they think the artist wanted us to see or feel when we looked at a particular color or image. The resulting discussions not only encourage children to consider the artwork from the perspective of the maker and the viewer, they can also tap into the feelings that art evokes, further serving as a foundation for developing interpersonal (social) understanding.

> *At small-group time, while using foam blocks and small plastic people, Sean describes how to get out of the jail he made. "You climb up here and slide down there. Then you scoot over to the other side, jump up and slide down the ramp so it bounces you over to here. Then you go through the hole and you're escaped."*

> *Monique paints a white streak in the sky and calls it a "jet stream." She tells her teacher, "I see jets. They fly over my house. They fly upside down and sideways. The pilots can't see me when*

Feeling Empathy: Teaching Strategies

Model caring behavior.

- Respond to the needs of children who are upset or angry, using spoken language, facial expressions, and body language.
- Individualize the type of comfort you provide, based on your observations and knowledge of children.

Acknowledge and label the feelings that children have in common.

- Focus on particular situations and point out that others have the same emotions under similar circumstances.
- In social problem-solving situations, help children understand the feelings of others in a nonjudgmental way.
- When children express concern about the well-being of others, label and acknowledge the children's observations and actions.
- While encouraging children to recognize shared feelings, be sensitive to children experiencing stress at home that may overwhelm them with negative emotions and make it difficult to act in prosocial ways. Be realistic in your expectations.
- While making it clear that antisocial responses to another's distress is not permitted, do not force prosocial behavior.

Create opportunities for children to act with empathy.

- At greeting time, discuss who may be absent and talk about what feelings that person may have about missing the day's activities.
- Encourage children to help one another.
- Encourage children to take care of plants and animals.

Practice perspective-taking in nonsocial situations.

- Help children practice taking different perspectives across a wide range of settings.
- Use art, science and nature, mathematics, reading, movement, and other types of activities to help children experience different viewpoints.

---

they're upside down." Her teacher asks what the upside-down pilots do see. Monique replies, "I think they see God up there."

In Conclusion

Empathy — the capacity to feel what another person feels and to act with their feelings in mind — is an emotional process with important social implications. Being able to put ourselves in someone else's place underlies many other social skills and values, such as appreciating diversity, negotiating interpersonal conflicts, and respecting the rights of everyone in a democracy. Our thinking about the development of empathy in young children is changing as exciting findings emerge from research and help to guide our practice. We do not want to overestimate how much preschoolers, who are still essentially egocentric, can understand and be responsive to in the emotional lives of others. On the other hand, we do not want to miss opportunities to help children develop this most human of capacities. To feel empathy, and to act on those feelings to improve the lot of others, makes svomeone a true "mensch." Promoting empathy in young children surely helps them become the "good" and caring individuals we want in our world.

Developing a Sense of Competence

At work time, while flattening a piece of play dough, Bianca shares her early morning experience:

Bianca: *I cried this morning.*

Sabrina: *Why?*

Bianca: *Because I didn't get a Pop-Tart.*

Jeremy: *Did you run out?*

Bianca: *No, I wouldn't get dressed.*

Teacher: *You took a long time getting dressed, so you didn't have time for a Pop-Tart?*

Bianca: *Yeah, I had to have a granola bar in the car. I wanted the Pop-Tart.*

The next day, at snacktime, Bianca talks to her teacher about what she was doing:

Bianca: *I'm only taking two crackers, because I had two Pop-Tarts for breakfast!*

Teacher: *You're not very hungry because you ate those Pop-Tarts.*

Bianca: *Yeah, I got dressed fast so I could pick that for breakfast.*

Definition

Feeling competent, also called self-efficacy, is "the belief that one can successfully accomplish what one sets out to do" (Kagan et al., 1995, p. 16). Albert Bandura, a pioneer in early social learning theory and research, established that a sense of personal competence is central to children's willingness to undertake learning at home and school (1977). Children who feel competent have the self-confidence to handle tasks and situations (such as getting dressed promptly in the above anecdote) with an expectation of success. To them, a challenge is something to be approached rather than avoided. Even after a setback, they quickly recover their sense of competence and attribute failure to a lack of knowledge or skill, which they believe they can acquire. "Such an efficacious outlook fosters intrinsic interest and deep engrossment in activities" (Bandura, 1994, p. 71).

A Sense of Competence

Children who feel *a sense of competence* (also described as feelings of self-efficacy), have the self-confidence to handle tasks and situations with an expectation of success. This involves acknowledging their limitations without a feeling of failure or any loss of self-esteem. They assume they can acquire the knowledge or skills needed to improve, and are thus willing to take on new challenges.

A sense of competence is a phrase often used interchangeably, if erroneously, with *self-esteem*. Although the research is inconclusive, it is widely believed that high self-esteem is related to success in school. Educators therefore regard high self-esteem, and adult steps to reinforce it, as a good thing. However, as early childhood specialist Harriet Egertson (2006) notes, this is a misleading assumption. Psychologists caution that there is a difference between *high self-esteem* and *healthy self-esteem* (Baumeister, Campbell, Kreuger, & Vohs, 2004).

Healthy self-esteem arises from a realistic sense of one's competence. Children develop healthy self-esteem when adults show them respect and support their attempts to try new things. Moreover, children with healthy self-esteem find satisfaction in their own efforts without the constant need for adult approval or praise.

> *Upon entering the classroom, Rosy tells her teacher, "This is my new sweatshirt. I know how to zip now!" Throughout work time, and again at outside time, she practices zipping and unzipping her sweatshirt.*

> *At work time in the toy area, as Brendan turns puzzle pieces to make them fit, he says to himself, "Me figure this out."*

Children with a healthy sense of themselves also acknowledge their limitations without a feeling of failure or any loss of self-esteem:

> *At outside time, Trevor jumps from the middle of the slide and says, "I jumped, I really jumped. I can do it from low and middle. I can't do it from high."*

> *At work time, Devon fills a cloth bag with blocks and tries to pick it up. He squats down and tries again. When the bag does not budge, he stands up and shrugs, then walks over to his teacher. "Can you help?" he asks. "It's just way too heavy for me."*

Healthy self-esteem can be high, but high self-esteem is not always healthy. Early childhood educator Lilian Katz warns that children with high self-esteem can also be self-absorbed and narcissistic, the antithesis of our goals for their social-emotional competence (1993). In fact, when self-esteem becomes inflated and is not tied to a comfortable and realistic self-assessment, it is not only unhealthy but can lead to poor outcomes, including taking unreasonable risks. Research shows, for example, that children who lead others into negative or dangerous behavior often have exaggeratedly high self-esteem (Baumeister, Bushman, & Campbell, 2000).

Feelings of competence — a sense of efficacy based on a confident but realistic view of one's abilities — thus arise from a healthy self-esteem. Children who feel competent are open to new challenges and tasks, are willing to try something without fear of failure, and are able to evaluate and take pride in their accomplishments without craving praise from adults. This does not mean adults are unimportant in the development of a child's sense of competence. Rather, it is by encouraging children's initiative, persistence, and ability to reflect on their efforts that teachers help them develop a realistic and healthy attitude toward their own competence.

Development

Differentiating the self from others. Newborns come without any sense of self. In their perception, they are "continuous" with the people, objects, and situations around them. But as they repeatedly become aware that events occur following their actions, they learn they are capable of producing effects on their environment. Infants who experience success in controlling events develop a sense of personal efficacy. Responsive adults are essential for this development to occur. If the infant's actions do not elicit a response, or worse, evoke a negative reaction, the child will not think of him or herself as a being whose behavior is capable of having a positive effect on the world (Meece, 1997).

Expanding capabilities. Young children broaden their sense of competence as their capabilities expand. At first they develop, test, and appraise their physical abilities; for example, bringing their hand to their mouth. As they mature, they try out their social skills (engaging a caregiver in a game of peek-a-boo), linguistic skills (asking for and receiving "more juice"), and cognitive capacity for understanding and managing the situations they encounter every day (retrieving a ball that has rolled behind the chair). Early exploratory and play activities, which occupy most of the very young child's waking hours, provide opportunities for the child to enlarge his or her repertoire of basic skills. The richer the materials and activities in this play environment, and the greater the freedom to explore, the more accelerated will be the child's intellectual development and growing sense of self-efficacy (Bandura, 1997; Meece, 1997).

A Sense of Competence: Development

Young children broaden their sense of competence as their capabilities expand. Exploratory and play activities provide opportunities for them to enlarge their repertoire of basic skills and their self-assessment of what they can do. Primary catalysts for children's development of social and cognitive competence are the home and family (including siblings), peers, and school.

The importance of early caregivers. Successful experiences in the exercise of personal control are thus central to the development of social and cognitive competence and the feelings of self-efficacy that accompany them. In a child's earliest years, these experiences are centered in the home and family and often in early care and education settings as well. Responsive parents and teachers set up reciprocal interactions through which children test and see the results of their behavior. The development of language, which takes place through these interchanges, provides children with the symbolic means to reflect on their experiences and the feedback others give them about their capabilities. Social interchanges thus expand children's self-knowledge about what they can and cannot do.

The role of peers. By toddlerhood, peers become increasingly important in the development of self-efficacy. It is in the context of peer relations that social comparison comes strongly into play. At first, the closest comparative age-mates are siblings, and one's birth order can affect one's sense of competence. That is, younger children typically compare themselves unfavorably with their more capable older siblings. Parents can mediate by minimizing comparisons and ensuring younger children experience success in activities that interest and motivate them.

In preschool, peers outside the family increasingly influence a child's sense of competence. As preschoolers play alongside one another, they inevitably compare what they know and what they can do to what other children are doing:

> *At work time in the toy area, Chelsea puts together a puzzle, points to another child, and says, "I did it faster than her."*

Although adults can help neutralize such comparisons (for example, by focusing on the fact that Chelsea feels good about completing the puzzle quickly, rather than commenting on her speed relative to others), it is important to remember that peers serve many other valuable functions in the development of a child's sense of efficacy (Bandura, 1994). A vast amount of social learning takes place with peers. They provide models of competence, and they judge and provide feedback to verify one's self-perceptions. Because children increasingly depend on peers to form their self-concepts, they tend to choose friends and playmates who share similar interests and values (Schunk & Pajares, 2001). Selecting peers on this basis will promote self-efficacy in some areas but may leave other areas of potential underdeveloped. Moreover, if children choose peers with similar interests but higher levels of skill, their own sense of self-efficacy may be undermined.

Negative or disrupted peer relationships (for example, being rejected by friends or ridiculed by classmates) can have other adverse effects on a child's developing feelings of competence (Schunk & Hanson, 1985). Feedback from peers that one is doing a poor job is often taken to heart. This connection can also work in reverse. That is, children with feelings of low self-worth may anticipate social rejection and withdraw. Conversely, an inflated sense of self-worth can also be alienating to other children. Although avoidance of "egotistical" classmates assumes prominence in early adolescence, even young children may not want to associate with peers whose high opinion of themselves makes them too bossy or directive in play scenarios. Aggressive children who get what they want by bullying others may also perceive themselves as highly efficacious.

The role of school. During late elementary school and beyond, the schools also take on a primary role in shaping a child's emerging sense of competence in both academic and social realms. School is where children

When adults support and value children's efforts, children come to see themselves as competent and capable learners.

acquire the knowledge and problem-solving skills necessary to function competently in the larger society. Their abilities are constantly being tested and evaluated, often in comparison with peers or some other external standard of success. As a result, students develop a sense of their intellectual efficacy. With today's pressure to master specific subjects at ever-younger ages, even preschoolers may start to think of themselves in terms of their academic competence. Consider this self-congratulatory claim by a four-year-old:

> *At work time, John says, "I'm really smart. I can write all the letters in my name."*

Schools contribute to the positive or negative development of a child's self-perception in two ways. First, educational settings provide opportunities for students to experience success or failure. The more classrooms and schools are set up to enable children to succeed (e.g., by letting children pursue topics of interest to them), the more the children come to see themselves as competent. Second, adults can either value each child's efforts or compare children to one another. In the former instance, children see themselves as learners on a par with their peers. In the latter (comparative) case, they will almost inevitably be rated "inferior" to others on one or more academic, social, or athletic dimensions. Unfavorable comparisons, or the absence of acknowledgment for those who seek recognition of their efforts, can cause students

to simply stop trying. The less they are motivated to do, the less opportunity they have to develop relevant skills, and feelings of incompetence become self-reinforcing. Research shows that cooperative learning situations, rather than individualistic or highly competitive ones, tend to promote more positive self-evaluations of capability and higher academic attainment (Bandura, 1994).

In sum, having an optimistic sense of one's own abilities is vital for a person's well-being. For children to develop healthy feelings of competence, they need to be supported by parents and siblings at home and by teachers and peers at school. Self-confidence lets them undertake challenges with the expectation of success and, if they face setbacks, to hold the belief that they can acquire the knowledge and skills to do better.

> *Casey sees a ball in the fenced area by the air conditioner unit. He stands on tiptoe and leans over the fence to get it out but drops it. He tries and drops it again. Casey walks away for a few minutes, then comes back and tries once more. This time he stays on tiptoe long enough to get the ball over the fence. He turns to his teacher and says, "I finally got it," and wipes his forehead.*

On balance, it is therefore best for children to think well of themselves, even if their self-assessment sometimes outstrips their abilities. In fact, researchers have shown that positive emotions and feelings of self-efficacy are found even in low-performing young children, who tend to overestimate their abilities (Stipek & Tannatt, 1984). Such unrealistically positive self-esteem shields them as the realities of the external world are integrated into their emerging self-concept (Kagan et al., 1995). Writer and comedian Steve Martin captures the idea that we sometimes benefit by thinking too highly of ourselves:

> *Through the years, I have learned that there is no harm in charging oneself up with delusions between moments of valid inspiration* (Martin, 2007, p. 52).

Compared with students who doubt their capabilities, those who feel efficacious participate more readily in school, work harder, persist at tasks longer, and achieve at a higher level (Schunk & Pajares, 2001). Another protective factor conferred by high levels of self-efficacy is that children do not give up when they encounter difficulties. They continue to engage with the world of learning, which in the end is the only hope for them to acquire the competencies that can lead to a more realistic yet positive self-evaluation.

Finally, when dealing with young children, it is important that adults judge "success" according to what the children themselves set out to accomplish, not by applying grown-up standards. For example, a child who feels competent to clean up after a spill may not wipe up as thoroughly as the custodian will do at the end of the day, but he or she can feel good about recognizing and accepting responsibility for the problem ("I spilled") and taking steps to resolve it. A competent response for a toddler may be taking a few swipes with a paper towel and throwing the towel in the trash. For a preschooler, it may include washing the tabletop with a sponge and rinsing the sponge as well. In the teaching strategies described in the remainder of this chapter, promoting the healthy development of a sense of competence relies on acknowledging, supporting, and extending each child's developmental capacities.

Teaching Strategies

Helping young children develop a healthy belief in their own intellectual and social competence is perhaps the single most important function of early childhood teachers. Children's sense of self-efficacy when they enter school determines their motivation to engage in learning and undertake challenging tasks. The strategies listed below can help establish a good early foundation for later social adjustment and academic performance.

Create a classroom space and schedule that promotes children's sense of efficacy and control. When the classroom areas and supplies are arranged and labeled so children can find, use, and return materials on their own, they gain confidence in their ability to carry out their intentions and achieve their goals. Establishing a consistent daily routine is also essential to giving children a sense of control over what happens in their environment. They can anticipate the order and content of the day's events,

feel good about their ability to predict what will happen, and participate appropriately. Clear expectations for behavior, in terms of how materials are handled and what to do during each segment of the day, also contribute to a young child's self-efficacy. Early childhood educator Lilian Katz (1993) suggests that children need an optimum mixture of acceptance, limits, and expectations about their behavior and level of effort to be able to build healthy self-esteem. An environment in which the space and time are organized, and choices provide flexibility within clear guidelines, helps young children regulate their own behavior, develop their independence, and gain self-confidence.

Encourage self-help skills in ways consistent with children's abilities and developmental levels. Young children need time to do things on their own, such as getting dressed, cleaning up spills, and sharing their ideas. It is therefore important to resist the temptation to perform tasks faster or better than children do, or to dictate how chores should be performed. Giving children ample time to carry out self-help skills and share their ideas for how best to accomplish them instills a sense of "I can do it myself!"

Allowing children to carry out tasks in their own way and at their own pace develops self-help skills and a sense of "I can do it myself!"

Accept a level of performance that is consistent with each child's capacity. Do not expect tasks to be executed in compliance with adult standards. Improvement will come with maturation and practice, but children who have been criticized or otherwise discouraged may no longer want to practice. Remember that the goal is not

Promoting Individual Feelings of Competence During Group Times

Children carrying out their own ideas are likely to feel a sense of competence. But we also want them to feel good about their abilities in situations when someone else plays a significant role in determining the activity. To develop feelings of competence during adult-led group times, teachers should consider children's interests, developmental levels, and degree of involvement. Here are some specific suggestions:

Think about what is interesting to your group of children. In many centers, group times are planned around a theme chosen by adults — such as "spring" or "zoo animals." But this theme may not be of interest to the children. We recommend instead that ideas for group times come from the children. For example, during home visits, the teachers at the High-Scope Demonstration Preschool learned that Scott, a four-year-old, was interested in building with wood and that parents of several other children did woodworking as a hobby. The teachers decided to develop a small-group time in which children worked with wood scraps and glue. After the wood scraps were introduced at small-group time, woodworking became a favorite activity of many children at work time (free play) over the next few weeks. During these times, children extended the range of materials they used along with the wood, sometimes using masking tape to connect wood pieces together and often painting their wooden creations. "The ideas these children came up with were incredible," commented one teacher.

Consider children's developmental levels when planning group activities. Activities that are too difficult for children often create management problems. Therefore, avoid games and activities with complicated rules. Some games are easily simplified. Most preschoolers can't distinguish left and right, but you can play "hokey pokey" by singing "Put your foot in, … put your foot out." Also, give children a chance to lead the activity. ("Tyrone, what body part should we put in next?")

A related issue is to **share control of group time by giving choices throughout the activity**. Although adults plan group activities, this doesn't mean that they dictate what happens during them. Adults provide a general context — a song, story, fingerplay, movement game, or a selection of materials to work with — but it is the children themselves who determine exactly how the activity will unfold. For example, an adult may set out collage materials but children decide what to create with them. As the children work, adults move around the group and talk with them individually to support and expand their efforts.

Once an activity is underway, **tune in to the involvement level of the children**. Group times are usually scheduled for 15 to 20 minutes; but be open to making them longer or shorter, depending on how children respond. To allow extra time for children who are very involved, schedule

> **Promoting Feelings of Competence
> (cont.)**
>
> something afterwards that doesn't require
> participation by the entire group — for
> example, large group or outside time — that
> children can join when they are ready. By
> the same token, if children grow bored or
> restless, cut the activity short and move on
> to the next part of your daily routine. Above
> all, if a group activity has not gone well, ask
> yourself why. Were there enough materials?
> Was the activity of interest to children? Were
> all the ingredients of active learning (materi-
> als, manipulation, choice, child language
> and thought, and adult scaffolding) present?
>
> — From *"Group Times: What Makes Them
> Work?"* (Perrett, 1996, pp. 71–76)

perfection but, rather, that children believe in their ability to take care of their own needs. It is also important that children not be limited in the amount they practice a task. Encourage them to repeat and rehearse their skills as often as they want, to achieve mastery of something that motivates them. Do not rush them or insist they move on to something else. Acknowledge how hard they are trying, and recognize each step along the road to competence in self-care.

Scaffold learning by introducing the next level of challenge when children are ready to move on. For children who lack the self-confidence to attempt the next level of performance, or who may wish to advance but are unsure how, you can provide examples and encouragement. One strategy is to coach or model ways to make everyday tasks easier or more efficient. Rather than giving explicit instructions — which can imply "I am better than you!" — offer indirect suggestions. For example, you might say, "Whenever I have trouble putting on my shoes, I try to loosen the laces first." Or give hints that help children discover solutions on their own.

At lunch, Joey tries unsuccessfully to open his graham crackers. He frowns and sits looking at the package.

Teacher: *It's hard to open.*

Joey: *(Nods) And I'm hungry!*

Teacher: *Show me what you did to get the box opened.*

Joey: *(Tries to lift the corner of the boxtop)*

Teacher: *I wonder if there's something on the side that would be easier to open.*

Joey: *(Looks at various places on the box and then sees the perforated finger hole) Here?*

Teacher: *Try poking your finger in there and see what happens.*

Joey: *(After two tries, pokes his finger in and pulls back the top) Whew! I was afraid I'd starve to death!*

It is also important to challenge children's thinking in ways that permit new insights and allow the children to adjust their conceptual understanding. If a child draws an erroneous conclusion or has trouble performing a task, help him or her consider another perspective. The more children solve problems on their own, the greater the resulting sense of self-efficacy. This process is especially important for children who are easily discouraged.

At work time in the block area, Austin tries several times to stack the cardboard blocks. They keep falling down. He crosses his arms over his chest and says, "I can't do it!" The following dialogue ensues when his teacher asks what the problem is.

Austin: *My tower won't stay up.*

Teacher: *Did you get any of them to stack?*

Austin: *Up to here. (Stacks three blocks, all the same size) But when I do this one on (he puts a larger one on top), they all fall down.*

Teacher: *(Aligns the first three blocks and puts the fourth block next to them) I see something different about that one. (Points to last block)*

Austin: *It's bigger. (Gets a fourth block the same size as the three smaller ones and successfully stacks them) Hey look!*

Teacher: *When you made the top one the same size as the others, you got it to stay up.*

A few days later, as Austin is building with the blocks alongside Jill, the teacher joins them.

Teacher: *Austin's tower has blocks that are all the same, but some of Jill's blocks are different.*

Austin: *(Looks at Jill's tower) Those (points to the two on the bottom) are bigger.*

Teacher: *I wonder how you could build a tower with different size blocks.*

Austin: *(Tries to add a bigger block on top of his tower; it falls down and he looks again at Jill's tower) I know! The big one goes on the bottom. (Stacks one big block and two small ones) There. I did it!*

Support children's ideas and initiatives. Encourage children to make plans and choices during work time (this part of the daily routine is called choice time or free play in some programs) and other *individual activities.* Provide opportunities for children to decide where they will play, what materials they will use and how they will use them, whether they will play on their own or with others (and if with others, who), and how long they will engage in their chosen activity.

> *At work time in the block area, Lute says, "I'm playing fire out." His teacher asks him how fire out is played. Lute explains, "You have to put the fire out at the hotel." He lifts the empty Tide container and says it has chemicals in it to put the fire out. "Can you show me how it works?" his teacher asks. Lute puts a length of plastic tubing in the box and makes "whooshing" sounds as he "sprays" chemicals on the hotel. "You put the fire out!" says his teacher. "It might start again," says Lute, and he keeps guard over the hotel.*

It is equally important for children to make choices and use materials in their own way during *group activities* (see pp. 50–51). When you welcome children's contributions to adult-initiated activities, you communicate that children's ideas are also valid. Encouraging children to share their ideas with peers sends the additional message that their ideas are good or interesting enough that others might want to try them. Further, referring one child to another puts the child in the role of teacher as well as learner.

Of course, all these strategies depend on children being engaged with the materials and activities that adults give them to work with. Initiative (and the feelings of efficacy that elicit it and result from it) flourishes when children are curious about themselves and their surroundings and have opportunities to investigate topics that capture their interest (Katz, 1993).

Acknowledge children's efforts and accomplishments. It is important for adults to show they are aware of children's efforts and what they are able to achieve. Reflect their self-pride, but don't be overly effusive. If you are interested in, but not "surprised" or unduly impressed by, children's accomplishments, you convey the message that you expect them to succeed.

At the same time you acknowledge children's efforts, be careful not to confuse praise with encouragement. Praise can make children depend on the judgment of others rather than developing and applying criteria for evaluating their work independently (Katz, 1993; Kohn, 1993/1999). By contrast, encouragement helps children look at the knowledge and skills they are gaining with positive self-regard. It is important to acknowledge children's own pleasure in their work instead of promoting the idea that their accomplishments are directed toward pleasing adults.

> *At work time in the book area, Ben walks up to Shannon (the teacher) and says, "Look." He finds the firefighter puzzle Shannon brought in after the class field trip to the fire station. After a few minutes, Ben comes back and says "Ta-da!" as he shows her the completed puzzle. Shannon says, "You look proud and excited that you put the puzzle together." Ben smiles and does the puzzle again.*

To encourage rather than praise young children, you can use the following strategies:

- *Watch and listen.* Paying attention to what children do and say lets them know they are engaged in meaningful and instructive pursuits. While conversing with children is essential to their language development, do not overlook the fact that sometimes being quiet — paying attention with our eyes and ears — is also an effective way to support early learning.

    During outside time, Christopher runs and dribbles the big red ball, saying, "Look, Mrs. Freire. When the grass is right here, I can go away." She watches as Christopher shows her how he moves the ball away from the edge and stays on the path with a continuous dribble.

- *Imitate their actions and repeat their words.* This shows you regard what they do as evidence of their competence and that you value their ideas enough to try them yourself.

    Jacey zips her coat without any help and says, "Teacher, look, I a big girl!" Her teacher replies, "You're a big girl because you zipped your coat all by yourself."

- *Comment on what they are doing.* Comments indicate you are observing children's actions with interest and are taking the time to reflect on what children are doing and learning. Commenting also serves as a model for children to engage in self-reflection, helping to develop this important aspect of their thought processes.

    Ashley pumps on a swing and states, "I'm making it go high by myself." Her teacher wonders how she makes the swing move. Ashley says, "My legs go up and down and I pull my body back and up."

- *Show (display) children's work to others, including peers and parents.* Displaying the work of all the children, without regard to adult standards of "quality," makes everyone feel equally valuable and avoids a situation in which children compare themselves (un)favorably with those whose work is (or is not) displayed. To involve parents in supporting their children's emerging sense of competence, send work home, share it at conferences and informally, and explain to parents what it reveals about their young child's learning.

At the parent-teacher conference, Simon's teacher shows his mother a fingerpainting he did the day before. "It looks muddy and there's a hole in the middle," Simon's mother comments. "Simon wanted to blend all the colors," explains his teacher, "and he worked on it so long that he rubbed a hole in the paper." His mother says with pride, "He really does stick with things when he's interested in them!"

Provide opportunities for children to be leaders. Being the leader helps a child see him- or herself as a capable person whose ideas are worth setting forward as an example for others. There are many opportunities throughout the day to acknowledge children's leadership capacities. For example, ask children to suggest movements at large-group time or how to transition from one activity to another. Referring children to their peers for help or ideas, as when Austin's teacher suggested he see how Jill built her tower (see pp. 51–52), benefits not only the individuals involved but sends a general message to the class that young children have valuable lessons to share.

Inviting children to suggest movements during an activity at large-group time gives them a chance to act as leaders and sends a message that their contributions are valued.

Children should not be forced or required to lead, but everyone who wants to lead should have the opportunity to do so. Be respectful of shy or reticent children who do not want to assume a leadership role. They may be more willing to lead if the opportunity is presented as a choice rather than a requirement. If such children do choose to share with the group, you may need to repeat or rephrase their ideas to make sure the ideas are heard

Developing a Sense of Competence: Teaching Strategies

Create a classroom space and schedule that promotes children's sense of efficacy and control.

- Arrange and label supplies so children can find, use, and return materials on their own.

- Establish a consistent daily routine.

- Make clear your expectations for behavior, in terms of how materials are handled and what to do during each segment of the day, providing flexibility within clear guidelines.

Encourage self-help skills in ways consistent with children's abilities and developmental levels.

- Avoid doing things for children simply because you can do them faster or better than they do; avoid dictating how chores should be performed.

- Give children plenty of time to carry out self-help skills, and don't limit children in the amount they can practice a task.

- Share ideas with children about how to best accomplish self-help skills, using yourself as an example or giving hints rather than explicit instructions.

Scaffold learning by introducing the next level of challenge when children are ready to move on.

- Provide examples and encouragement for children who lack the self-confidence to attempt the next level of performance, for example, by coaching or modeling.

- Challenge children's thinking in ways that permit new insights and allow the children to adjust their conceptual understanding.

Support children's ideas and initiatives.

- Encourage children to make plans and choices during work time and other individual activities.

- Encourage children to make choices and use materials in their own way during group activities.

  ○ In choosing an activity, think about what is interesting to your group of children.

  ○ Take children's developmental levels into account when planning group activities.

  ○ Share control of group time by giving choices throughout the activity.

  ○ Once an activity is underway, determine its length by tuning in to the involvement level of the children.

- Welcome children's contributions to adult-initiated activities.

- Encourage children to share their ideas with peers.

Acknowledge children's efforts and accomplishments.

- Show you are aware of children's efforts and what they are able to achieve. Reflect their self-pride, but don't be overly effusive. Convey the message that you expect them to succeed.

Teaching Strategies *(cont.)*

- Encourage rather than praise children, and acknowledge children's own pleasure in their work.

  - Pay attention to what children do and say.

  - Imitate children's actions and repeat their words.

  - Comment on what children are doing.

  - Show (display) children's work to others, including peers and parents.

Provide opportunities for children to be leaders.

- Ask children to suggest movements at large-group time or how to transition from one activity to another.

- Refer children to their peers for help or ideas.

- Do not force or require children to lead, but make sure that everyone who wants to lead has the opportunity to do so.

- Be respectful of shy or reticent children who do not want to assume a leadership role.

and are clear to the other children. Encouraging young children to act as leaders allows them to make meaningful contributions to the group and see themselves as socially competent individuals.

> *As he dances to the music at large-group time, Jabiari says, "I can jump high. See how high I am jumping!" Later, as he claps his hands to the beat, Jabiari says, "I can clap my hands!" His teacher says, "I wonder if we can all clap our hands," and Jabiari smiles as the others take up his action.*

In Conclusion

"Self-efficacy beliefs determine how people feel, think, motivate themselves, and behave … A strong sense of efficacy enhances human accomplishment and personal well-being" (Bandura, 1994, p. 71). Helping young children develop a positive self-appraisal is a vital factor in their ability to see themselves as competent social-emotional, intellectual, physical, and creative individuals. If they see the world as beyond their control and if they feel powerless to achieve meaningful goals, children will not engage with the wide range of people, ideas, and opportunities around them. If, on the other hand, they possess a healthy sense of competence, young children will welcome challenges, be less vulnerable to setbacks, and explore life with optimism and enthusiasm.

Recognizing and Labeling Emotions

At small-group time, while coloring and listening to a piece of music, Lily says, "It's sad when no one plays with me." Francine (the teacher) says, "This song makes you feel sad and makes you think of when kids don't want to play with you?" Lily nods her head yes and says while moving her body, "I'm just showing you my sad moves so you will understand." When listening to another song and drawing with a crayon in each hand, Lily says to Francine, "This is my happy look, like going to the museum or stuff like that."

Definition

Emotional awareness is understanding that one has feelings as distinct from thoughts; being able to identify and name those feelings; and recognizing that others have feelings that may be the same as or different from one's own. Developmental psychologist Susanne Denham (2006) explains that emotional competence has three main components, and being able to recognize and label emotions plays a direct or prior role in each:

- *Emotion expression* is the experience and display of emotional states. To explain its importance in early development, psychologists often take a functional view. That is, they ask, "What does the expression of an emotion do or accomplish for the child?" Emotions, when properly understood and expressed, can facilitate the child's attainment of goals, both social and cognitive.

- *Emotion regulation* is the ability to identify and control one's emotions. The first step in self-regulation is labeling emotions with greater specificity and clarity. For example, feeling "bad" can mean feeling angry, sad,

bored, and so on. Without knowing which emotion one is feeling, one cannot take steps to deal with it.

- *Emotion knowledge* is understanding how emotions affect individual behavior and social relationships. School is hard for young children because peers, unlike adults, are not as adept at regulating emotions. So, opportunities for conflict and misunderstanding multiply when children move from home to school. As emotion knowledge increases, children gain control over the situations they create and respond to.

> ### Emotional Awareness
>
> *Emotional awareness* is understanding that one has feelings as distinct from thoughts; being able to identify and name those feelings; and recognizing that others have feelings that may be the same as or different from one's own.

Young children are gaining knowledge and skills in all three areas of emotional competence. They learn to send and receive emotional messages, use emotional knowledge and self-regulation to negotiate interpersonal exchanges and form relationships, and maintain positive emotional states that make them open to learning about their world. Emotionally competent young children "experience and begin to express a broad variety of emotions, without incapacitating intensity or duration; understand their own and others' emotions; and deal with and regulate their emotions — whenever emotional experience is 'too much' or 'too little' for themselves, or when its expression is 'too much' or 'too little' to fit with others' expectations" (Denham, 2006, p. 86).

Development

Influences on development. Emotional development is influenced by many factors, which accounts for its complexity and variability, even in infants. According to professors Cybele Raver, Pamela Garner, and Radiah Smith-Donald (2007), research on innate *temperamental differences* shows that by the time young children enter school, they already have stable bio-behavioral profiles of emotional reactivity and regulation. Some are more vulnerable to negative emotions (anxiety, anger, inhibition) while others are more positive (sociable, adventurous, drawn to novelty).

Cognition (perception and knowledge) also regulates emotion, and emotion may in turn regulate cognition. For example, high levels of negative arousal make it difficult for a child to encode and retrieve information, while positive emotions can facilitate learning. Children who feel positively about school stay more engaged, persist in tasks, and perform better than those with negative emotional states (Raver et al., 2007).

Language development also contributes to emotional competence by helping children identify and label their feelings. Further, because teachers regularly rely on emotion-based language to create positive school environments and democratic classrooms, children who lack the necessary verbal skills may be at a social and academic disadvantage (Raver et al., 2007).

Finally, a significant body of research demonstrates that emotional competence is influenced by *socialization* forces such as modeling (the way children see others handle emotions), reactions to the child's emotions by adults and peers, depictions of emotion in the media, and discussion and teaching about emotions at home, in school, and in the community and society as a whole.

Development of emotion identification. Although children experience emotions from birth, recognizing and labeling them corresponds to the emergence of language. Beginning in the second year, children use *internal-state*

Recognizing and Labeling Emotions: Development

Emotional development is influenced by many factors, including innate temperamental differences, cognition (perception and knowledge), language development, and socialization. Although children experience emotions from birth, recognizing and labeling them corresponds to the emergence of language. Preschoolers' ability to form mental representations allows them to imagine and act on solutions to emotion-based problems. Research shows that children who understand and regulate their own emotions, and know how to deal with the emotions of others, do better academically and socially.

---

language to describe their own and other's feelings (Raver et al., 2007). They can make simple statements such as "I angry" or "Want toy now!" The ability to identify one's own and others' emotions improves with age. Consider how articulate this preschooler is as he describes his feelings and the type of situation that provokes it:

> *At work time in the art area, Trevor is waiting to use the red paint pump and the child using it says, "Be patient." Trevor says, "My grandma always says, 'Hold your patience' and it just makes me get stressed."*

Not only does their increasing vocabulary help preschoolers differentiate emotional states, but their ability to form mental representations allows them to imagine and act on solutions to emotion-based problems. For example, three- and four-year-olds can picture the sand timer running out and envision themselves then getting a turn to play with a desired toy. A child distressed by the absence of a parent can find comfort in imagining his or her return, particularly if the child is beginning to sequence time:

At outside time (just before dismissal), Penina is looking around and Wendy (the teacher) asks what she is thinking. Penina replies, "I'm thinking about my mommy and how I love her. She's coming soon."

Development of emotion regulation. Thus, mental images (such as the sequence of events or the outcome of certain actions) allows the immediacy or "right now" of toddlerhood to give way to the deferred gratification — "soon," "later," "after" — of preschool. Being able to label feelings and imagine solutions helps young children regulate emotions. It may even have an impact on their brain development. Research on the effects of the stress hormone cortisol shows that repeated trauma can hinder neural growth, while being able to release these feelings — for example, by labeling them and letting them go — can help children cope with intense experiences and emotions (Perry, 1994). Of course, the more intense the emotion, the more difficult it is for children to use their emerging ability to control it. Nevertheless, repeated experience in resolving problems, and "emptying out" the stressful feelings and harmful biological reactions associated with them, can support both cognitive growth and emotional self-regulation.

As young children learn to label their feelings and mentally picture how they might solve problem situations, they are better able to regulate their emotions and delay gratification.

Emotional development and social relationships. Children with better emotion knowledge are also more likely to form friendships and get help and support from adults in negotiating social relationships. Conversely, children who have trouble with emotion regulation may also be less competent at acquiring emotion knowledge from peers or adults. They may overidentify negative emotions, especially anger. Contrast the responses of these two preschoolers to anger-evoking situations:

At outside time, when Erik hits him, Jabiari says, "Hands on your own body. I don't like that." When Erik later hits Jabiari's friend Mac, Jabiari says to him, "Don't hit my friend." Then he walks over to Mac and says, "Are you all right?" He puts his hand on Mac's shoulder.

At work time, Luis and Perry are playing alongside one another with magnet tiles. When his magnet tile "rocket" falls apart, Luis points at Perry (two feet away) and says, "He broke it. I'm not playing anymore."

Research shows that approximately 20 percent of preschoolers may be at risk for moderate to clinically significant social and emotional difficulties, with those from low-income families at greater risk (Raver et al., 2007). Fortunately, studies suggest there is considerable plasticity in the neurological systems involved in emotion regulation and emotion knowledge, especially in the preschool years, which means early intervention can be effective. Psychologists caution, however, that interventions should focus on more general school readiness, such as preliteracy skills, rather than explicitly trying to "teach" about emotions. Children who feel competent and in control of events (see Chapter 5, "Developing a Sense of Competence") may in turn develop the cognitive skills and motivation to better regulate their emotional states.

In sum, helping young children learn to identify and label their emotions is an important foundation of emotional health. Children who can understand and regulate their own emotions, and know how to deal with the emotions of others, do better academically and socially. They are more engaged at school, better able to sustain attention and persist at tasks, and have positive dispositions toward learning. Emotional competence promotes social development by allowing successful interactions that involve listening, cooperation, and negotiation. Positive affect contributes to initiating and sustaining relationships; negative affect works against the young child. "Quite simply, happier children fare well, and angrier or sadder children worse" (Denham, 2006, p. 88).

Teaching Strategies

Although having emotions is inborn and instinctual, knowing what they are, what they mean, and how they are labeled is a learning process. Because the emotions of young children are so close to the surface, there are many natural opportunities throughout the day when adults can help them acquire specific knowledge and skills in this area. Moreover, since preschoolers are capable of forming mental representations, they can think about situations apart from the here-and-now to further understand emotional experiences and terminology.

By using the teaching strategies described below, you can help young children begin to understand the complex world of emotions with a growing sense of their ability to express themselves and deal with others. And although we take it for granted that educating preschoolers about negative emotions serves a useful function, these examples also recognize that positive feelings can — and should — comprise a significant part of the young child's day.

Accept children's full range of emotions as normal. It is important not to judge children's emotions as good or bad. Although adults need to stop hurtful or unsafe behavior that may result from strong negative emotions (see Chapter 11 "Resolving Conflicts"), children need reassurance that it is the behavior and not the underlying feelings upon which you are placing limits. Children — like adults — can learn to control how they behave in response to their feelings, but they should not be led to think they have to control the emotions themselves.

When children express their emotions, it is important to show acceptance through words, facial expressions, and gestures. We know as adults how frustrating or demoralizing it can be to share our feelings with others — our pleasure as well as our pain — and not get any recognition

in response. Other techniques for letting children know you have observed and considered their feelings include making (but not forcing) eye contact, remaining still and patient as children get their feelings out, nodding, and getting down on children's physical level.

Gaby's teacher writes down Gaby's plan to make a card for her mother, who is out of town. Working in the art area, Gaby folds a piece of blue paper vertically and asks her teacher to take dictation on the inside of the card, writing, "I love you, Mommy." Gaby decorates the front, back, and inside, tracing around stencils and symbols. At recall time, she tells the group, "It's to let my Mom know that I'm thinking about her." Gaby's teacher encourages her to tell the other children about the words and pictures on the card.

At work time in the science area, Jacob's teacher kneels beside him as Jacob (whose mother is incarcerated) talks about the mother and baby hamsters in their cage. "She's loving them," he says about the mother. He puts his head on the teacher's shoulder and she holds him and strokes his back.

Not all children can or do show emotions, and it is important to accept children's current expressive level. They may have been discouraged from showing feelings at home if doing so is regarded as personally or culturally unacceptable. Children with emotionally restrictive backgrounds need time to develop a sense of security and learn that emotions are regarded as natural in the classroom and can be expressed in socially acceptable ways. Teachers should be especially gentle and patient in such cases, neither pressuring children to exhibit emotions before they are ready, nor overreacting — even positively — when they do. Sometimes it is easier for children to express emotions indirectly, through role play, than it is for them to state their feelings directly, as the following anecdotes illustrate:

At work time in the block area, while sitting in the "puppy house," Amelia says, "Ruff, ruff, the puppy is lonely and now it's mad. It needs to go on a walk."

At breakfast, Madison says her bagel person has a "frown." (She turns a half-bagel with the ends pointing down.) "He's sad because he misses his mommy and daddy."

Teachers can also help parents understand, in respectful and nonthreatening ways, that children benefit from identifying and expressing feelings appropriately. If a discrepancy between home and school remains in this area, teachers and parents can negotiate what is acceptable in each place. Preschoolers are capable of understanding that different rules apply in different settings and, although it may not be easy at first, adults can work together to help children transition back and forth. In fact, learning where, when, and how to express emotions is itself a part of the emotional education that takes place during childhood.

Name or label children's emotions as well as your own. By preschool, most children have learned the words for a few basic emotions, such as "angry," "happy," and "sad." Increasingly, early childhood programs are also introducing sign language for words, including emotions, to help preverbal children (infants, toddlers) and those with hearing impairments, speech and language delays, autism, or other special needs, express their thoughts and feelings (Daniels, 2000). (For a dictionary of American Sign Language [ASL], with video clips illustrating the signs, visit the American Sign Language Browser Web site, 2000.)

Adults can encourage young children to use familiar labels for emotions, and adults can then repeat these so other children can hear the names of emotions in context. It also helps to expand simple statements to clarify which labels children are attaching to the feelings and experiences they commonly encounter.

At planning time, Aubrey looks in the mirror and says, "I'm happy today." Milton, his teacher, looks in the mirror so their faces show side by side. Milton smiles and says, "I'm happy, too."

At greeting circle, Sean says, "I hate my mom because she always puts my toys away so I can't get them." His teacher repeats, "You get mad when your mom puts your toys where you can't reach them."

At planning time, when Kiley makes a plan that does not include Jermaine, Jermaine says of his friend, "I get sad when he makes bad choices." The teacher responds, "You feel sad because Kiley wants to play something different today."

At recall time, Gabrielle says, "I was excited at the computer because I was looking at the sand timer." Her teacher repeats in a questioning voice, "You were excited looking at the sand timer?" Gabrielle explains, "It made me glad I didn't have to give Jalessa a turn yet. I was excited to play on the computer more."

At work time, Chad scowls and kicks the blocks when his tower falls down. His teacher makes the sign for angry ["The fingers pull away from the face to show the wrinkles on the face of the angry person"; ASL Browser, 2000]. Chad nods and makes the sign back to her.

As their vocabularies expand in general, children also begin to learn and use more sophisticated terms for their feelings. You can introduce new vocabulary words to describe feelings, especially terms the children may have heard before but may not have connected to their own emotions. If they hear these words in the context of a situation that is meaningful to them, they are more likely to add them to their own emotional vocabularies. In the following anecdote, the teacher helps make explicit the connection between Bianca's hearing the clock beeping and her concerns about being late.

Reporting to the group at greeting time, Bianca says, "I'm glad I'm not late today. I heard the beeps in the Pepper Café when I was eating breakfast with my Mom." Her teacher acknowledges, "When you heard the clock beeping, you worried you would be late." Bianca replies, "I worried I would miss greeting time."

You can also introduce words to help children deal with the feelings aroused by social conflicts. Having these words at their disposal can help children communicate the reason for the dispute and negotiate a solution. However, it is best not to attempt vocabulary lessons when emotions are running high. If children are upset, they are too distracted to absorb what you are saying. Wait until the crisis or conflict has passed and everyone can talk about it calmly. Remember that preschoolers' ability to mentally represent events in their lives means they will be able to recall the situation and apply the words to the feelings that were prevalent at the time. This is useful not only for the children directly involved in the incident, but for others who witnessed it. (See additional examples and discussion in Chapter 11.)

To expand children's emotional lexicon, you can also introduce new words before conflicts arise; for example, while reading a book in which feelings play a central role in stating or resolving a problem. A book such as *Where the Wild Things Are*, by Maurice Sendak (1963), can open up a discussion about anger or a child's fear of losing someone's love when they act "bad." If the characters' emotions are familiar to the children but not currently highly sensitive for them, the children can more readily process the new information and apply it in their own lives later. (Also see the teaching strategy "Incorporate discussions about feelings into daily events" on pp. 63 and 65.)

Adults can open up a discussion about feelings by reading storybooks with children in which emotions play a key role in the characterization and narrative.

It is also valuable when you label your own emotions as you interact with children. Acknowledging and naming your feelings helps children learn that everyone has emotions and that the nature and range of your feelings is comparable to theirs. By seeing how you deal with your emotions — again both positive and negative — children

will learn how they can handle emotions with the same names and characteristics in themselves.

Finally, remember that when you label your feelings, you may be providing children with information they already have! Young children sometimes surprise — and even embarrass — us by the degree to which they are tuned in to the emotional states of the parents and teachers they depend on for care. Often their astuteness manifests itself in their role playing, as in the following anecdote:

> *At work time in the house area, Roxanne puts on the feathered hat and takes her keys out of the blue purse. She places her hands on her hips and announces to Sean: "Hurry up or we're gonna be late, you slowpoke. We're always late. It makes me furious! Next time I'm just gonna leave for the movie without you."*

Call attention to the feelings of others. Although preschoolers are increasingly able to take perspectives other than their own, they do not always do so automatically. Drawing their attention to the feelings of others helps to increase their awareness that emotions are universal. It also helps the children see how others express their feelings in ways that are both similar to, and perhaps different from, their own.

Children can better resolve conflicts when they are sensitive to the feelings of others. As noted above, it may be difficult to orient them to how others are responding to the situation when they are caught up in their own feelings. However, once you have calmed things down (see the initial steps in conflict resolution in Chapter 11), you can help children consider how the other players in the scenario feel. When you sense a child is ready to listen, you might simply repeat, for example, "Erika said it made her angry when you grabbed the toy." Here is another example:

> *Jeremy and James argue over a book at greeting time. Jeremy tells James, "You can't be 'grrr' all day, because I don't like that." The teacher comes over, takes the book in her own hands, and sits down calmly between them. When the boys relax a bit, she asks them what the problem is. Jeremy says, "I had it first, and he tried to take it." The*

teacher turns to James and asks him what happened. "I want that book!" he answers. "So, you both want to look at this book and you are both angry that you can't have it," she summarizes. The two boys nod. After some discussion, they decide the teacher can read the book to both of them while they take turns turning the pages.

Adults can also be effective mediators by interpreting children's emotions for one another. Just as in reading, children need to learn the meaning of emotional signs or symbols in the same way they learn the appearance and sounds of letters. Describe and interpret for children the significance of emotional indicators such as body language (clenched fists, jumping for joy, walking away, gentle stroking), facial expressions (grins, scowls, downcast eyes) and verbalizations (growls, yelling, angry words, soothing hums). Adult interpretation is especially helpful for children who are not (yet) adept at picking up these cues themselves. It is also valuable when children are too overwhelmed and self-involved at any moment to notice others' feelings. At such times, keep it simple and focused. Calling attention to one or two indicators is sufficient to get the message across.

Comment conversationally on the emotions children express throughout the day. Casual remarks about feelings brings them into the realm of ordinary life. The world of emotions then becomes just one of the many content areas — along with reading, mathematics, science, art, and so on — that children learn about every day. In the following example, a child converses easily with her teacher about the emotional roller coaster of being sick and then getting better. Note how the teacher helps connect Rosy's feelings with the things Rosy is doing to treat her illness, thereby strengthening the idea that emotions are something we can regulate through our actions.

Rosy draws a figure with a happy expression.

Rosy: *I made a happy face because I'm feeling better.*

Teacher: *The doctor gave you medicine for the bronchitis.*

Rosy: *I'm taking a lot of medicine at night. And I'm drinking a lot of soup with chicken inside it. My Mom put Vicks on my tummy and back so I don't*

cough too much. I only took the pink one last night. I don't like the purple one. Sometimes I mix it with the white one that doesn't show. Then I drink water.

Teacher: *So you don't like to take all the medicine but you are happy that it makes you feel better.*

Emotions that might otherwise be overwhelming for young children do not seem as scary or unmanageable when they are treated as part of normal, daily experience. Feelings such as sadness, anxiety, and anger do not threaten to escalate out of control when an adult's remarks indicate they are normal and acceptable.

At work time in the art area, Michelle says, "My sister is so mean to me. She broke my necklace. I just can't believe it! It was my most special one! She goes to day care now." Her teacher comments, "When I was growing up, my little sister did the same thing and it made me really angry too! I'm happy for you that your sister will have other things to play with in day care."

What is additionally noteworthy about the above anecdote, which took place in the spring, is that Michelle was diagnosed as having a speech and language impairment at the beginning of the school year. She was seen weekly by a speech therapist, who noted how much Michelle's language had improved during the program because she was encouraged to talk and express herself in the classroom every day.

In conversing with children about their feelings, as with all facets of emotional development, it is important to notice and remark on positive as well as negative feelings. For example, you might comment at greeting time, "You look sad this morning," "What a big smile! I think you're very happy today," or "You sound excited that you played at Sally's house after school yesterday." Once again, the more wide-ranging the topics of conversation, the more the children will come to understand the common presence of feelings in our lives.

Incorporate discussions about feelings into daily events. Because of their growing ability to hold ideas and images in mind, preschoolers can begin to talk about emotions in the abstract. However, it still helps to tie

Recognizing and Labeling Emotions: Teaching Strategies

Accept children's full range of emotions as normal.

- Do not judge children's emotions as good or bad; reassure children that it is the behavior and not the underlying feelings upon which you are placing limits.

- Show acceptance of children's feelings through words, facial expressions, and gestures; for example, by making eye contact, remaining still and patient as children get their feelings out, nodding, and getting down on children's physical level.

- Accept children's current expressive level; respect personal and cultural differences; be gentle and patient, neither pressuring children to exhibit emotions before they are ready nor overreacting — even positively — when they do.

- Recognize that children who have difficulty expressing feelings may be better able to express their emotions indirectly, through role play.

- Help parents understand, in respectful and nonthreatening ways, that children benefit from identifying and expressing feelings appropriately; work with parents to help children understand what is acceptable for expressing feelings at home and at school.

Name or labels children's emotions as well as your own.

- Encourage young children to use familiar labels for emotions and then repeat them so other children can hear the names of emotions in context.

- Introduce new vocabulary words to describe feelings and social conflicts, especially terms children may have heard before but may not have connected to their own emotions.

- Introduce new words after a conflict or crisis has passed, when everyone can talk about it calmly; preschoolers will be able to remember the incident and attach the new words to the emotions they and others were feeling at the time.

- Introduce new words before conflicts arise; for example, while reading a book in which feelings play a central role in stating or resolving a problem.

- Label your own emotions as you interact with children, and remember that when you label your feelings, you may be providing children with information they already have.

Call attention to the feelings of others.

- Draw children's attention to the feelings of others to increase their awareness that emotions are universal.

- Use the initial steps in conflict resolution (see Chapter 11) to help children consider how the other players involved in the conflict feel.

- Mediate children's conflicts by interpreting children's emotions for one another; describe and interpret both body language and verbalizations.

Teachng Strategies *(cont.)*

Comment conversationally on the emotions children express throughout the day.

- Treat the role of emotions as part of normal, daily experience; learning about feelings is no different from learning about reading, math, art, or science.

- In conversing with children about their feelings, note and remark on positive as well as negative feelings.

Incorporate discussions about feelings into daily events.

- Look for ways to tie children's explorations of feelings to something concrete; the activities that occur at small-group time often offer appropriate conversational openings.

- Use storybooks to initiate conversations about emotion; help children relate the feelings and reactions of the characters to comparable events in their own lives.

- Use art as a springboard for expressing and talking about feelings; encourage children to talk about the artist's feelings behind his or her creation and/or the emotions that the artwork evokes in the children themselves.

these explorations to something concrete. Although it does not work to plan a small-group time specifically to talk about feelings, the activities that occur at small-group time often offer appropriate conversational openings.

For example, children can discuss the reactions a storybook character has to a particular situation, especially if you help the children relate it to similar experiences they have had. Common emotion-provoking experiences and story plots include the birth of a sibling, a pet's death, going to the doctor, or the anger of a parent or friend.

> *When Mrs. Mel reads* Where the Wild Things Are *by Maurice Sendak (1963), Chelsie asks, "Why is his mommy angry?" Timmy suggests it is because Max gets his wolf suit dirty. Jonah offers that his mother takes away his dinner because he won't eat his vegetables. Mrs. Mel asks what other things might make a parent mad. The children talk about getting into fights with their siblings, being "pokey" at bedtime, and not putting away their toys. When they get to the end of the book, Chelsie points to the food waiting in Max's room. "His mommy is angry but she still loves him and gives him his dinner," says Mrs. Mel.*

Art can be another stimulus for expressing and talking about feelings. In the opening anecdote, for example, Lily listens to music and paints pictures to illustrate how different situations evoke different emotions — in her case, feeling sad or happy. In the following anecdote, we see that, drawing on the common experiences that make children in her class feel angry, one teacher uses a story as the basis for an expressive art activity:

> *To begin small-group time, the teacher tells a story about a boy who is mad because his friend doesn't want to play with him. The children talk briefly about the things that make them angry and then the teacher gives them each paper and crayons to draw what it feels like to be mad. As they work, the children talk about angry colors, mad faces, and mad actions. One child draws herself breaking toys; another says, "I stomped so hard I made a hole in the paper!" Some children even describe and draw the clothes they*

*wear when they feel angry — "A really, really
red tee shirt" and "A zipper I close all the way
to the top."*

Preschoolers are also avid art appreciators. They enjoy
looking at works of art and talking about the artist's feelings behind his or her creation and/or the emotions that
the artwork evokes in them. Even in small-group activities where learning about emotions is not the focus, there
are often opportunities to attach names and descriptions
to the feelings children express — the satisfaction of
duplicating a pattern, the frustration of not getting two
pieces of clay to stick together, the gratification of helping
a friend solve a problem. By planning these learning opportunities, and being alert to serendipitous ones, you can
help children expand their knowledge of the labels and
modes of expression that characterize our emotions.

In Conclusion

Emotions are part of the complex and sometimes confus-
ing array of characteristics that distinguish human beings.
As in any other content area, young children are learning
the vocabulary of feelings and developing the skills to deal
with their feelings. Being able to recognize and label emotions in turn gives them the foundation for meeting other
developmental tasks. They can channel positive feelings
toward exploring, discovering, and establishing satisfying relationships. And they can control negative feelings
and redirect them toward constructive problem solving.
Helping young children master the lexicon of emotions
thus works in the service of learning across the curriculum
content of the classroom and the opportunities and challenges of life beyond it.

Part Three

SOCIAL DEVELOPMENT

Developing a Sense of Community

Martin is playing between the cubbies when a parent volunteer says to him, "I'm worried someone will get hurt back here." Martin says, "Don't worry. I'm strong and will protect everyone because I have some muscles." During work time, he makes a cape out of butcher block paper and string, and he asks his teacher to help him write the words "Class Protector" on the front.

Definition

A community is a social group whose members have common interests based on one or more shared attributes, such as their geography, age, education, social status, values, or goals. Having a sense of community means seeing oneself as belonging to the group and sharing all or a significant number of its characteristics, beliefs, and practices. The early childhood classroom is a community whose members share an age range, educational interests, time, and friendship. In a community, the members receive and give one another support for individual and group undertakings. Through their interactions with peers in the classroom community, and the families and school of which they are a part, young children also deepen their understanding of broader social norms and conventions.

Educator Nancy Meltzoff (1994) offers weaving as a metaphor for the structure and function of the classroom community. Each individual strand, such as shared environment, distributed leadership, communication, and cooperation, interacts with the others to form an integrated whole. If one element is missing, or becomes frayed, the whole system can unravel. But when all the components are present and smoothly interlocked, the community provides beauty, warmth, and protection, just as a well-constructed cloth does for its wearer.

A Sense of Community

Having a *sense of community* means seeing oneself as belonging to a group and sharing all or a significant number of its characteristics, beliefs, and practices. A sense of community involves actions as well as feelings, such as giving help and support to other members. The early childhood classroom is a community whose members share an age range, educational interests, time, and friendship.

A sense of community is related to, but also differs from, the ideals of justice or democracy (see Chapter 13, "Creating and Participating in a Democracy"). Psychologists F. Clark Power and Tatyana Makogan (1995) point out that a sense of community is based primarily on attentive responsiveness. That is, we feel part of a community when we are open to the personal experiences of others and care about them as individuals and as group members. Democracy, by contrast, sometimes requires us to act impersonally and impartially for the good of some higher cause. Community generally puts compassion and empathy above fairness. Democracy may reverse these priorities. Ideally, the two are not in conflict; but when they are, we may be faced with a moral dilemma. Fortunately for young children, such disparities rarely emerge. When they do, however, choices based on concrete and personal experience will make more sense to them than will abstract principles.

Development

Psychologists agree that belonging to a community is central to social and emotional health. "Educational practices that ignore the reality of children's deep need for a sense of community are educationally unsound; they do not provide the conditions that promote immediate or long-term optimum social and cognitive development or emotional well-being. The absence of a sense of belonging to a community may have a deep effect on a child's development socially and neurologically" (Katz & McClellan, 1997, p. 17).

> ### Developing a Sense of Community
>
> Because young children are essentially social beings, communities are meaningful and attractive to them. Young children belong to more than one community, with their initial encounters generally being with their immediate and extended families and perhaps with nearby playmates. The early childhood program is usually their first community beyond those mediated by their parents. How children interact with one another helps them internalize new information and shapes the way they think. Collaborative activities allow them to learn from and teach one another.

Children's first communities. Because young children are essentially social beings, communities are meaningful and attractive to them. Although infants and toddlers may have a limited ability to become community members because of their less-developed cognitive and social abilities (see Chapter 2, "An Overview of Child Development and Teaching Practices"), by preschool, children are able as well as eager to join. Young children belong to more than one community, with their initial encounters generally being with their immediate and extended families and perhaps with nearby playmates. The early child-

hood program is usually their first community beyond those mediated by their parents. But while preschoolers want to be part of the community, joining it is a learning experience for them. The abilities necessary to form a community — knowing and abiding by its rules, caring about others as well as satisfying one's own needs, and so on — are just beginning to emerge during this period.

The classroom as community. The idea of the classroom as a community has its roots in different developmental and educational theories. One is the social constructivist perspective of Vygotsky (1934/1978), which maintains that how students talk and interact with one another helps them internalize new information and shapes the way they think. At all levels, including early childhood, collaborative activities provide students with a language-rich environment in which they learn from and teach one another (Douville & Wood, 2001). Community is thus the social context that enriches and enhances children's engagement in the learning process.

Another school of thought combines individual and social psychology and promotes the idea of establishing a "caring community" in classrooms and schools. This model has been field-tested in the Child Development Project at the Developmental Studies Center in Oakland, California (Battistich, Solomon, & Watson, 1998). The theory, supported by research, says that satisfying individual needs is the most effective way to promote broader social membership. That is, active participation in a caring community meets children's personal needs for autonomy, belonging, and competence, which in turn results in their attachment to the classroom and motivation to adopt and abide by its norms and values. If we support autonomy by offering choices, promote belonging by making everyone welcome, and foster competence by enabling achievement, then children's membership in the group will follow. In sum, young children will be more inclined to adopt the values of the community and respond to community members in a caring way if their own needs are being met.

The melding of these individual and group concerns is especially relevant in preschool, because it means we can build on young children's natural egocentrism (concern with their own well-being) to invest them in a community that helps them as individuals while simultaneously benefitting all the members. Put another way, contributing to the group helps children feel validated, competent, and important as individuals. By paying careful attention to children's emotional learning (see Chapters 3–6), we enable them to become part of the social learning that occurs in the expanding communities in which they find themselves.

Young children are more inclined to adopt the values of the community and respond to other community members in a caring way if their own needs for autonomy, belonging, and a sense of competence are met first.

Early learning in a community context. In a community-centered classroom, children make the bridge from "me" to "we" by collaborating with peers who have equal status. They learn the importance of paying attention to others and negotiating compromises. These are skills children cannot learn individually (Battistich et al., 1998). They must encounter similarities in others to cement aspects of their own identity. For example, a child likes to play with blocks; other classmates like blocks, too; together they make a community of block-players. And children must face competing perspectives to understand, resolve, and finally integrate themselves into a larger social milieu. For example, a child wants to sit next to the teacher as she reads a book, and so does another child; if the children sit on either side of the teacher, they can both see the book.

While respecting children's intentions and capacities, proponents of early childhood communities nevertheless recognize that preschoolers' peer interactions are seldom optimally collaborative. Active monitoring and involve-

ment by knowledgeable and supportive adults is essential to creating and sustaining classroom communities. Teachers can intervene to promote a problem-solving approach to conflict, which is more effective than a system of reward and punishment, as well as being more consistent with the ethic of a caring community described above (see Chapter 11, "Resolving Conflicts"). Adults can also point out opportunities for collaboration that preschoolers may not have considered on their own, as we see in this example:

> *At work time, walking past the sand table, Ashley notices sand on the floor. She goes to the teacher and says, "Someone might fall. But it's just too much to clean up myself!" Her teacher replies, "How could you solve that problem?" Ashley says, "I could get someone to help me." "Who?" asks the teacher. Ashley suggests Veronica, but when the teacher asks, "What do you think she'll say?" Ashley sees that Veronica is engrossed at the easel and might not want to interrupt her painting. Then Ashley's eyes light upon Solomon, who is watching a group of children in the block area. "Hey, Solomon," Ashley calls. "Wanna help me clean up all this sand?" Solomon races to get the broom and dustpan. He holds the dustpan while Ashley sweeps. They play together at the sand table for the rest of work time.*

Beyond a respect for other individuals, part of establishing a sense of community is cultivating feelings of responsibility for the classroom as a whole. Developmental psychologists Rheta DeVries and Betty Zan (1994), at the University of Northern Iowa, say adults often underestimate the amount of responsibility young children are willing and able to accept. Since they use the materials and furnishings in the classroom every day, children can observe what happens when these are not well-cared for. For example, children can see that markers dry up when the tops are not replaced or that someone gets hurt when a spill is not wiped up. When such results are tied to concrete examples, preschoolers can understand the implications of their actions — for others as well as for themselves — and alter their behavior with a mental image of consequences and the associated feelings in mind.

The cognitive capacity for connecting cause and effect thus helps to create the social phenomenon we call community.

Teaching Strategies

As noted above, strategies that first help children feel validated as individuals can help them become members of the community. Teachers can also explicitly adopt strategies that create a sense of comfort and coherence for the entire group and make the classroom a welcoming place where children feel a sense of belonging. The following practices will help you establish a supportive classroom community that preschoolers will readily join.

Create an atmosphere in which children are expected to be kind and supportive to one another. The emotional tone in a classroom creates an environment in which all areas of learning — social and cognitive — take place. Jan Randolph and Pansy Gee (2007) at the Center for Education at Rice University say a positive community sets the stage for each child to feel good about school and be a successful learner. When children feel known, safe, loved, and accepted, then they feel connected to the learning community of the classroom. And they feel emotionally and socially allied with the adults and peers with whom they share that setting.

In a supportive community, children assume responsibility for taking care of one another. While it may involve empathy (see Chapter 4, "Feeling Empathy"), community-mindedness goes beyond understanding someone else's feelings. One can empathize with another without establishing a connection or being motivated to act on their behalf. A sense of community, by contrast, involves actions as well as feelings. It is about helping individual members, and the group as a whole, feel good and function well as a cohesive unit. In young children, this means being aware of what their classmates need or want to achieve personal goals. It may also involve assisting one individual so that the larger group benefits.

> *At work time in the art area, Ashley overhears the teacher say that Ben is looking for the book* Monkeys Jumping on the Bed. *Ashley stops what she is doing, goes to the book tub, pulls out the book, and gives it to the teacher. "Here's the book Ben wants," she says.*

> *As the class gets ready for outside time, Casey sees Noam trying to snap his snow pants. Casey walks over to Noam and says, "Want help?" Noam answers "Yes," and Casey snaps Noam's pants for him. "Now we can all go outside and make snow angels," Casey announces to the other children nearby.*

Although it should go without saying, it is still important to state the following unequivocally: Never shame children, and never blame or humiliate children in front of others or criticize their personal attributes (appearance, intelligence, background, and so on). When children make mistakes — because they have not yet learned how to behave differently — use problem-solving techniques that strengthen your relationship with them; allow them to learn by working through problems; and build their sense of competence and self-esteem (Zieger, 2007; see also Chapter 12, "Creating and Following Rules").

Listening is perhaps the single most important component in establishing a supportive community — not only how the teacher listens to children but also how the teacher encourages children to listen to one another. To feel supported, children must first and foremost know that their needs and ideas are being heard and that their membership in and contributions to the community are being acknowledged. Adults should also express their own pleasure at being part of a classroom in which everyone treats all the members with kindness and respect.

Arrange the room so different size groups can gather. Communities come in all sizes, and children need opportunities to interact in pairs, meet in small groups, and all come together in large groups. Research (Cummings, 2000) repeatedly shows that how the classroom is arranged affects the interactions that take place within it. Although educators typically focus on room arrangement in terms of discipline and academic learning, the spaces we create in the classroom are equally important in creating — or discouraging — a feeling of sociability and community among the students. An early childhood setting should include open areas where large groups can assemble and small, enclosed areas with comfortable furniture for intimate interactions.

When spaces are tight and have restricted access, children are forced into solitary play and have no choice but to work on their own or in very small groups. Limiting the number of children who can work in a given area can also create competition among them and contradicts the notion of the classroom as a community. For example, if the computer is in a corner with only one chair, then working there becomes an activity for a single child while everyone else is excluded. If, on the other hand, the computer is located in an open space with two or more chairs, working at the computer can be a shared activity, with children using the keyboard, contributing ideas, and talking about what they see on the screen.

Conversely, when the classroom is one big and undivided space, it is easy for children to feel overwhelmed by how impersonal (and often how noisy and bustling) the setting is. Though some children may thrive in this beehive of activity, others may experience difficulty finding their place in this undifferentiated community. Even children who do well in large groups may now and then want to curl up alone with the teacher and look at a book, or work quietly at a small table to make a collage with a friend.

An early childhood classroom should include open areas where large groups can assemble, as well as enclosed areas for intimate interactions, so children can seek and find different levels of community throughout the day.

Including a variety of intimate and open spaces in the room allows children with different temperaments to find a setting that is right for them. Such an arrangement acknowledges that the same child will seek different levels of community at various times during the day, depending on his or her mood and needs. Teachers can also interact

with children one-on-one or in small and large groups, again depending on what they sense is called for at any given moment.

Including open pathways between the different learning areas further enhances the sense of community. Opportunities to be part of a subgroup ("the book readers" at work time) or to interact with the group as a whole ("the scarf wavers" at large-group time) permits fluidity in how children express their membership in the classroom. A supportive community provides variety and access to gathering places.

> *At work time in the block area, when the other children are not able to get to the block shelf because so many blocks are on the floor, Gina clears a path for them to walk through. Dee and Chloe each carry a small block back to the house area where they sit on the couch and feed their dolls wooden "popsicles." Together with Gina, four other children continue to build a hockey rink on one side of the path. Justin takes a long block that he calls his "police flashlight" and sits inside the chairs-and-blanket tent he constructed with Rona, looking at the photographs of the camping trip he took with his family.*

Establish a consistent daily routine. Just as the room arrangement creates a sense of community through space, so does a consistent daily routine establish a community through time. When everyone is engaged in the same type of activity at the same time each day, it creates a feeling of commonality and togetherness.

It is important to emphasize that participating in the same *type* of activity does not mean that everyone does the same thing. All children can be equally engaged, but in different activities, during work time or free-choice time. As noted above, choice promotes children's sense of autonomy, which in turn makes their voluntary membership in the group authentic. Similarly, at small- or large-group time, children use the same set of materials or engage in movement and music activities, but each is free to use materials, body, and voice in his or her own way. What all the children share at such periods is a commonality of purpose — learning through experience — that is taking place at the same time and within the same routine structure.

Another aspect of the daily routine that can promote community is for each activity to proceed at an unhurried pace. A relaxed schedule lets people enjoy one another's company instead of leading them to feel pressured to finish a task. Whether young children work together or engage in conversation with adults and peers while carrying out parallel activities, freedom from time constraints helps them ease into the camaraderie of community.

Cleanup time and rotating chores, when part of a consistent routine in the early childhood classroom, can also establish a sense of community. When all the children respect the designated time for cleanup, they are pooling their efforts to make the classroom a smoothly functioning environment.

> *At work time in the block area, Aubrey walks up to Ms. Bev and asks, "When it's cleanup time, can I turn the lights out? Then everyone will know it's time to put things away."*

It also helps to develop a system for class jobs that involves every child. Having all the children pitch in results in a sense of ownership among students and a feeling that it is everyone's classroom — not just the teacher's (Zeiger, 2007). Maximize the number of jobs — even if you have to "invent" some — to ensure that all children have a chance to feel they are contributing members of the classroom community.

> *At snacktime, Jacob asks the teacher if he can do the snack basket the next day. She gives him the snack chart and says that he can sign up. Then Jacob asks her, "Could we have applesauce tomorrow? I want to do the spoons." After she agrees, he asks the others at the table, "How many like applesauce? Raise your hands." Jacob counts: "One-two-three-four-five-six. Six spoons. That's everybody!"*

Call attention to activities the whole class participates in. There are many whole-class activities throughout the day, including greeting circle, transitions, and outside time, as well as the period specifically designated as large-group time. Children may not always be aware of the "togetherness" of these periods, but if teachers point it out, preschoolers will become conscious of the fact that everyone is joining in to participate as a group. In addition to activities that are routine ("We got everything put away at cleanup so we can find them tomorrow at choice time"), you can call attention to special activities that everyone looks forward to and shares, such as field trips and follow-up activities ("Look at all the shells we gathered at the beach. I wonder what we could do with them") and holiday celebrations ("I wonder if we'll all recognize one another tomorrow in our Halloween costumes").

An effective and concrete way to support the awareness of whole-class participation is to take photos and write simple captions of group activities. These can be posted for students and parents to see and/or put in a class album in the book area. In talking about the photos, or recalling class activities in general, you can further reinforce the idea of community by referring to children and adults in the classroom with phrases such as "our class," "all of us," "our group," and "all together." These simple words, heard repeatedly, communicate the unity of the group. They also help young children acquire concepts related to number and classification.

Organize activities that foster participation with others. Although communities can emerge spontaneously, they also need to be consciously created. Plan activities that promote interaction and provide options for each child to participate in a way that is comfortable for him or her. Even children who tend toward solitary play can feel safe in groups that are noncompetitive and do not call attention to the individual. By keeping whole-group activities relatively brief (10–20 minutes), preschoolers can maintain their attention and involvement.

The primary focus of such activities should be building relationships, never whole-group instruction, which is neither appropriate nor effective with young children. Educator Jan Zeiger (2007) cautions that teachers often jump right into "instruction" without first taking the time to establish a community atmosphere that promotes learning. Pressure to cover curriculum content, long prominent by the late elementary grades, is increasingly creeping into the early childhood years as well. Says Zeiger, "The teacher who spends time nurturing relationships between students and teaching classroom expectations may get into the curriculum later, but wastes less time on behavior management throughout the year. Children are more eager to cooperate when they feel comfortable in their classroom and connected to their teacher and classmates. They are more willing to take risks as learners when they feel safe in their learning environment and know what to expect each day."

Reading the message board at greeting time is one type of organized activity that is especially effective in promoting a sense of community among children. You can use this communal activity to inform children about upcoming events, visitors, and new materials in the classroom. Children can contribute their own hypotheses about a "mystery" symbol on the message board or talk about their ideas for something everyone is looking forward to, such as a field trip the next day. They can also share ideas or new materials to benefit the group.

Raphael guesses the picture on the message board means there are new brushes in the art area. He and Viktor make a plan to use the brushes to "paint a sign for our garage," and they accept Susan's offer to help them tape it up. Over the next few days, several children use the new brushes to make signs (tea café, monster cave, skate store). The following week, the class takes a walk in the neighborhood to look at the signs on their block.

Bria races into the classroom, telling her teacher, "I brought a book to read. My Mom read it to me. Now you read it to my friends!" They agree, and draw the new book on the message board.

Other planned group times, such as greeting circle or small-group discussions also provide an opportunity for children to talk about and solve problems in their community (such as running in the classroom or not helping at cleanup time). You can introduce the problem for discussion using typical strategies for beginning a small-group time; for example, telling a story, reading a hidden message, or using props such as puppets or pictures to

focus on the problem to be addressed. After children offer solutions, the group can decide which one(s) to try out, implement the solution(s), then revisit the problem later to see whether their ideas worked or need further modification. The satisfaction of dealing with issues as a group ("We solved the problem!") further builds the children's sense of belonging to a vital and meaningful community.

To address a recurring problem over sharing, a teacher shows a small group of preschoolers a picture of two children pulling on a garden hose. They talk about what they think is happening and agree the children in the picture are mad. Asked how they think the problem can be solved, the group offers various suggestions, which the teacher writes down: "Share it"; "Take turns"; "Give it back and forth"; "Ask for it" (for example, saying "Could I please have that?"); and "Both quit and do something else." The children are engaged in the discussion (despite several interruptions) and feel good about all the solutions they propose (**Adapted from Evans, 2002, pp. 259–263**).

One additional caveat, offered by DeVries & Zan (1994) is to not overorganize peer interaction. Sometimes teachers assign children rotating play or work partners because they are concerned about a child who rarely interacts with others or because they want to promote an awareness of diversity by bringing together children of different backgrounds. However well-intentioned, this misguided approach lessens children's natural social motivation and is not respectful of their preferences. The authors say community cannot be purchased at the price of the individual's initiatives and friendships, and that coercion can operate against the establishment of children's feelings of ownership of the classroom. Whether and how to participate in activities with others should always be optional. The teacher's role is not to force or require it but, rather, to create the supportive circumstances that make group activities something each child can look forward to joining.

Involve children in the community beyond the classroom. It is important to help children become aware of the community beyond the classroom, including the neighborhoods where their homes and schools are located

Developing a Sense of Community: Teaching Strategies

Create an atmosphere in which children are expected to be kind and supportive to one another.

- Encourage children to assume responsibility for taking care of one another.

- Help children become aware of what their classmates need or want to achieve personal goals. Assisting one individual can often benefit the whole group as well.

- When children make mistakes, use problem-solving techniques that strengthen your relationship with them; allow them to learn by working through problems; and build their sense of competence and self-esteem. Never shame children, and never blame or humiliate children, or criticize their personal attributes.

- Listen to children and encourage children to listen to one another.

Arrange the room so different size groups can gather.

- Design your early childhood setting to include open areas, where large groups can assemble, and small, enclosed areas with comfortable furniture for intimate interactions.

- Include open pathways between different learning areas to further enhance the sense of community.

Establish a consistent daily routine.

- Provide opportunities for children to engage in the same type of activity at the same time each day, always allowing choice within these activities.

- Establish a routine that allows each activity to proceed at an unhurried pace.

- Involve everyone in cleanup and develop a rotating system for class jobs that involves every child.

Call attention to activities the whole class participates in.

- Point out the "togetherness" of whole-class activities throughout the day so children become conscious of the fact that everyone is joining in to participate as a group.

- Take photos and write simple captions of group activities to increase children's awareness of whole-class participation.

- Use a variety of phrases to talk about the group doing things as a community (e.g., "all of us," "all together"); these terms can also help children acquire concepts related to number and classification.

Organize activities that foster participation with others.

- Plan activities that promote interaction and provide options for each child to participate in a way that is comfortable for him or her.

- Keep whole-group activities relatively brief (10–20 minutes) to maintain preschoolers' attention and involvement.

- Keep the primary focus of group activities on building relationships, never whole-group instruction.

Developing a Sense of Community: Teaching Strategies *(cont.)*

- Use communal activities such as reading the message board at greeting time to inform children about upcoming events, visitors, and new materials in the classroom.

- Involve children in small-group discussions to talk about and solve problems in the classroom community.

- Avoid overorganizing peer interaction. Do not assign permanent or rotating play or work partners. Allow children to choose the peers they wish to interact with.

Involve children in the community.

- Validate the community experiences children have with their families by showing interest and encouraging children to share them with their classmates through conversations and role-playing.

- Plan children's participation in community projects such as recycling classroom materials.

- Take neighborhood walks to draw children's attention to how residents decorate the buildings where they live and what shopkeepers display in storefronts.

- Plan field trips to local establishments such as the public library or farmers' market. Take part in community events such as street fairs and parades.

- Clip newspaper photos of familiar people, places, and events in the community, write simple captions for them, and post them near the door so children and families can see and discuss them at drop-off and pick-up times.

- Invite community members into the program on a regular basis, giving children a chance to learn about their guests and what they do, as well as to play host to the visitors.

- Use stories, poems, songs, and chants as a way to feature people and practices common in the community beyond the classroom.

- Make sure that the focus of community-oriented endeavors for children is collaboration and not competition (e.g., seeing how many recyclables the group or school as a whole can collect rather than encouraging individual children or classrooms to compete to collect the most).

and other places they are likely to frequent. Preschoolers often participate in activities, such as movies or sporting events, with their families. You can validate these experiences by showing interest and encouraging children to share them with classmates through conversations and role-playing. Bringing outside activities into the classroom helps children become aware that they and their families are participating in the life of the community around them.

Reading the message board at greeting time to inform children about visitors, absences, new materials, or upcoming events helps foster a sense of the classroom as a community.

> *At work time in the block area, while playing "dog show," Lute says to his teacher, Sue, "The 'mission is free." She replies, "The admission is free." Lute explains that it means you do not have to pay. Sue asks if his family had to pay when they went to the dog show the day before. "No," says Lute, "Monarch [his aunt's dog] was in the circle, so we got free tickets." He tells Sue how the hair spray made his mother cough so they had to leave early. "We got DQ and then we drove to the park and I saw the ducks," he says. "You went lots of places in the city yesterday," Sue comments. "Yes," says Lute. "I fell asleep in the car on the way home."*

In addition to doing things with their families, preschoolers are also ready to join their classmates in activities and ideas that connect the group to the wider community, such as the school or neighborhood. They can participate in community projects such as recycling classroom materials. A neighborhood walk can draw their

attention to how residents decorate the buildings where they live and what shopkeepers display in storefronts. Children can talk about similarities and differences in their own homes and the places their families frequent.

You can also expand young children's sense of community by doing the following:

- Visiting local establishments such as the public library or farmers' market and by taking part in community activities such as street fairs and parades.

- Clipping newspaper photos of familiar people, places, and events in the community, writing simple captions for them, and posting them near the door so children and families can see and discuss them at drop-off and pick-up times.

- Inviting guests into the classroom. Children in well-organized and regularly scheduled programs may delight in welcoming visitors, taking them around to all the learning centers (areas) or telling them what will happen next in the daily routine. Playing "hosts" reflects children's sense of ownership in their community, especially when it is a place where they know where things are and when things happen.

Stories, poems, songs, and chants are another way to feature people and practices common in the community. For example, children attending a program in a rural farming community loved to sing "Old MacDonald," substituting in the repeating verses the kinds of livestock their families raised. Private programs with a religious affiliation may use stories and songs to help children learn about the practices of their group. The same holds true for the beliefs and traditions of various ethnic groups, cultures, and nationalities. Music, dance, and narrative all provide a means for expressing community norms and participating in communal activities.

The focus of community-oriented endeavors for children should always be collaboration, not competition. As an alternative to many traditional activities, staff at the Developmental Studies Center in Oakland, California (Battistich et al., 1998) work with school coordination teams to reexamine their competitive nature. Often these activities pit one child or classroom against another (e.g., who can achieve the best attendance or sell the most candy to benefit the PTA). They encourage schools to redesign these activities so everyone participates on an equal level and contributes to the success of the project as a whole. As more local districts and state departments of education establish pre-kindergarten programs in elementary schools, shifting the focus of communal activities toward collaboration becomes increasingly important. Not only do such efforts make preschoolers' involvement more appropriate, they also remove the win-lose pitfalls for older children and help to integrate children across all grade levels into the life of the school.

For example, instead of a contest to see which classroom collects the most canned goods for a food drive, the planners might set a target goal for the entire building, with a central drop-off point in the lobby. A rotating group of representatives from each classroom would take turns counting the total each week and reporting the results to everyone; for example, with a chart on the bulletin board or the school's Web page. (Preschoolers could be paired with older children to take part in the counting.) No individual or classroom would be singled out as "best" or "the winner." Instead, the school would take collective pride in achieving a common goal. Even the youngest children could see themselves as equal contributors to this community activity.

In Conclusion

Being part of a community is an important aspect of human existence. It gives individuals a sense of security while simultaneously expanding their horizons to include others who are both similar and different in essential ways. Preschoolers are socially and cognitively ready to join the community of the classroom, but they depend on adults to create a supportive environment that allows each of them to participate in their own way. A good experience in their early childhood community can pave the way for children to eagerly anticipate becoming a member of other learning communities during their school years, as well as the many work and social groups they will join over the rest of their lives.

Engaging in Cooperative Play

At work time in the toy area, Gabrielle, Mariah, and Ellie are playing dogs. Gabrielle says she is the teacher and she is teaching her dogs how to do tricks. Mariah does a somersault and Ellie rolls over.

At snack time, Zachary wants to get the attention of the child next to him, so he uses his teddy grahams to pretend to talk to the other child. "Yum, yum, I like honey," Zachary makes his bear cookie say. "Me, too," says the other child's teddy. They giggle and pretend to lick honey off the hands of their teddy grahams.

Definition

Cooperation is defined as acting together toward a common goal. Cooperative (also called collaborative) play in early childhood means playing and working with others and includes sharing toys, space, friends, attention, conversations, resources, skills, and ideas.

Within the school readiness dimension of social and emotional competence, the National Education Goals Panel (NEGP; Kagan et al., 1995) says social competence in dealing with peers has two dimensions. First is having the skills necessary to cooperate with others, and second is the ability to form and sustain reciprocal friendships. Cooperating implies understanding the rights of others, interacting without being overly directive or submissive, differentiating intentional versus accidental actions, treating others as you would like to be treated, and balancing your own needs with those of others (National Center for Clinical Infant Programs, 1992). The formation of reciprocal friendships is characterized by mutual acceptance

> ### Cooperative Play
>
> *Cooperative play* in early childhood means playing and working with others and includes sharing toys, space, friends, attention, conversations, resources, skills, and ideas. The National Education Goals Panel (Kagan et al., 1995), which includes social and emotional competence in its dimensions of school readiness, say cooperating with others is one component of social competence with peers. The other is the ability to form and sustain reciprocal relationships.

and preference and provides opportunities for giving and receiving affection, intimacy, companionship, and instrumental support and help.

> *At outside time, Gabrielle is waiting to get on the swing. Ellie is swinging and Gabrielle says, "I want to swing with you. You're my friend."*

Cooperative play and friendship are more likely to emerge when a child is emotionally secure with parents and teachers and can approach others with the expectation of positive interactions. Engaging in these relationships also depends on the ability to solicit and listen to other points of view and to detect another person's needs in order to provide the appropriate help and support. As described below, the capacities for collaborative play and friendship undergo impressive development between the infant-toddler and preschool years, and both are dependent not only upon social experiences but cognitive and linguistic changes as well.

Development

Although parent-child relationships have long been a focus of early childhood research, only in recent decades have psychologists recognized that age mates also play a significant role in the formative years of development (Ladd, Herald, & Andrews, 2006). The period between birth and age five is a particularly sensitive time in setting the stage for later behavior and adjustment, and "the adequacy with which a child gets along with other children may well be the single best predictor of adult adaptation" (Hartup, 1991, p. 6).

Peer sociability. Evidence of peer sociability emerges in infancy. Infants orient toward peers by 2 months of age, make simple gestures by 3–4 months, and direct smiles and vocalizations by 6 months to try to get the attention of others. By 9–12 months, babies begin to imitate one another. This imitation is the beginning of infant play, as though they are saying "I know what you're doing, so let's do it together!" (National Research Council, 2000b).

These sequential actions with peers in the first year are followed by parallel play in the second year, and cooperative, or reciprocal, play in the third year. The length of these interactions and their reciprocity also increase with age, indicating that by toddlerhood there is an awareness of the "intent" of others and a growing ability to take turns. These emerging capacities for perspective taking and turn taking lay the groundwork for later coordinated play. Language development also helps. Throughout the preschool years, children who speak more clearly and communicate their ideas better have an easier time starting and keeping play going, says play researcher Carollee Howes (1988).

Peer preferences and friendships. As early as age two, children show peer preferences (indicate who they would rather play with) and begin to form friendships (a voluntary, two-way, positive bond). Friendships are

Cooperative Play: Development

The early years set the stage for later peer relationships and adult social adaptation. Evidence of peer sociability emerges in infancy. During the first year, typically developing infants follow a progression of orienting toward peers, making simple gestures, then directing smiles and vocalizations toward others to elicit attention, and imitating one another. In the second year, children engage in parallel play (playing alongside rather than actually "with" one another), and in the third year, they engage in cooperative or coordinated play. Throughout preschool, especially as children's language skills grow, the length and reciprocity of these interactions increases.

unique — even toddlers adjust their style of play to each friend. The more two children play together, the greater the complexity and compatibility of the play. Toddler friendships are often sustained into preschool, and preschool friendships are often multiyear (Ladd et al., 2006). By preschool, friends share a level of intimacy as shown through self-disclosure and nurturing behavior, especially in make-believe (fantasy or role-taking) play. Preschoolers have the conceptual and verbal ability to reflect on and describe their friendships, including their reasons for liking their friends or disliking others. They commonly cite shared interests and desirable traits, such as being funny or kind, as the basis for their preferences. Preschoolers can also identify behaviors that are antithetical to their forming friendships.

Destiny says, "I plan to go to the block area with Caitlin, Matthew, and Tia because we need to build our big castle. Then we'll have a queen, a princess, and Matthew can be the king we need. I like Matthew 'cause he always wants to play king."

At work time in the house area, when Dosia grabs a toy that Alpha is using, Alpha says, "Dosia's not my friend and I don't play with her anymore. She's mean and she always takes our toys."

Peer conflict. Other social patterns are also evident in preschool, including peer acceptance or rejection (the degree to which a child is liked or disliked) and aggressor-victim relations (whether an individual or subset of children delivers or receives aggression to/from the group). A certain amount of conflict among children is normal, of course, and can play a positive role in development (Hartup, 1991; Piaget, 1950; Vygotsky, 1978). Aggression and arguments indicate something is wrong and challenge children to figure out how to get the play back on track.

Preschoolers may be inclined to be physical or to walk away from conflicts, but appropriate adult intervention can help them sort out and solve social problems that disrupt the flow of their play (see Chapter 11, "Resolving Conflicts"). With age, children — especially friends — are more likely to try resolving a conflict so they can continue to play together. Growing cognitive and language abilities, along with improved emotional self-regulation (see Chapter 6, "Recognizing and Labeling Emotions"), help young children work through social problems and sustain episodes of collaborative interaction.

Diversity and complexity of play. Cooperative play also becomes more diverse in the preschool years. It increasingly involves pretense (role playing and fantasy) and becomes less dependent on specific props. By age five, most children can make almost anything stand for something else (Howes, 1988).

At work time in the house area, Kayleigh is making a cake by stirring yellow foam pieces in a pan. She gives the spatula to Sue (her teacher) and asks her if she wants a taste. "I think it needs more sugar," says Sue. Kayleigh shakes a small red block over the pan and says, "Try it now."

Pretend play means acting "as if" and transforming the here and now, the you and me, into another time and/or place that is populated by different characters. Fantasy play

involves holding mental images in mind, whether remembering something from before or anticipating something yet to be. Pretenders know what is real and not real; they can differentiate between "acting as if" and "acting in error." This requires cognitive, linguistic, and affective abilities (such as separating intentional from accidental behavior) that first come together during the preschool years (Kavanaugh, 2006).

The number of children who can play together in a group also increases between the ages of three and five (National Research Council, 2000b). A younger child may play well with one other person, but the addition of a third — with more competing ideas and interpersonal interactions — is too difficult to manage. Over the next two years, this same child can initiate and sustain complex play patterns with groups of peers.

The complexity of cooperative play, and number of children who can collaborate on a common goal, increases during the preschool years.

Cognitive neuroscientist Adele Diamond (2006) says that in social pretend play, children must not only keep track of their own role but also those of their peers. As the pretend-play story evolves through interaction, children must adapt their play. The plot may change in ways they did not anticipate and may not even like, and they have to negotiate. Thus, shared imaginative play simultaneously depends on and builds social and cognitive flexibility.

An increased capacity for cooperative play does not come "naturally" to children, however. Although their desire for sociability may be strong, their interactions can be quite fragile. Distractions, frustrations, or misinterpreted cues can easily break up their play. For these reasons, adults are very important in structuring an environment that determines how much, how long, and how well children play together. Despite concerns that increased time in child care might slightly elevate young children's aggression, an important finding of the National Institute of Child Health and Human Development (NICHD) Early Childhood Care Research Network (Belsky, 2002; NICHD, 2006) is that higher-quality child care is generally related to more competent peer relationships during early childhood and into the school years. Below are strategies you can use to help promote the frequency and quality of preschoolers' cooperative play.

Teaching Strategies

Learning to play with others happens through watching and imitating and by trial and error. Preschoolers' growing ability to converse, understand different perspectives, and imagine things beyond the here and now all contribute to their capacity to play cooperatively with others. Because they are social beings, children are also intrinsically motivated to master the complex techniques needed for human interchange.

Nevertheless, it would be a mistake to assume that young children engage in role playing and collaborative behavior without adult intervention. Teachers are vital in encouraging children to take risks and negotiate the intricacies of interactive play. Through careful attention to space and time, their own behavior with children, and the support they provide for children's interactions with one another, teachers create a secure environment in which children can develop the capacity for cooperative play with confidence, competence, and enjoyment. The following strategies will help you establish such an environment:

Promote interaction through the arrangement of space and materials. How the room is arranged, and the kinds of materials you stock it with, can have a big impact on the way children play with one another. In terms of space, limiting clutter makes it easier for children to congregate and act out their play scenarios without feeling crowded or worrying about bumping into or breaking things. Do not arbitrarily limit the number of children

who can play in a given area, because doing so models exclusionary behavior. Allow children to spread their play into adjoining areas and to carry materials from one area to another.

At work time in the house area, Aubrey is playing with two other girls. She takes dishes out of the cupboard and says, "Okay, kids. We have a big day today. We're moving." As they begin to stack dishes, Aubrey puts her hands on her hips and says, "What on earth can we pack these in?" She goes to the block area, empties a plastic crate, and tells the boys playing there she needs it for moving. Two of them volunteer to be the movers. "Come on," says Aubrey, "we gotta finish and get there before it gets dark!"

Choose materials that inspire group role play (such as dress-up clothes) and outdoor equipment (such as long, multiwheeled vehicles) that requires two or more children to operate. Large and heavy objects, such as oversized blocks or water-filled pails, also encourage children to work in teams to carry out their play ideas. Whenever possible, provide enough of the same type of materials so children can use them side-by-side and together. If children are preoccupied with having access to materials, they are less likely to think about how to share them in joint play activities. If space or supplies are limited (for example, the classroom has only one couch or two computers), problem-solve with the children about ways to accommodate everyone who wants to use them. For example, put the computer in an open area with several chairs around it. Research (Clements, 1999) shows that children enjoy working together at the computer, especially with open-ended programs that let them share ideas about what to do next, talk about what they see and hear on the screen, and problem-solve when their actions produce unexpected results. (See Chapter 7, "Developing a Sense of Competence," for more on room arrangement to accommodate joint play and Chapter 11, "Resolving Conflicts," for individual and group problem-solving ideas.)

Create opportunities for collaborative interaction. During work (choice, free-play) time, children may choose to act alone or with others. If they choose to be with peers, or inadvertently find themselves in a collaborative situation, allow ample time for them to elaborate on their ideas. Play narratives often emerge slowly as children struggle to find the words to express themselves or to identify the materials they need to carry out their plans. You may even find an unexpected bonus when the time finally arrives for free play to end. Yale psychologist Dorothy Singer (1990) says children who engage in complex make-believe play (as opposed to structured activities) are more likely to clean up independently after a free-choice period in preschool. They take on that responsibility with greater willingness, and assist others in doing so, without teacher prompting.

Teachers are sometimes concerned about developing social skills in those children who always choose to play alone at work time. But by building group times, as well as individual choice times, into the day's routine, even children who otherwise prefer to play alone have a structured and safe opportunity to interact with others. Typical group activities include greeting time with a message board, small-group time, large-group time, transitions, meals or snacks, and outdoor time. Children whose inclination is toward solitary play will find it easier to risk being with others when group times are a familiar and repeated part of the day and are mediated by adults.

Remember that children should never be forced to join in the group activity but should be welcomed at any level of involvement. It is not uncommon to see children first observing from the sidelines, then gravitating toward the fringes, and finally participating wholeheartedly as they settle into the routines and social milieu of the program.

You can also explicitly encourage cooperation in some activities by suggesting that children work with a partner or in teams if they choose. (Never assign partners or require that children work with others.) For instance, you can plan activities that naturally involve children working in twos and threes. Examples include children moving or dancing as partners; two children moving a large container of toys from the hallway to the playground and back; and children gathering data where one (or more) collects information while others record it. Referring children to one another for assistance is another good

---

Build Collaboration by Referring Children to One Another for Assistance

At small-group time, the children are exploring play dough. Callie, the teacher, notices that Kyle is having trouble and refers him to Gabriella for help:

Callie: *Kyle, you look frustrated. What do you want to do with your play dough?*

Kyle: *I'm trying to make it go down but it won't.*

Callie: *You want your play dough to go down. You want to make it lie flat on the table?*

Kyle: *Yes, but it's not staying.*

Callie: *Show me how you are using your hands to make it stay flat.*

Kyle: *(Shows Callie how he presses down on the play dough)*

Callie: *Gabriella, I see your play dough is lying down flat. Can you show Kyle how you did it?*

Gabriella: *Look Kyle, I used this roller to push it. I think there's another roller in the bucket. (She gets a roller and gives it to Kyle.)*

Kyle: *(Tries the roller but still does not get the effect he wants)*

Gabriella: *You have to push down really, really hard. (Puts her hands over Kyle's and pushes down with him)*

Kyle: *Hey, it's working. Let me try. (Tries it and the play dough stays flat)*

Gabriella: *There. You got it to go way down.*

Kyle: *I did it! I made it flat like a pizza. Here, Gabriella, I'll slice you a piece.*

— From *The Intentional Teacher* (Epstein, 2007, p. 78)

way to encourage collaboration, and it establishes a precedent for children to seek help from peers without always turning to the teacher. Referrals benefit the "receiver," who learns from a classmate, as well the "giver," whose skills are acknowledged.

Help aggressive or withdrawn children join their peers. Some children need extra help before they can negotiate cooperative play on their own. While some may push their way into the play setting, others are fearful of approaching their peers at all. It is important to remember that such children are not (mis)behaving willfully or with negative intent. Like children engaged in social conflict, they have not yet learned how to become part of a group play situation. You can help forceful or shy children learn the necessary skills in several ways.

For example, you can coach children who enter a group too aggressively. Observe with them from the sidelines, validate their desire to join the play, and discuss their ideas on how to do this or offer ideas of your own. Suggest noninvasive strategies by saying something like "Maybe if you help carry blocks, they'll let you build the tower with them." Make comments or ask questions that help them consider the consequences of their ideas.

At work time in the house area, Cassandra says, "I could go for some Chinese!" She adds, "I'll be the orderer" and tells the others where to sit at the table. Martha (a teacher) sees Alix approaching from the toy area. The previous day, Alix had been rebuffed by this group. Martha kneels beside Alix, acknowledges that she really wants to play restaurant, too, and talks about how she might do that. "I want to be the orderer," says Alix. "Cassandra's the orderer," says Martha, "but maybe you can ask if they need someone to be something else." "I could be the cook," suggests Alix. "That might work," says Martha. "Would you like to try?" Alix approaches the group and Cassandra agrees, adding "You can be the cook who fries the shrimp in the pan."

Calling attention (in a noncompetitive way) to how other children successfully enter a play situation can also help the child who has difficulty being accepted. In the following example, the group listens intently as a teacher and preschooler recall how roles were adjusted in a play scenario to accommodate new children:

Kelly: *I was working with Giselle. Andrea and Nicholas came. We were all playing with beads. I was pretending to be the mom first and Giselle's friend.*

Teacher: *Was there a problem?*

Kelly: *When Andrea came, she wanted to be the mom. So I was the friend.*

Teacher: *I saw you move to the vanity.*

Kelly: *We had a party. Nicholas came as a witch. We ate pizza.*

Teacher: *I heard Andrea ask Nicholas what kind of food he wanted. You told him to make the pizza. I didn't know that it was a party.*

Kelly: *He needed to help her cook pizza in the kitchen.*

Teacher: *I saw you talking on the phone.*

Kelly: *I was calling people to make sure they were coming to the party.*

Teachers can coach aggressive or withdrawn children to successfully enter a play situation.

At the other end of the social continuum are children who may be so fearful of rejection that they do not even attempt to enter into cooperative play. As noted above, regular and nonthreatening (noncoercive) group times can help some children overcome their anxiety. But sometimes withdrawn children benefit from concrete (physical) aids that give them the "power" to be part of the group. A device such as a "talking stick," for example, can embolden those who are shy or quiet. Consultant Emily Vance (personal communication, 2004) offers the following example, in which a talking stick is used:

At greeting circle, the teacher invites children to tell the group about something they saw on the class walk. She gives the first child a "talking stick" and each child passes it to the next one who wants to speak. Those who do not want to speak are not pressured to do so. However, the teacher notices that even children who are often shy or reserved feel "empowered" when they hold the talking stick and take a turn speaking before passing it to a peer.

Allow children to discover the consequences of their actions. Not all social conflicts require adult intervention or even the formal steps of problem solving (covered in Chapter 11). So, provided no one is being hurt or endangered, and the children have not reached an impasse, wait and see if they can adjust their own behavior accordingly. Here's an example, recorded by a preschool teacher, of self-correcting social behavior:

Jim brings his new fire truck to school and announces that no one is allowed to touch it. When he brings it over to where Zack and Maggie are playing with toy cars and ramps, they tell him he cannot join their game. This continues for two days. On the third day, Jim puts his truck on the ramp and says to Maggie, "You can push it if you want." She does and then gives it to Zack. Maggie asks Jim, "Do you want to play racing cars with us?" Jim says yes and joins their play, letting his friends take turns with his truck.

In this instance, the teacher did not jump in to give directions, offer opinions, or solve a social problem for the children. If the teacher had told Maggie and Zack to let Jim play with them, Jim might not have figured out how to change his behavior. However, teachers can point out the beneficial consequences of cooperative actions to encourage children to continue or increase them. When working with a child in such a situation, the focus should be on how the behavior makes the child feel rather than whether (or not) it pleases the adult. In the above exam-

ple, the teacher could observe, "You're having fun racing cars together," rather than saying "It makes me happy to see you sharing your truck."

Play as partners with children. Teachers model cooperation when they act as partners in children's play. To join in their activities, get down on the children's level, imitate their use of materials, and follow their ideas. Whether you are imitating or becoming part of an extended role play, give children conversational control. Listen, describe their actions, and comment on what they say or do. Do not overload them with questions.

By getting down on children's level and following their leads, teachers model cooperation and collaboration.

To make sure you let children take the lead, act out the roles and portray the attributes they assign you. Be careful not to take over and direct the themes or characters. For example, if a child says, "You're the dog and you chase me," then that is what you should do — don't decide to be a monster or say you're tired of being the chaser and it's the child's turn to catch you. You can extend the play by asking whether you should be a certain type of dog or make a particular chasing sound. If the child wants you to carry out the chase in a different way (faster or slower, in another area of the room), she or he will let you know. You can try a small variation (growling or running toward the book area), but be sensitive to the response. The child may elaborate on the idea and take the lead in extending it. But if the child objects, or does not pick up on your innovation, drop it and continue playing according to the directions established by the child.

Engaging in Cooperative Play: Teaching Strategies

Promote interaction through the arrangement of space and materials.

- Limit clutter in order to make it easier for children to congregate and act out their play scenarios.

- Do not arbitrarily limit the number of children who can play in a given area.

- Choose materials that inspire group role play, such as dress-up clothes, and outdoor equipment (such as long, multiwheeled vehicles) that requires two or more children to operate.

- Provide enough of the same type of materials so children can use them side-by-side and together.

- If space or supplies are limited, problem-solve with the children about ways to accommodate everyone who wants to use them.

Create opportunities for collaborative interaction.

- During work (choice, free play) time, when children are in a collaborative situation, allow ample time for them to elaborate on their ideas.

- Build group times, as well as individual choice times, into the day's routine in order to provide children with a safe and structured opportunity to interact with others.

- Do not force children to join in the group activity but welcome them at any level of involvement.

- Plan activities that naturally involve children working in twos and threes (e.g., children moving or dancing as partners; two children moving large containers of toys from one place to another). Never assign partners or require that children work with others.

- Refer children to one another for assistance as another way to encourage collaboration.

Help aggressive or withdrawn children join their peers.

- Remember that children are not misbehaving when they push their way into playing with others or express reluctance to join the group.

- Coach children who tend to enter a group too aggressively by observing with them from the sidelines, validating their desire to join the play, and discussing their ideas on how to do this (or offering ideas of your own). Suggest non-invasive strategies and make comments or ask questions that help them consider the consequences of their ideas.

- Call attention (in a noncompetitive way) to how other children successfully enter a play situation.

- Provide withdrawn children with concrete tools that empower them to be part of the group (e.g., a "talking stick" that children use to take turns talking to the rest of the group).

Teaching Strategies *(cont.)*

Allow children to discover the consequences of their actions.

- When children have social conflicts, provided no one is being hurt or endangered and the children have not reached an impasse, wait and see if the children can adjust their own behavior accordingly.

- Avoid giving directions, offering opinions, or solving a social problem for children; instead, point out the beneficial consequences of cooperative actions.

- When working with a child having a social conflict, focus on how the behavior makes the child feel rather than whether (or not) it pleases the adult.

Play as partners with children.

- To join in their activities, get down on the children's level, imitate their use of materials, and follow their ideas; give children conversational control.

- Listen, describe children's actions, and comment on what they say or do; do not overload them with questions.

In addition to work time, there are many other opportunities throughout the day to act as a partner and encourage children to be partners in cooperative interactions. For example, you can solicit their ideas for a rotation system to pass out snacks or share other classroom chores. You can also let children choose a song or propose an action at large-group time. Knowing they will have an opportunity to lead not only removes the sense of competition (especially helpful for shy children), it also enables children to follow others without feeling they are being relegated to a lesser position. This kind of give-and-take is essential to sustained collaborative play.

In Conclusion

The roots of cooperative play appear in infancy and expand during the toddler and preschool years. Successful interactions with others depends on the simultaneous emergence of many related cognitive, language, and psycho-social abilities. The capacity to collaborate cannot develop in isolation. Not only do children need social experiences with playmates, they also depend upon adults to facilitate and mediate their interactions. Early childhood programs offer children an opportunity to negotiate collaborative relationships beyond those in their immediate family. By providing a safe and secure, yet interesting and challenging, environment, teachers encourage young children to expand their social networks through cooperation and reciprocity. These are skills that will serve children well into their school years and throughout their adult lives.

Valuing Diversity

At work time in the house area, Amber asks Margie (her teacher) if she knows she (Amber) is an Indian. When Margie says she does, Amber asks how she knows. Margie says Amber's mother told her. Amber continues to talk with her teacher about being an Indian:

Amber: *We went to the powwow. I danced and shaked the beads and my grandma made fry bread.*

Margie: *How do you make it?*

Amber: *You cook the bread and you fry it up and it gets all hot. Can we have it for snack?*

Margie: *Your grandmother is picking you up today. I'll ask her if she'd like to come to school and show us how she makes fry bread. We could ask her to stay and eat snack with us.*

> ### Valuing Diversity
>
> *Valuing diversity* means seeing differences in personal or group attributes as normal and positive. Attributes include gender, ethnicity, age, religion, family structure, ability levels, body build, other physical traits, ideas, and aesthetic preferences. Respecting diversity means treating people as individuals, not as stereotypes, and recognizing that individuals can simultaneously share some characteristics and differ on others.

Definition

Valuing diversity means seeing differences in personal or group attributes as normal and positive. Attributes include gender, ethnicity, age, religion, family structure, ability levels, body build, other physical traits, ideas, and aesthetic preferences. Respecting diversity means treating people as individuals, not as stereotypes, and recognizing that individuals can simultaneously share some characteristics and differ on others. This recognition involves classifying on more than one attribute, something preschoolers are just beginning to do.

Multicultural education is aimed at helping children understand and appreciate the diversity in our increasingly pluralistic society. Professor Patricia Ramsey (2006) says, "Multicultural education emphasizes the positive, adaptive value of cultural pluralism and encourages children to be competent in more than one cultural system. It typically involves using images, books, and toys (e.g., plastic foods, cooking utensils, dolls) that represent a wide range of cultural and racial groups. The underlying premise is that exposing children to a wide range of values and life styles will help them appreciate their own and other groups" (p. 280).

The Anti-Bias Curriculum, developed by Louise Derman-Sparks (1989), was one of the earliest attempts to foster children's individual identities (also see Chapter 3, "Developing a Positive Self-Identity") and intergroup respect. In the past several decades, as various social rights movements have come into prominence (for example, the women's movement, the rights of the disabled), the term *multicultural* has expanded to include any group other than the "majority" or the "mainstream."

In practice, however, there is often very little discussion in educational settings, including preschool, of the values and beliefs that make people different. Children's exposure to differences is typically superficial, limited to cultural artifacts such as holidays, foods, clothing, and artwork. Moreover, multicultural education does little to help young children of different backgrounds develop understanding and respect for themselves or the characteristics of others. At an even deeper level, we as educators rarely take the time to examine our own beliefs and practices and how they shape young children's identities, attitudes, and behaviors (Gonzalez-Mena, 2008; see below and also Chapter 14, "Preparing Ourselves to Be Role Models").

Development

Ideals versus reality. Our attitudes about a young child's ability to value diversity often reflect ideals rather than reality. We tend to romanticize children and say they are born accepting of others and without bias. Think of the lyrics in the song from the musical *South Pacific* (Rodgers & Hammerstein, 1949) that say, "You've got to be *taught* to hate and fear." But we also know that very young children sort things into "same" and "different" and may conclude that things that are the same as them are better. (Only later in preschool do they begin to sort on more than one dimension.) When we combine this natural tendency of young children to categorize (classify) with the stereotypes they encounter in their communities and the media, encouraging respect for diversity becomes quite a challenge in the early childhood classroom.

Sources of children's ideas and attitudes. Summarizing the research, psychologist James Banks (1993) noted that preschoolers have already internalized the ethnic and racial attitudes of their culture, preferring "in-group" over "out-group" members, even when they themselves are members of the out group. Many of their ideas initially come from their families and the immediate community, and they increasingly are affected by news and entertainment media, toys, and popular culture, all of which are highly stereotyped (Levin, 2003). Evidence further shows that the older children get, the harder it is to influence or change these attitudes. Thus, says professor

Valuing Diversity: Development

Preschoolers have already internalized the ethnic and racial attitudes of their culture, preferring "in-group" over "out-group" members, even when they themselves are members of the out group. Many of their ideas initially come from their families and the immediate community, and they increasingly are affected by news and entertainment media, toys, and popular culture. How young children think about similarities and differences also reflects their general developmental level and thought processes as they begin to classify people as well as objects, and they may conclude that one group is "better" than another.

Lourdes Dias Soto, "early childhood educators have the best opportunity to positively influence the racial and ethnic attitudes of children" (1999, p. 244).

Early thought processes. How young children think about similarities and differences also reflects their general developmental level and thought processes as they begin to classify people as well as objects, and they may conclude that one group is "better" than another. Summarizing child development research, educator and media expert Diane Levin (2003) identifies the following characteristics of the infant-toddler and preschool years (pp. 70–71):

- *Children begin to construct ideas about similarities and differences when they are very young.* The process begins essentially at birth (differentiating a parent from a stranger) and allows children to navigate their world. Gender labels begin around age two, ideas about race and special needs at age three.

- *Young children tend to focus on one thing at a time — usually, in this case, the most salient and visible aspects of similarities and differences among people.*

So, for example, they will focus on skin color rather than lineage for race, clothing or hair length rather than genitals for gender, or assistive aids (guide dog, crutches) rather than physiological bases for disabilities.

- *Young children tend to think in dichotomies.* To young children, something is either one thing or the other, or like me or not like me. It is hard for them to think of things as being both, as being similar in some ways but different in others. That leads to stereotypical thinking, but does not necessarily reflect bias (judgment).

- *Young children generally think egocentrically and concretely — relating what they see and hear about similarities and differences to themselves and their own experience.* They draw conclusions about others based on themselves. Again, this is their basis for developing ideas, not a reflection of bias.

  Jacey says, "I have green eyes. Just can't change them into blue eyes. Latrelle and Jonah have brown eyes. Brown skin too. They can't change them either."

- *Static thinking can make it hard for young children to understand logical causal relationships or the permanence of physical characteristics.* Unlike Jacey in the above example, young children may not yet realize that some traits are unchangeable. For example, they may think dark skin color can be washed away or that gender can change by chance or design:

  Sherelle says, "When I grow up I'm going to be a daddy so I can have tickly whiskers."

- *Children's ideas about diversity and how they learn to respond to it are influenced by what they see and hear in the world around them about similarities and differences.* It can therefore be hard to sort out what children see and hear (and repeat) from what they really think.

Teaching Strategies

Teachers are often uncomfortable with children's remarks that sound biased to our adult ears; for example, "You can play with the chocolate baby [the dark-skinned doll]." Our responses range from the laissez-faire to the directive. If we assume children get such ideas from home and we are powerless to change them, we do nothing. At the other extreme, we may attempt to lecture children about equality and treating everyone with respect. Neither approach takes into account children's concrete and hands-on way of constructing ideas about the world, and neither helps children engage personally and meaningfully to be a member of one or more diverse groups.

Children's ideas about diversity come from family, community, media, and popular culture and also reflect their developmental level and thought processes.

Effective teaching practices lie between these extremes. Our first role is to create a classroom environment in which children have positive interactions with a variety of adults and peers. These experiences can help them develop an appreciation for diversity on their own. However, because preschoolers have often encountered and possibly internalized harmful stereotypes outside of school, teachers also need to actively help them embrace diversity. You can use the following strategies to encourage young children to understand and value differences.

Work with program administrators to enact non-discriminatory recruitment and admissions policies. The classroom is one part of an organization (an agency, a school district), so the stage for respecting diversity should be set in this larger context. Consider where and how you advertise your program and whether you are reaching families from all the neighborhoods in the community (or communities) you serve. Look at the language(s) and images in your promotional materials; do they reflect the range of participants you want to attract? Pay attention to whether the terms used to address family members show respect, and honor cultural norms for age, gender, and status. For example, norms vary on whether adults like the informality of being called by their first name or prefer being addressed by their title and last name.

Office furnishings and staff clothing and demeanor can also make a difference in whether families and visitors from different backgrounds feel welcomed in your program. Together with the members of your teaching team, ask yourselves if the places where you meet with parents are clean, attractively decorated, and have comfortable seats that invite family members to stay and talk. The style of dress may be casual — most places that work with children are not formal — but staff attire should still be neat and should respect local norms of propriety. Look and listen to make sure that everyone on staff, regardless of position, is friendly and never appears too harried or busy to be "bothered" by a parent or visitor.

Model respect for others. If we want children to treat others equally and fairly, we should demonstrate this behavior ourselves (see also Chapter 14). Listen to and accept the ideas and feelings of everyone — not only the children in your care but also their parents and your colleagues. The climate of respect we create in the classroom will carry over into children's dealings at home and in the community.

Disrespect for differences is often rooted in fear. Children, like adults, are uncomfortable in the presence of something unfamiliar. What we do not know we often label as "bad," and our natural response is to actively reject or passively avoid anything perceived as negative. By making the exploration of differences a part of everyday classroom interactions, teachers can help young children learn not to equate "different" with "bad." In the following anecdote, Lily's comments reflect how children in a supportive classroom atmosphere learn to accept each other's differences rather than labeling them.

Jared is a preschooler with a speech and language delay, enrolled in an inclusion classroom. At outside time, Lily, a very verbal child, says to her teacher, "Jared said 'Hi' to me and he also said don't fall down because it's dangerous.

He knows that word, too. He is learning lots of words." Lily's teacher responds, "Yes, Jared says many words."

To model and encourage a healthy examination of diversity, make sure children feel "safe" when differences are addressed. Step in when necessary to reframe hurtful statements (see Chapter 11, "Resolving Conflicts"). Protect the recipient of negative remarks, but remember that the young speaker is not ill-intentioned, either. He or she is just trying to understand the nature of people; and, as with all social learning, children make honest mistakes.

When children do express stereotypes, it is okay to challenge them (Levin, 2003). Pointing out contradictions helps children reexamine their thinking — the same process that results when you use this strategy to scaffold their reasoning in math or another area. Don't correct children or say they are "wrong"; merely observe when something they say or think is at odds with another aspect of the experience. For example, if a child says that "all old people smell bad," you might ask children around the table if their grandmothers and grandfathers (or the gray-haired cook) smell bad. Negative responses can help the child reconsider the validity of the initial statement. At the same time, don't feel you have to "fix" children's stereotyped ideas or answer all their questions directly. Encourage them to explore ideas with one another and arrive at conclusions through their own experiences.

Finally, just as we treat children with respect, they should observe us acting respectfully toward other adults. Don't justify judging or dismissing people based on status. In a preschooler's classification system, people are either grown-ups or children. If they see a supervisor being impatient with a teacher, or a teacher being curt with a parent, children will not rationalize such behavior on the basis of hierarchies. They will simply see rudeness or disrespect among grown-ups and learn that it is an acceptable — even a mature — way to act. So, when it comes to respecting diversity, our behavior as well as our statements must reflect an inclusive respect.

Focus on similarities and differences without judgmental comparisons. Since children are inherently curious about differences, use their observations as learning opportunities. Acting as though differences do not exist will not help children come to understand and live with them. Instead, treat differences among people as you would differences among materials and events — a natural part of the world to be accepted and explored. As long as you and the children study differences without bias, the children can learn to value, not denigrate them.

> *At snacktime, Jamaica says, "My sister is heavy. I'm not." Her teacher comments, "We come in all different sizes."*

To acknowledge differences, comment on specific attributes and accomplishments without labeling one as better than the other. For example, you might observe that "Yolanda is wearing red ribbons and Nicole's braids have blue ribbons." If you say to Yolanda, "I like red ribbons," Nicole may infer there is something wrong with her blue ones. Focus on both similarities — what brings people together and what they share — as well as distinctions between them. For example, note that everyone eats but that they do so in different ways; they may use different utensils or eat with their fingers, and they enjoy different foods. Since preschoolers are concrete, comment on things they can see, hear, taste, touch, and smell. Connect your observations to their experiences; for example, that families refer to relatives by different titles and names, that children exhibit different likes and dislikes at snacktime, or that the friends and cousins they visit have different types of houses, toys, and rules for meals and bedtimes.

> *At work time in the art area, Abby says to Deirdre (her teacher), "I have a dad who doesn't live with us." Then she tells Deirdre about her visits with him:*
>
> **Abby:** *He picks me up here. His car is bigger than my mommy's.*
>
> **Deirdre:** *I see his big car when he comes to get you. It's dark green.*
>
> **Abby:** *He has a special seat for me in the back. And we go shopping on the way to his apartment.*
>
> **Deirdre:** *What do you buy?*
>
> **Abby:** *Spaghetti, every time spaghetti. And donuts. My mommy doesn't let me eat donuts.*

> **Deirdre:** *Mommies and daddies sometimes have different rules.*
>
> **Abby:** *My daddy also lets me watch one extra television show. But not too much. And he reads to me before I go to sleep, just like at home with my mommy.*

Whenever possible, draw on the diversity in the classroom to help children appreciate differences. Even if some traits (such as ethnicity) happen to be homogeneous, point to differences in other attributes such as gender, color preferences, and family composition. If important variations are lacking in your classroom (for example, there is no racial or economic diversity), find other meaningful and concrete ways to introduce them to the children. For example, use books, photographs, artwork, computer programs, field trips, and visitors to expand children's firsthand experiences with the diversity in their community and the larger society.

Adults can counteract gender, racial, and other stereotypes by encouraging all children to work with the diversity of materials in the classroom.

Include diversity in every classroom area and activity. It is not enough to have a kimono in the dress-up area, serve hummus at snacktime, or invite a parent to talk about Kwanza. "Special" clothes, foods, or celebrations, while valuable additions to the classroom, do not simultaneously address the fact that diversity is an everyday and everywhere occurrence. Our goal as educators is to incorporate diversity throughout the environment, activities, and interactions of the program day. Only then does difference become the norm, not the exception.

When and How to Celebrate Holidays

Celebrating holidays can pose a dilemma in early childhood programs. Holidays are usually happy occasions and are a natural way to honor diversity. However, if they are also religious observances, publicly funded programs must adhere to laws regulating separation of church and state. Further, families that don't observe that holiday may feel excluded. There is also the danger that holidays that are a "big deal" for grown-ups may hold limited interest for young children. Or conversely, that holidays adults have long since crossed off their calendars continue to engage children's imaginations and dominate their role playing.

In the following story, two preschool teachers (the "we" in the narrative) not only resolved the problem of how to celebrate holidays but even expanded their definition of celebrations. Both adults and children learned something in the process.

—•••—

"Rosie celebrates Christmas, Irene celebrates Santa, and I celebrate Hanukkah!"

This comment, made by three-year-old Eli, illustrates the importance that holidays and other special celebrations can have for a young child. Like many preschoolers, Eli was already becoming aware that individuals and families have many different ways of observing these special events.

If being interested in celebrations is natural for young children, why do so many adults feel panicky when deciding whether or how to support holiday-related experiences in their early childhood setting?

We used to feel this concern every time a holiday was near. Until we thought through our approach to these special occasions, the word "celebration" left us feeling uneasy and unsure. We questioned ourselves: How did we decide what to celebrate? What experiences with holidays and special events had the children in our classroom participated in? Would we offend some families by celebrating holidays that have a religious basis? How would we support the child in our classroom who did not celebrate any holidays due to their religion? And, if we did decide to bring such celebrations into our classroom, how could we use what we knew about active learning to enhance these experiences?

It would have been easy to "bury our heads in the sand" and have no holiday celebrations. Then again, we could have taken the "holiday of the month" approach and celebrated every holiday on the calendar. Neither option [was acceptable.] Instead, we decided to find a middle ground: In the holiday-related experiences we planned, we tried to show the value we placed on the traditions, rituals, and beliefs of the children and families in our classroom, without losing sight of the fact that these traditional celebrations raised sensitive issues for many families.

Here are some of the steps we took as we explored this issue:

Defining celebrations. Special occasions seemed to us to be divided into two categories: The first included the standard ways of observing holidays that had religious, cultural, or ethnic origins; the second

When and How to Celebrate Holidays *(cont.)*

we called "life's little celebrations." This second category included traditions and rituals that were less oriented to specific groups or days on the calendar — things like Kyle's family having a shower for a new baby, Jessie's grandmother teaching her how to make paper towel butterflies, and the arrival each summer of ripe red tomatoes in the preschool garden. We also remembered other kinds of special occasions — the arrival of new siblings, riding a "two-wheeler" for the first time, attending community art fairs and carnivals, and losing a tooth.

We then recalled how excited Lauren was about being a flower girl in her aunt's wedding. We celebrated with Lauren by sharing her excitement, listening to her stories of the wedding, and eventually adding veils and flowers to the house area for her to reenact the wedding. In a similar way, we celebrated with Lakisha when she made piles of toys in the house area and said, "I'm packing for my trip to Grandma and Grandpa's house." Lakisha's family always took a trip to her grandparents' house for Thanksgiving weekend. To support Lakisha's family tradition, we added suitcases and a car steering wheel to the classroom.

Recognizing why celebrations are important. We discovered several reasons why celebrations are important: (1) Celebrations add excitement to everyday life. (2) They make children and families feel important and special. (3) They introduce children to new routines and rituals. (4) They pass on family cultures and traditions. (5) They expose children to differences among people. (6) They offer opportunities for people to recognize their similarities.

(7) They help children connect with the communities in which they live.

Using families as resources.
Through home visits, family surveys, casual conversations with family members at drop-off and pick-up times, parent-teacher conferences, and family potlucks and gatherings, we had already established an open relationship with our families. We resolved to use these ways to learn more about how they observed holidays and family traditions. For example, one day Katie's mother mentioned at drop-off time that Katie had made and taped paper Easter eggs to the walls in the living room. She also mentioned that their family would be dyeing Easter eggs and she would be happy to bring eggs and help dye them with the class. We invited Katie's mom to dye eggs with the children at small-group time and added colored plastic eggs and baskets to the house area. In the days that followed, the children invented a "hide-the-egg" game.

Since we have adopted our new approach to holidays, the word "celebration" no longer evokes panic and uneasiness for us. We invite you to try this approach in your own early childhood center. As your starting point, **know the families in your classroom,** and **keep your children's interests in mind.** Most of all, understand — as Eli did — that we all celebrate in our own way and that's okay!

●●●

— Adapted from "Amazing Days: Celebrating With Children and Families" (Lucier & Gainsley, 2005, pp. 433–441)

Valuing Diversity: Teaching Strategies

Work with program administrators to enact nondiscriminatory recruitment admission policies.

- Evaluate your program's promotional materials to see whether they reflect the range of participants you want to attract. Pay attention to whether the terms used to address family members show respect and honor cultural norms for age, gender, and status.

- Evaluate whether office furnishings, staff clothing and demeanor, and other features of your program will make families and visitors from different backgrounds feel welcomed.

- Make sure the places where you meet with parents are clean, attractively decorated, and have comfortable seats that invite family members to stay and talk.

Model respect for others.

- Listen to and accept the ideas and feelings of everyone — not only the children in your care but also their parents and your colleagues.

- Make the exploration of differences a part of everyday classroom interactions.

- Step in when necessary to reframe hurtful statements; protect the recipient of negative remarks but remember that the young speaker is not ill-intentioned, either.

- Remember that, when children do express stereotypes, it is okay to challenge them by raising contradictions in their thinking; in doing so, you scaffold children's reasoning. At the same time, don't feel you have to "fix" children's stereotyped ideas; encourage children to explore ideas with one another and arrive at conclusions through their own experiences.

- Model respectful behavior toward other adults; don't justify judging or dismissing people based on status.

Focus on similarities and differences without judgmental comparisons.

- Treat differences among people as a natural part of the world to be accepted and explored.

- To acknowledge differences, comment on specific attributes and accomplishments without labeling one as better than the other.

- Whenever possible, draw on the diversity in the classroom to help children appreciate differences. If important variations are lacking in your classroom, find other meaningful and concrete ways to introduce them to the children (e.g., through books, photographs, artwork, computer programs, field trips, and visitors).

Include diversity in every classroom area and activity.

- Incorporate diversity throughout the environment, activities, and interactions of the program day.

- Make sure equipment and materials represent human diversity and reflect the homes, communities, and special needs of children and their families.

Teaching Strategies *(cont.)*

- To avoid stereotyping, make sure all materials are equally accessible and that all children receive equal encouragement to incorporate them into their play.

- In the reading area, feature books, magazines, and catalogs with illustrations and photographs of diverse cultures, people performing nonstereotypical jobs, families of varying composition and backgrounds, and people of different ages portrayed in a realistic light; make sure the images in computer programs also reflect this diversity.

- Hang reproductions of artwork in diverse media from around the world at eye level throughout the room.

- Include simple instruments from different traditions in the music area.

As you survey the equipment and materials in your program, make sure they represent human diversity and reflect the homes, communities, and special needs of the children and their families. For example, in the dress-up area, provide everyday clothes as well as holiday costumes from the countries represented by the families and teachers in the program. The house area might contain work clothes and tools used in different types of jobs (families can often contribute used items from home), cooking utensils and empty food containers from many ethnic cuisines (especially those represented in the classroom), and equipment (such as crutches and magnifiers) used by people with various disabilities. To avoid stereotyping, make sure all materials are equally accessible and that all children receive equal encouragement to incorporate them into their play.

At work time in the house area, Megan tells Mikey and David that "Women can be firepeople, too, because I saw it on TV." Then she puts on a fire hat and joins them putting out fires.

Serve food from the families' cultures and religions at snacktime on a regular basis, and offer special treats associated with holiday times. In the reading area, feature books, magazines, and catalogs with illustrations and photographs of diverse cultures, people performing nonstereotypical jobs, families of varying composition and backgrounds, and people of different ages portrayed in a realistic light. Make sure the images in computer programs also reflect this diversity. Hang reproductions of artwork in diverse media from around the world at eye level throughout the room. In the music area, include simple instruments from different traditions.

Plan activities that reflect diversity; for example, encourage families to bring seeds for their favorite vegetables and flowers to plant in the school garden, listen and move to music from different cultures and genres, eat foods of different regional or ethnic cuisines, take field trips to neighborhood stores and outdoor markets that cater to the local population, and celebrate holidays and traditions that are observed by families in the program and are meaningful to the children (see the sidebar on pp. 96–97). Go to local places and attend events that showcase diversity, such as food and craft shops, fairs, and concerts. Visit sites ahead of time or preview materials to make sure that places the class might visit are not biased and to anticipate any questions children might have about the individuals and groups portrayed. Let staff at the sites know you are coming and, whenever possible, arrange to be hosted by someone who is prepared to welcome and interact with young children.

In Conclusion

Young children are naturally curious about differences. One way they make sense of the world is to sort it into different categories. At the same time they divide objects or actions or people into groups, they are also trying to separate right from wrong and good from bad. Their intent is not to judge but merely to organize a complex and challenging environment. However, this mode of thinking can sometimes lead young children to label anything that differs from them as negative or undesirable. Our responsibility as educators is to support their fascination with differences while helping them understand that diversity is normal and not inherently good or bad. By addressing and valuing the differences among ourselves and the children and families in our programs, we can encourage the acceptance of diversity among the children who turn to us as an example.

10

Developing a Framework for Moral Behavior

The psychologist Jean Piaget (1932/1965) interviewed children about acts such as stealing and lying. When asked what a lie is, younger children (early preschool) answered that they were "naughty words." When asked why they should not lie, they again could not explain it beyond citing the forbidden nature of the act: "Because it is a naughty word." However, older children (later preschool) were able to explain, "Because it isn't right" or "It isn't true." That is, they cited simple moral reasons. Even older children (beginning primary grades) indicated intention as being relevant to the meaning and judgment of an act: "A lie is when you deceive someone else, but to make a mistake is just when you make a mistake."

Definition

Morality is a system for evaluating human conduct. It is the internal sense we have of right and wrong apart from any external censure or punishment. Moral development, also called having a conscience or a superego, is a long process. It begins in toddlerhood with concrete ideas, such as that it is wrong to hurt others, and extends well into adolescence and even adulthood as people form abstract moral values, such as the concept of equality and how it should govern our behavior. How people use moral values to define themselves, and their decision-making, is known as their moral identity. Moral identity addresses the question, "What kind of person do I want to be?" A person who is motivated to "make the world a better place" has a strong moral identity.

Moral Behavior

Morality is a system for evaluating human conduct. It is the internal sense we have of right and wrong apart from any external censure or punishment. How people use moral values to define themselves and their decision making is known as *moral identity*. Moral identity addresses the question, "What kind of person do I want to be?"

Development

Theory and research. Piaget (1932/1965) was among the first psychologists to study moral development in children, and he did so based on his observations of how children develop rules for games and construct ideas about behavior such as cheating and lying. He concluded that in earlier stages of moral reasoning, children are "heteronomous" — focused on outcomes rather than intentions — and bound by rules and obedience to authority. As children increasingly interact with their peers, they become more "autonomous" in their moral reasoning — that is, able to consider behavior from other perspectives and selectively apply rules based on mutual respect and reciprocity. Thus, social interactions, especially those in which cooperation is stressed, lead to more advanced moral reasoning.

Beginning 50 years ago, developmental psychologist Lawrence Kohlberg elaborated on Piaget's work and

Older preschoolers can also begin to grapple with the motivation behind an action, and they can attempt to differentiate harmful behavior that is "accidental" from that which is "intentional." For example, they can recognize that knocking over a block tower because you weren't paying attention when you ran past is not the same as knocking it over because you are mad at the builder. While children sometimes claim "It was an accident" as a way of denying responsibility or avoiding punishment (merely mimicking adults), they are also genuinely interested in classifying the root causes of potentially hurtful behavior into the two categories of "intended" (deliberate) and "unintended" (accidental). This ability to differentiate intent is still fragile — preschoolers still focus primarily on the consequences of their actions — but it does emerge along with other classification skills.

Influences on moral development. Families and communities also play a significant role in children's moral development. The capacity for empathy has some biological basis, according to genetic psychologist Nancy Eisenberg (1989). Yet an inborn sense of empathy is just a starting point, emphasizes developmental psychologist William Damon (1990). Parenting is also critical. Everybody starts off feeling good when other people feel good and feeling bad when other people feel bad, so the question is, "What goes wrong?" when children old enough to know better behave immorally. Family variables that work against the development of healthy morality include child abuse (the child sees a hostile world as the norm), the model of using violence rather than negotiation to settle conflicts (between peers, between parents), exposure to inappropriate role models (aggression glorified on television and in video games and music), isolation (lack of exposure to people who are different so there is no opportunity to learn tolerance), and lack of guidance (no direction on how to act even when feelings of empathy are triggered).

Friends also have an influence on moral development, but parents are a more powerful force. According to Damon, children with a stable parental influence usually choose peers who share their family's moral sense. In the absence of diligent parenting, children are more susceptible to peer influences that lead them to engage in troublesome behavior. Other adults can solidify the moral thinking instilled by parents. And since most young children these days attend early care and education settings, teachers and caregivers play an increasingly important role in children's moral development. Fortunately, the growing body of research on development and practice can help us adopt practices that are both appropriate and effective in promoting moral reasoning.

Teaching Strategies

As described above, children's moral sense develops to a great extent from the examples set by significant others in their lives. The home setting begins to shape a child's beliefs about right and wrong. Later, the behavioral models in the classroom, and the ways in which adults exemplify and articulate moral principles, lay the groundwork from which children continue to build their own value systems. To support children as they construct a moral framework, you can employ the strategies described below.

Be consistent and fair-minded. Children will learn the principles of equality and fairness when you establish and act upon clear expectations for their behavior. As you strive for consistency in these rules, however, it is important to emphasize problem solving rather than blame or punishment. (Also see Chapter 11 for a problem-solving approach to conflict resolution.) DeVries and Zan (1994) offer the following advice, illustrated with examples from the author:

- *Avoid sanctions and punishments.* If children cannot see the logic in the consequences, it puts the responsibility on the adult, not the child.

  For example, if an adult says that Chris, who knocked over Pat's block tower, cannot join the group at story time, this "punishment" is not likely to make sense to Chris. It is the adult who is making an (arbitrary) connection and hence taking responsibility for establishing cause and effect. A more logical outcome, such as helping to rebuild the block tower (especially if Chris and Pat arrive at this solution together), allows Chris to take responsibility for the action by helping to solve the resulting problem.

• *When children suggest a consequence that is too severe, ask the wrongdoer to say how he or she feels about it.* Support this child's feeling. Young children will often make punitive suggestions because it fits within their system of logic without their having the ability to completely think through (or empathize with) the consequences for the one being punished. The teacher can help point out what the full consequence of the punishment would be and ask children for a less extreme alternative.

For example (in the above incident), Pat may suggest that Chris "can never play with blocks again." Chris might say, "But I need the blocks to build a racing ramp." The teacher might also ask Pat, "What if you needed help carrying a big block to build a ramp for your cars and Chris offered to help you. Could Chris use the blocks then?" Pat may concede that this would be permissible. By posing a series of such real-life examples, the teacher can validate everyone's feelings and help children reconsider the solutions they propose.

• *Avoid indefinite or abstract consequences.* The closer the time connection, the more likely the child is to see the relationship between an act and its aftermath. If the consequence drags on, or its relationship to the action is unclear, it takes on a life of its own and the cause-effect relationship is lost to the child.

For example, if the consequence in the above example was that Chris had to help put away blocks every day for a week (regardless of whether Chris actually played with them each day), the connection between knocking down the tower and shelving the blocks at cleanup time would be lost after the first day. But if Chris and Pat agreed that Chris should help Pat put away the blocks at cleanup time that day, the connection would be direct and would occur within a timeframe the young children could grasp. Likewise, a solution focused on the blocks *per se*, rather than some other behavior, would be concrete and meaningful. If Chris had to do something else "nice" for Pat — such as drawing a picture — it would be abstract and disconnected from the incident.

Teachers can help children see the consequences of their actions by pointing out cause-effect relationships with simple, nonjudgmental statements.

Verbalize in simple terms the reasons for actions and decisions that involve moral matters. Lengthy or abstract statements of moral rectitude will go right over children's heads. But simple explanations in concrete terms will make sense to them. So, for example, you might say, "I'm making sure every child who wants birthday cake gets a piece before giving out seconds. It isn't fair if someone gets two pieces before every child has one." Imitating you as their model, children will also benefit from hearing themselves and others offer straightforward moral reasons for their behavior. You will hear these explanations stated not only in terms of their actions toward other people, but often in consideration of how to treat animals and plants:

> *At snacktime Madison says, "Next time I'm never ever going to take all the crackers because now there aren't too much left for everyone else."*

> *While playing in the grass yard, Casey finds a roly-poly. He moves it, saying "If we don't move it, somebody is going to step on it."*

> *At outside time, Jazlyn tells Paris, "You don't touch bird eggs or the mama won't come back."*

Another reason to verbalize cause-effect relationships is that children may not see them on their own. A simple statement is usually enough to raise children's awareness. Call their attention to the problem in a factual, nonjudgmental way. For example, suppose it wasn't just Chris, but several children who unintentionally demolished Pat's block structure. You might say, "When we run fast, we sometimes don't see things in our path. Then we accidentally knock things down, like Pat's tower. Pat worked really hard on that tower and feels bad because now all the pieces are on the floor."

Such statements also open the door to problem-solving. For example, the children who ran and knocked down the tower might suggest they help Pat rebuild it. Although our instinct is sometimes to prevent such behaviors, it can also be helpful to selectively allow natural (nondangerous) consequences to occur. So, don't be too quick to "rescue" children or they will lose an opportunity to construct a cause-effect relationship and thereby solve a problem or prevent it from recurring.

Teachers can also help children differentiate between rules that reflect moral issues and those that reflect social conventions (see the discussion of "domain theory" above). Consider this excerpt from an interview with a four-year-old girl who witnessed different types of transgressions at her preschool (Office for Studies in Moral Development and Education, 2007):

Moral issue:

> Interviewer: *Did you see what happened?*
>
> Girl: *Yes. They were playing and John hit him too hard.*
>
> Interviewer: *Is that something you are supposed to do or not supposed to do?*
>
> Girl: *Not so hard to hurt.*
>
> Interviewer: *Is there a rule about that?*
>
> Girl: *Yes.*
>
> Interviewer: *What is the rule?*
>
> Girl: *You're not to hit hard.*
>
> Interviewer: *What if there were no rule about hitting hard, would it be all right to do then?*
>
> Girl: *No.*
>
> Interviewer: *Why not?*
>
> Girl: *Because he could get hurt and start to cry.*

Conventional issue:

> Interviewer: *Did you see what just happened?*
>
> Girl: *Yes. They were noisy.*
>
> Interviewer: *Is that something you are supposed to do or not supposed to do?*
>
> Girl: *Not do.*
>
> Interviewer: *Is there a rule about that?*
>
> Girl: *Yes. We have to be quiet.*
>
> Interviewer: *What if there were no rule, would it be all right to do then?*
>
> Girl: *Yes.*
>
> Interviewer: *Why?*
>
> Girl: *Because there is no rule.*

Helping children understand in simple terms the reasons behind what is asked of them is especially important as they navigate different situations. For example, preschoolers can understand that we speak more quietly when others read or listen to music, but that when children are engaged in noisy activities outdoors, it is okay to shout and yell. Similarly, children are often confronted with conflicting rules in different settings — for example, they can paint with their fingers in preschool but must use brushes in day care; mommy only permits juice in her house although daddy allows soft drinks at his apartment. If children understand that alternative standards for behavior reflect social conventions, they have a basis for adapting their behavior accordingly. If something is labeled as a moral absolute, however, children know the rule applies regardless of the setting or the people involved.

Acknowledge when children have acted morally. A common mistake adults make is thinking that if children feel good about themselves, they will do the right thing. But a child's moral development does not stem from self-esteem. In fact, says developmental psychologist William Damon (1990), it is the reverse. Children who do the right thing feel good about themselves. By acknowledging (not praising) children's moral behavior, they become more aware of what they did and its positive effects on others. (For more on praise versus encouragement, see the teaching strategies in Chapter 5.)

At small-group time, while doing puzzles at the table, Jerzy says, "I want to help Christian with the panda (puzzle)." He moves next to Christian, but when Christian shakes his head to indicate he does not want any help, Jerzy sits back down and begins working on another puzzle. His teacher says, "You paid attention to Christian when he showed that he did not want help."

In the same vein of helping children act morally in order to regard themselves positively, DeVries & Zan (1994) emphasize the importance of making sure the solution is something the child truly wants to do — whether it is a verbal statement ("You can play with the truck after I have two turns on the sand timer") or an action (one child hands over the truck after playing with it for a few more minutes). If the solution to a problem is coerced, no one benefits. Moreover, it perpetuates the idea that morality is externally imposed rather than being a set of principles generated and followed from within.

When adults acknowledge children's moral behavior, children become more aware of their actions and their positive effects on others.

Involve parents to achieve as much congruence between home and school values as possible. As noted above, parents play a critical role in their children's moral development. Teachers can support parents in their attempts to raise moral and ethical children and acknowledge their concerns that messages from the media often make this a challenging task. It is important to remember that parents and other family members are a child's first and most important example of moral behavior. What they do and say leaves a big impression.

Parents can also provide indirect (noncoercive) instruction to young children on how to take the perspective of their playmates and understand their emotions, says psychologist Nancy Eisenberg (1989). Research shows that a parental comment, such as "When you hit your sister, it made her sad," is related to positive social and moral development. In this respect, parents and teachers can provide parallel and consistent messages. Share ideas with parents on noncritical ways to help children understand the consequences of their actions.

When home and classroom beliefs diverge, explain clearly and simply to children and families why this is so. Accept rather than judge differences, and problem-solve any potential conflicts in how situations are handled in the two locations. Oftentimes differences reflect variations in social conventions, while the underlying moral principle is the same. For example, parents and teachers may hold different views about eating. They share a moral value that grown-ups are responsible for feeding children healthy food. However, the healthy food served at home (such as cooked carrots) is eaten with utensils, while the healthy food served at school (such as cheese cubes) can be eaten with one's fingers. Clarifying both the commonality and the differences in this case can help you reach a mutually acceptable resolution. (See Chapter 14, "Preparing Ourselves to Be Role Models," for additional ideas on how to bridge cultural divides between parents and teachers.)

Sometimes children's statements or role plays give teachers insights that something they may consider "immoral" is occurring in a child's home. Except in cases where abuse or neglect is suspected (and must be reported), teachers need to acknowledge their limits in enforcing or imposing their own standards for moral behavior. In the following two examples, children reveal their own sense of what is morally fair and socially acceptable, respectively:

At breakfast, Justin says, "My mom's life is boring. She just watches TV and plays games. I have to clean the whole house. It's no fair. I have to cook dinner every night, too. I cook mac and cheese. I put it in a bowl and put in the microwave. I'm bored of mac and cheese."

Developing a Framework for Moral Behavior: Teaching Strategies

Be consistent and fair-minded.

- Establish and act upon clear expectations for children's behavior; emphasize problem solving and avoid blame or punishment.

- When children suggest a consequence for wrongdoing that is too severe, ask the wrongdoer to say how he or she feels about it and support this child's feeling.

- Avoid indefinite or abstract consequences.

Verbalize in simple terms the reasons for actions and decisions that involve moral matters.

- Phrase explanations in simple and concrete terms that will make sense to children; verbalizing cause-effect relationships helps children learn to see them.

- Call children's attention to a problem in a factual, nonjudgmental way.

- Selectively allow natural (nondangerous) consequences to occur (e.g., children running and knocking down another child's tower) to give children an opportunity to construct a cause-effect relationship and solve the problem.

- Help children differentiate between rules that reflect moral issues and those that reflect social conventions.

- Help children understand in simple terms the reasons behind what is asked of them so they understand that different conventions apply in different situations

(e.g., they speak quietly when others are reading but they can speak loudly when everyone is playing outside).

Acknowledge when children have acted morally.

- Acknowledge (rather than praise) children's moral behavior to help them become more aware of what they did and its positive effects on others.

- Make sure the solution to the problem is something the child truly wants to do, whether it is a verbal statement or an action. A coerced solution benefits no one.

Involve parents to achieve as much congruence between home and school values as possible.

- Support parents in their attempts to raise moral and ethical children and acknowledge their concerns that messages from the media often make this a challenging task.

- Remember that parents and other family members are a child's first and most important examples of moral behavior.

- To provide parallel and consistent messages, share ideas with parents on noncritical ways to help children understand the consequences of their actions.

- When home and classroom beliefs diverge, explain clearly and simply

Teaching Strategies *(cont.)*

to children and families why this is so; accept rather than judge differences, and problem-solve potential conflicts.

- When teachers have insights that something they may consider "immoral" is occurring in a child's home, except where abuse and neglect is suspected and must be reported, teachers should acknowledge their limits in enforcing or imposing their own standards for moral behavior. They can, however, acknowledge and validate children's feelings about their home lives.

Model moral behavior in instructional interactions with children.

- Act as a role model to help children see themselves as self-initiating and competent learners.

- Employ inquiry-based learning methods rather than direct instruction.

- Ask open-ended rather than closed-ended questions.

Rebecca and Justin are in dress-up clothes, talking on the phone. Rebecca says, "I'm calling him poop. I call him poop 'cause he didn't take a shower for a week; that is my ex-husband." Rebecca looks at her teacher and adds, "I'm just pretending."

When teachers witness such behavior, sometimes the best strategy is simply to acknowledge and validate the child's feelings (in the first case) or respect their need to protect the integrity of their families (in the second). Comments such as "You're upset because you think it's not fair that you have to cook," or "I know you're just pretending," communicate your own moral values — that is, that you care about children's feelings.

Model moral behavior in instructional interactions with children. People generally think moral education is what happens when adults encourage children to treat others fairly or kindly. So, while teaching methods are typically examined in terms of their behavioral or academic effectiveness (task-orientation, knowledge and skills), their moral implications are rarely analyzed. Yet *how* we engage children in learning also affects their moral development. Psychologist Cary Buzzelli (1996) says it is therefore legitimate to ask how "morally" teachers treat their students in their instructional interactions.

Teacher-child discourse is one way that teachers, often inadvertently, convey their own moral values and act as role models. In early childhood programs, how adults talk and act with children determines whether children see themselves as self-initiating and competent learners who are treated with dignity and respect by adults *or* as blank recipients and objects of learning whose role is to absorb what authority figures transmit to them.

As an example, consider the following instructional strategies:

- *Direct instruction versus inquiry-based learning.* In the former mode, children receive information from the adult. What they are told is presumed to be accurate — it comes from an authoritative source — so children are not encouraged to question it. Mistakes are labeled as wrong and are corrected by the teacher. In the latter instructional style, children actively discover and generate knowledge. They pose and answer questions through a combination of adult guidance and their own investigative efforts. They are typically encouraged to share ideas and be challenged by their peers. Children may make mistakes, but with appropriate adult scaffolding, they can reexamine their own conclusions and (self-) correct their ideas.

- *Closed- or open-ended questions.* By asking closed-ended questions, the teacher controls the dialogue, allowing children to contribute only what the teacher asks for. In the open-ended style of questioning, the control is shared. Children are given an opportunity to express and expand on their own ideas rather than conforming to the adult's definition of what is relevant and the response(s) that are considered right and wrong.

These teaching strategies can not only affect children's mastery of specific subject matter, they also influence their moral development. Direct instruction and closed-ended questions establish a model in which rules are imposed from outside and followed because of external controls. Authority is not questioned. Someone else, rather than the individual, takes responsibility for the learning. Children who learn this way do not have an opportunity to engage in the higher realms of reasoning that contribute to advanced moral development. That is, they do not have experiences beyond the level of "following orders."

By contrast, when learning is inquiry-based and teachers ask open-ended questions, children take responsibility for their own education. They express ideas and receive feedback from adults and peers alike. Teachers act as mediators for children's inquiries and problem-solving but they do not take over or impose solutions. In this type of learning, children have a model for contributing to forming and enacting moral principles.

In Conclusion

"Conceptualizing teaching as inherently a moral activity means that we, as early childhood educators, must consider the moral implications of all the activities that occur in our classrooms" (Buzzelli, 1996, p. 534). We should therefore acknowledge and nurture children as capable and enthusiastic learners, encourage them to pursue knowledge in creative ways, and help them build connections between what they know and what they have yet to learn. By following these goals, we will help young children become adults whose thinking and behavior toward people and the environment is guided by fundamental moral principles.

Resolving Conflicts

At work time, when Andre bumps into cups that Justin is stacking, Justin stands up, puts his face inches from Andre's, and yells, "You stupid. Why did you do that?" Later, when Andre sits in the computer chair before Justin can, Justin says, "You're a brat!" Andre replies, "I'm not a brat. A brat is a crying kid."

At work time in the art area, Amber says, "Teacher, she (another child) took my tape." When asked what she could do, Amber replies, "Say I don't like that." Then Amber gets the other child another roll of tape.

At outside time, Makenna gets off the bicycle to look at a turtle. Becky asks her, "Could I ride your bike while you look at the turtle? I'll give it back in a little while."

Definition

Conflict resolution is the use of appropriate, nonaggressive strategies to settle interpersonal differences. It is also referred to by other names such as social problem solving, behavior or anger management, and classroom discipline. To emphasize that children are not misbehaving but, rather, making mistakes as they learn how to act appropriately in conflict situations, whatever words are used should not be value-laden or describe children's behavior in negative terms.

Development

Sources of conflict. Because children are egocentric and focused on their own needs, they often get into conflicts with others. They do not intend harm, nor do they mean to be selfish; they are simply goal-oriented. For example,

> ### Resolving Conflicts
>
> *Conflict resolution* is the use of appropriate, nonaggressive strategies to settle interpersonal differences. It is also referred to by other names such as social problem solving, behavior or anger management, and classroom discipline. To emphasize that children are not misbehaving but, rather, making mistakes as they learn how to act appropriately in conflict situations, avoid words that are value-laden or describe children's behavior in negative terms.

they want to play with a toy or sit next to the teacher while she reads a story. When they act aggressively, children may also simply be imitating the behaviors they see elsewhere — at home or in the media — without having learned that violence or verbal abuse are not acceptable ways of dealing with social problems in the classroom and elsewhere.

Resolving conflicts when needs and emotions run high is a complex process and involves a great deal of learning. The anecdotes that open this chapter show how young children's behavior can range from name calling (Justin), to using language to defuse a situation (Andre), to saying and acting upon a solution (Amber). In the last example, a preschooler (Becky) even shows empathy when she anticipates how another child (Makenna) will react to her behavior and takes steps (says she will return the bike) to prevent a conflict.

Resolving Conflicts: Development

Because young children are goal-oriented and focused on their own needs, they often get into conflicts with others. They may also simply be imitating behavior they have seen elsewhere — at home or in the media. Children's capacity to resolve conflicts is highly dependent on their emotional and social abilities in other domains. Because conflicts elicit strong emotions, children must be able to recognize, label, and regulate their feelings and see situations from more than one perspective. Developing skill at conflict resolution also involves feeling empathy, developing a sense of community, engaging in cooperative play, valuing diversity, and developing a framework for moral behavior.

Given that even adults are not always effective at social problem solving — because we, too, are overwhelmed by feelings and/or have not learned how to manage or mediate conflicts — it is no wonder that this area poses a substantial challenge for young children. It is also cited as a primary concern among practitioners, many of whom have not received child development information or training in how to deal with this daily occurrence.

The influence of other social-emotional skills. Children's capacity to resolve conflicts is highly dependent on their emotional and social abilities in others domains. Because conflicts elicit strong emotions, children must be able to recognize, label, and regulate their feelings (see Chapter 6, "Recognizing and Labeling Emotions"). Finding solutions to interpersonal problems involves seeing situations from more than one perspective and hence draws upon the emerging capacity for empathy (see Chapter 4, "Feeling Empathy"). The desire and means to negotiate and act on a mutually determined resolution further draws on a broad set of social behaviors, includ-

ing creating community, working cooperatively, valuing diversity, and being guided by moral principles (discussed in Chapters 7 through 10, respectively). Thus, the mastery of conflict resolution skills is not a separate strand of development but, rather, reflects the trajectory of growth already described in those earlier chapters.

Within those other domains of emotional and social development, however, there are certain features that are particularly salient when young children encounter and attempt to resolve interpersonal disagreements. The following is a summary of these major points from previous chapters in the book:

- *Feeling empathy* (Also see Chapter 4) — To understand another person's viewpoint, children must be able to "decenter"; that is, take a perspective other than their own. This ability requires the mental capacity to imagine thoughts, feelings, and actions that are beyond oneself and not tied to the here and now. This ability is just beginning to emerge in preschool, so it is unrealistic to expect younger children to engage in conflict resolution without adult facilitation. However, young children can see the effects (consequences) of their actions on others and, with adult help and support, modify their behavior to bring about a different result.

- *Recognizing and labeling emotions* (Also see Chapter 6) — Before being able to resolve a conflict, children must identify and self-regulate (control) their emotions. This is difficult for young children, but preschoolers are developing two abilities that assist them in this process. First is their emerging facility with language, which allows them to label and describe their feelings. The very act of attaching words to feelings can help them calm down. Second is the preschoolers' ability to defer gratification, at least for short periods of time. They are able to do this because they can imagine (again, mentally picture) how and when their desires will be fulfilled.

- *Developing a sense of community* (Also see Chapter 7) — Children are motivated to get along with members of their community. Sometimes other desires get in the way — for example, they want a toy someone else is using or the immediate attention of an adult.

However, the need for social acceptance helps them weigh the risks of being exclusively self-centered against the benefits of simultaneously fulfilling their own and others' wishes. Preschoolers are able to meld these individual and group concerns and thus make the transition from "me" to "we." This capacity allows them to engage in conflict resolution, in which those on both sides of the dispute get their needs met.

- **Engaging in cooperative play** (Also see Chapter 8) — Preschoolers can also collaborate with others to reach a common goal. While turn taking in the form of give-and-take imitation appears as early as infancy, it is not until preschool that children engage in coordinated play with others. These interactions involve paying attention to playmates and delaying one's own actions — a form of self-regulation. Pretend play also entails imagining what you and others might say and do. Similarly, dealing with conflict requires one to picture "what if" in order to arrive at a solution. The same skills involved in role playing — I do this and then you do that — also apply to sharing materials and friends. In the end, common goals such as building a tall tower, or sitting close enough to the teacher to see and hear the storybook, are achieved through a comparable set of collaborative behaviors.

- **Valuing diversity** (Also see Chapter 9) — Conflicts arise because people perceive things differently. To agree on a solution, both parties have to accept that the other person's needs or opinions are as valid as their own. This world view of equality is also at the heart of valuing diversity. With their growing ability to classify objects and actions, preschoolers can see in simple terms what each party in a conflict wants and describe what each person did to satisfy that need. As long as adults can help them avoid labeling these contrasts as "good" or "bad," young children can then begin to develop a solution that respects their differences as normal and positive.

- **Developing a framework for moral behavior** (Also see Chapter 10) — Young children's growing appreciation for both moral principles and social conventions assists them in resolving conflicts. Preschoolers are concerned with the treatment of others; they have internalized the principle that hurting someone else is not right. They also have rudimentary ideas about fairness, such as "everyone should get the same." Likewise, they have been in enough social situations to become familiar with social norms; for example, a timer is an accepted way of keeping track of turns while impatience is not. As they confront conflicts, therefore, preschoolers can resolve them by calling on their dual knowledge of moral principles and socially accepted ways of achieving them.

Children's ability to resolve conflicts when emotions run high is closely tied to their emotional and social abilities in other domains.

Teaching Strategies

Adults are often uncomfortable with young children's social conflicts and are eager to get them over with quickly. Early childhood specialist Sandra Lamm and her colleagues in practice and research (Lamm, Groulx, Hansen, Patton, & Slaton, 2006) identify three common teacher responses to children's disagreements: *pleading* (begging children to take turns or to "be nice and share"), *directing* (telling children not to take toys from others or to "use your words"), or *punishing* (assigning children time-outs or withdrawing privileges). These strategies may impose short-term solutions — sometimes no more than momentary ones — but they do not bring about long-term changes or build children's social problem-solving competencies.

Instead, teachers can see children's social mistakes as learning opportunities. When a conflict arises, you can use the occasion to help children solve it by practicing the emotional and social skills described above. Once the crisis is past and things have calmed down — or when reading about or discussing similar situations — you can also use the lessons learned to help children avoid and resolve social problems in the future.

Learning the strategies for resolving conflicts takes a great deal of patience and repetition, but preschoolers can begin to implement problem-solving behavior on their own. Rather than intervening, you can guide the process with appropriate modeling and support. Research shows that children can master the steps in conflict resolution; moreover, when they do, there is a 40 percent decrease in challenging behaviors, including crying, tattling, and physical aggression (Lamm et al., 2006).

Below are the strategies you can use to help preschoolers avoid social conflicts and deal with them when they inevitably arise. Adults who use these techniques also report that their own ability to solve interpersonal problems at home as well as with colleagues in the workplace improves. When you and your children learn and practice the steps of conflict resolution, disagreements can cease to be a source of threat and become an opportunity for learning and building bridges of peace and respect.

Establish a safe classroom environment with clear limits and expectations. A teacher's first job is to create a positive and safe environment in the classroom. Psychologist Diane Levin (2003) says children need to know that the following four things are safe: their bodies; their feelings; their thoughts, ideas, and words; and their work. Reassure children that you will not allow them to be physically or verbally hurt and that you will immediately stop any harmful or dangerous behavior, including aggression, name calling, and rejection. Your words and deeds should also reassure children that adults will not physically punish or shame them or deprive them of basic needs.

In addition to overall safety, children need to know strategies for calming themselves down so they can feel "safe" with their emotions. Pointing out strategies that you know work with particular children will help them identify these activities for themselves. These might include pouring water or sand at the texture table, hugging a teddy bear, or working with play dough or other sensory materials. Some programs create a "peace place" (Kreidler & Whittall, 1999), a quiet spot where children can calm down. Furnish this refuge with materials that provide comfort and encourage the safe release of emotions: rugs and pillows, pinwheels to blow, mirrors in which to examine facial expressions, art and building supplies, puppets with which to act out scenarios, relaxing music, and books about feelings. Invite children to share ideas about what to include, and encourage parents to set up a peace place at home. If there is no room to establish a permanent peace place in the classroom or at home, create a temporary one — for example, with a soft chair in the corner — when you sense children need one.

A positive program environment for preventing and dealing with social conflicts also includes these elements:

- *Consistent daily routine* — Children need and appreciate order and consistency. A predictable daily routine helps them know what is happening next and approximately how long things will last. It is reassuring, for example, to know a parent will pick them up after outside time, which happens right after large-group time. Or that they can resume working on a painting the next day because work time happens every day at the same time.

A consistent routine eliminates the "surprises" that can cause anxiety and in turn provoke children to act angrily or disruptively. Sharing a routine with others also helps children feel like members of the classroom community, which in turn provides an incentive for social problem-solving. At those times when routines are changed — for example, when there is a field trip — give children ample warning and support, reassuring them that the normal routine will resume afterwards. Also remember to be flexible, within limits, when minor change can help avoid frustration. For example, allow a child to finish a project at small-group time rather than insisting on washing up and going to the snack table immediately.

- *Organized and labeled room arrangement* — A room in which work areas are organized and labeled gives children a sense of control over their environment, which in turn can help them maintain emotional self-control. Open traffic patterns and lack of crowding and clutter keep them from bumping into one another and knocking over others' work. Too much openness, however, such as having all the furniture pushed up against the wall, can encourage running and accidents. Children need large areas to spread out (for example, to work on an art or construction project), as well as cozy and intimate places where they can be alone or meet in pairs and small groups for quiet activities. Rooms arranged to meet these multiple needs — for group and solitary play, for noisy and quiet activities — allow children to use the environment to achieve their own ends and can help to prevent or minimize social conflicts.

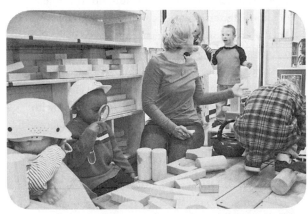

An organized classroom with ample and diverse materials gives children a sense of control over their environment and reduces conflicts over sharing.

- *Ample, diverse, and appropriate materials* — Inappropriate toys — such as those substantially above or below children's developmental levels, or with only one "correct" way they can be played with — may lead to frustration and boredom. Children should be able to easily access the materials they need to carry out their plans and ideas. Organizing and labeling materials in logical areas of the room helps them find, use, and return supplies in the classroom. Whenever possible, provide multiple sets of materials, especially popular ones, to avoid conflicts over sharing. Give children

tools, such as various types of timers, that will help them find workable solutions to using equipment and materials that must be shared (such as computers).

> *At work time in the block area, Michala and Christopher are arguing over who will play with the toy animals. Michala says, "I'll make you a deal. You can have these and I can have these."*

> *At lunch, while waiting for the girls to return from the bathroom, Charles and Amir start to argue over a chair. Charles says, "There's lots more choices."*

- *Minimum number of planned and short transitions* — Transitions can be hard for children, just as they are for many adults. To help children deal with shifts in activity or location, use the following strategies: Give warnings shortly before an activity ends (encourage children to help you — for example, by flicking the lights); minimize waiting time (prepare materials beforehand, start an activity as soon as children begin to arrive); allow adequate time for transitions so children do not feel rushed or pressured, and provide reasonable choices to keep children engaged (for example, moving in different ways from large-group time to the snack table). As with the daily routine, be flexible whenever possible so children can finish what they are doing before transitioning to the next activity. (For additional strategies on handling transitions, see *I Know What's Next: Preschool Transitions Without Tears or Turmoil* by Betsy Evans, 2008).

- *Clear and consistent limits* — Just as having a predictable schedule and space helps children feel in control, so does knowing what behaviors are (and are not) acceptable. Let children know what you expect of them in simple and concrete language that they can understand. For example, say "Hitting hurts" rather than "I cannot allow violence in the classroom." Simple rules can also be written and posted using a combination of pictures and words.

Rules should be kept to a minimum, and they work best if children have brought up the problem and helped to create the solution (see Chapter 12,

"Creating and Following Rules"). Once expectations are set, be consistent about implementing them and following through on consequences. Share them with parents, and solicit their input, so they can work with you in explaining and supporting classroom expectations with their children.

Use a multistep approach to conflict resolution. Several individuals and organizations have developed procedures to help young children resolve conflicts. All these programs have in common a sequence of adult-guided steps to help children deal with their feelings and come to a peaceful resolution of their disagreements. They also recommend professional development to help teachers understand and implement the multipart process. HighScope's six-step process for resolving conflicts follows this overall model and is summarized below and in the sidebar on pages 118–119. For a complete description of the social problem-solving process, see the book *You Can't Come to My Birthday Party! Conflict Resolution with Young Children* (Evans, 2002) and the videotape *Supporting Children in Resolving Conflicts* (HighScope Educational Research Foundation, 1998).

1. *Approach calmly, stopping any hurtful actions.*
   During a conflict, adults should stay calm in voice, body language, and facial expression. (Note: Be aware of personal triggers beforehand to help prevent over-reacting during an emotional situation.) Stop behavior that might cause injury, whether hurtful words or actions. Show concern for the children and their situation, but not alarm. When children sense the adult is in control, it helps them regain or maintain self-control. If you are calm, it communicates the message that feelings need not be scary. Remaining calm also focuses attention on solving the problem rather than on being upset with or critical of the individuals involved.

   At work time in the house area, Ella and Kevin both reach for the large wooden spoon at the same time. Ella slaps Kevin's hand and yells, "I want it." Kevin makes a fist. José, their teacher, comes over and kneels down. He gently takes the spoon from Ella and says, "Let me hold this while we solve this problem." He puts one arm around

   Kevin and strokes his hand. Kevin leans into him and relaxes his fist. José puts his other arm around Ella. José says, "We can't hit because it hurts. But we can talk. Tell me what happened." He listens calmly as the children each express their intentions to stir the "bear soup" with the spoon.

2. *Acknowledge children's feelings.* Young children live in the here-and-now and their feelings are all-encompassing (Lamm et al., 2006). Therefore, it is critical to deal with children's emotions, which can often run high during a conflict. Ignoring or denying them invalidates children and does not help them learn that emotions are normal and can be addressed like any other area of learning. Begin by soothing children who are upset, using the strategies known to be effective with the individual(s) involved. Ask to hold any disputed objects to "neutralize" them and allow children to focus on the discussion, not the object. Acknowledge and respect children's feelings. Name or label emotions. Encourage children to name their own emotions; repeat the words they use. Interpret children's feelings for one another. (Also see Chapter 6, "Recognizing and Labeling Emotions.") Act and speak with sincerity. For example, make eye contact with all the children involved. Use a warm and concerned voice. Touch or hold children in nonthreatening ways to reassure them and help them regain self-control.

   Sydney and Olivia tug in opposite directions on the beanbag chair. When their teacher, Amy, comes over, Sydney says she wants to sit in the chair and read a book to her baby doll. Olivia says that Sydney, who is younger, "is too little and dumb to read" and that she wants the chair to look at a book herself. Sydney yells, "No!" Amy says, "It sounds like you are both upset because you each want to sit in the chair." The girls nod. Amy sits on the floor a slight distance away from the chair. Sydney sits down a few inches from her, while Olivia sits right next to Amy and puts her head on her shoulder. Acknowledging that each child seeks comfort in a different way, Amy smiles directly at Sydney and puts her arm around Olivia. She turns to Olivia and says, "Sydney is upset because she wants to read to her doll." She turns to Sydney and says, "Olivia is upset because she wants to read in the chair, too. Let's see how we can solve this problem." After problem-solving, the girls agree they can sit in the chair together and take turns reading to the doll.

3. **Gather information.** Observe behavior and collect information to arrive at an insightful interpretation of the situation. Do not jump to conclusions or make assumptions about what triggered a conflict. Pose simple questions, such as "What happened?" or "What is the problem?" Listen actively to what children say, and be patient if it takes them a while to find the words or gestures with which to express themselves. Remain neutral as you gather information from the children involved or bystanders (who are learning at the same time as the active participants). Never assign blame or take sides. Find out, for example, whether a child has knocked down a block tower as a misguided attempt to enter play or because the child is angry with the peer who built it. Knowing what is behind children's feelings helps you guide them toward a solution that meets their needs.

Marcus stands alongside the "tunnel" he's built with Jamal, gripping a red car in his clenched fist. Jamal kneels on the floor, his back turned to Marcus, shooting the blue and yellow cars through the tunnel. "Is there a problem?" their teacher, Lucy, asks. "He's making them go too fast. They'll crash," answers Marcus. "It's a race," says Jamal. Franklin, standing nearby, says "Marcus took the red car. Jamal had it first." Lucy looks at Marcus, who says, "Because he was gonna crash it."

Lucy asks the boys if she can hold the cars and then summarizes, "It sounds like Marcus wants the cars to race fast and Jamal wants them to go slow." "Not slow," corrects Jamal, "just not crash." Lucy amends, "So it's okay if they go fast, but not so fast that they crash?" Jamal nods yes. "I can make 'em go fast but they don't crash," says Franklin. "Is it okay if Franklin shows us how he does that?" asks Lucy. Marcus and Jamal

agree and Lucy hands Franklin the cars. The three boys race cars "Franklin's way" until it is time to clean up.

By calmly acknowledging and labeling this child's feelings, the teacher reassures him and helps him regain self-control.

4. **Restate the problem.** Make sure you correctly understand the problem by restating it in simple terms and checking with the children. Say something like "So the problem is that you both want to be the bus driver." Be open to changing your statement if the children correct you, as Lucy was, above, when Jamal clarified his objection to the speed at which Marcus was racing the cars ("fast" was okay as long as the cars did not crash). If necessary, rephrase children's hurtful statements.

Devon points at Matthew and says, "He's stupid!" Their teacher says, "You are angry at him because he kicked over your tower." Devon says, "I'm really mad. I worked on it all morning!"

5. **Ask for ideas for solutions and choose one together.** Solicit the children's ideas for resolving the conflict. If they do not offer any on their own, suggest one or two.

At work time in the block area, Ben and Mariah want to sit in the same chair on the "pizza truck." Their teacher asks what they can do to solve the problem. Christian, standing nearby, says, "They could have two chairs." The teacher asks if that is okay and Ben and Mariah agree. Together Ben and Mariah bring over a second chair, which Ben sits in, and then Mariah takes the first chair.

Steps in Conflict Resolution

Children learn how to solve social problems when adults model a consistent and systematic approach to conflict resolution. Adult mediation and repetition are essential in this learning process. With time and practice, however, preschoolers can begin to solve problems on their own. Recommended approaches to conflict resolution vary somewhat, but they all contain the same basic elements. Here is one six-step procedure for conflict mediation with children, developed by preschool teacher and HighScope trainer Betsy Evans. The list of steps is followed by an example in which the first two steps set the tone for the rest of the process.

Six Steps in a Problem-Solving Approach to Conflict

1. **Approach calmly, stopping any hurtful actions.**

   Place yourself between the children, on their level.

   Use a calm voice and gentle touch.

   Remain neutral rather than take sides.

2. **Acknowledge children's feelings.**

   "You look really upset."

   Let children know you need to hold any object in question.

3. **Gather information.**

   "What's the problem?"

4. **Restate the problem.**

   "So the problem is … "

5. **Ask for ideas for solutions and choose one together.**

   "What can we do to solve this problem?"

   Encourage *children* to think of a solution.

6. **Be prepared to give follow-up support.**

   "You solved the problem!"

   Stay near the children.

Conflict Resolution Begins by Acknowledging Children's Feelings: An Example

Shari is feeding her doll a bottle. Daniella grabs it away and says "I need that." When Shari takes it back, Daniella punches her in the arm and says, "I hate you, you stupid baby!" Their teacher, Tom, comes over and kneels down between the two girls.

Tom (to Daniella): *You're angry because you want to feed the bottle to your doll. But you cannot punch Shari or call her stupid.*

Tom (to Shari): *Let me hold the bottle while we talk about this (Takes the bottle to "neutralize" it during their discussion).*

Shari: *I had it first.*

Tom (to Shari): *You're upset because you were using the bottle and Daniella grabbed it away from you.*

Shari: *(Nods yes)*

Tom (to Shari and Daniella): *So you both want to feed this bottle to your dolls. How can we solve this problem?*

As the children calm down, the teacher takes them through the rest of the problem-solving steps. Each child describes in her own words what happened; Tom

---

Conflict Resolution (cont.)

repeats and verifies their statements, then asks them to suggest solutions. The girls decide to make another bottle. Shari holds a block while Daniella tapes on a red Lego "nipple." Shari uses the original bottle while Daniella uses the one they made together, happy because "My bottle is bigger." When Tom checks back later, the dolls are taking a nap in the carriage and Shari and Daniella are building a cradle out of blocks.

— Adapted from *You Can't Come to My Birthday Party! Conflict Resolution With Young Children* (Evans, 2002, pp. 117–118)

At work time at the sand table, Ashley and Christian want the same funnel. Their teacher, Sue, asks for ideas to solve the problem, and Lili says, "Ashley can have mine when I'm done, and Christian can keep the other one." Sue asks Ashley if that is okay. When Ashley hesitates but is unable to say why, Sue asks, "Do you want to know when Lili will be done?" Ashley nods and Lili says, "I'll get the sand timer and turn it over once. Then you can have it." Sue turns to Ashley, who nods her okay.

Respect children's ideas about "fairness" in the solutions they offer. Their ideas may differ from those of adults, but as long as all the parties involved agree upon the solution, it should be accepted and carried out. If children propose unrealistic solutions, you can help them explore the implications and encourage them to find alternatives (See Chapter 10 for teaching strategies when children offer unrealistic or harsh suggestions):

Jacob and Sam are having a disagreement over the new necklaces in the house area. When the teacher asks what they can do to solve the problem, Jacob says, "We need more new necklaces."

Since it is not possible to get more necklaces, the teacher is about to ask the boys for another idea. To her surprise, however, Sam says, "Yeah!" and then goes to the art area to get leather thongs and beads. The boys spend the rest of work time making necklaces and wristbands with hidden "spy phones" inside.

6. ***Be prepared to give follow-up support.*** Shortly after children begin to carry out the agreed-upon solution, check back to see if it is working. Acknowledge their efforts with a simple observation, such as "You're sitting side-by-side in the chair and looking at the house book." If conflicts reemerge, repeat the problem-solving strategies until all the children appear settled and reengaged in play.

Lane and Brian agree it will be Lane's turn at the computer after Brian has used it for two flips of the sand timer. As the end of the second flip nears, their teacher looks toward the computer area to make sure the changeover happens as agreed. Brian says, "Here, Lane," and switches chairs to watch and offer his ideas. Lane and Brian continue to take turns at the computer and talk for the next 15 minutes.

Help children reflect on problem-solving strategies apart from actual conflict situations. It may be easier for children to absorb information when emotions are not running high — so revisiting a conflict after a crisis has passed is helpful. Children are better able to understand the process — and acknowledge their successful role in solving the situation — if you review the episode later; for example, during snacktime or as you dig alongside them at outside time.

You can also deal more generally with the idea of conflict resolution by reading books and sharing songs and tales about people coping with similar social conflicts. For example, using a technique called a "social story," a common problem can be introduced at greeting circle and children can share their ideas about how to solve it. The following is an example of how teachers can use a social story with children to help solve a common toy-sharing problem.

Resolving Conflicts: Teaching Strategies

Establish a safe classroom environment with clear limits and expectations.

- Reassure children that you will not allow them to be physically or verbally hurt and that you will immediately stop any harmful or dangerous behavior.

- Point out strategies you know will help children calm themselves and restore a sense of safety (e.g., pouring water or sand at the texture table, hugging a teddy bear, or working with play dough or other sensory materials).

- Create a "peace place" — a permanent or temporary quiet spot where children can calm down. Furnish this area with materials that provide comfort and encourage the safe release of emotions (e.g., rugs and pillows, pinwheels to blow, mirrors in which to examine facial expressions, art and building supplies, puppets with which to act out scenarios, relaxing music, and books about feelings).

- Create a positive program environment that includes these elements: Consistent daily routine; organized and labeled room arrangement; ample, diverse, and appropriate materials; minimum number of planned and short transitions; and clear and consistent limits.

Use a multistep approach to conflict resolution, such as the six-step sequence developed by HighScope.

- Approach calmly, stopping any hurtful actions. Stay calm in voice, body language, and facial expression. Show genuine concern, but not alarm.

- Acknowledge children's feelings. Sooth children who are upset; hold disputed objects to "neutralize" them; help children name their emotions; reassure them their feelings are okay and that you can help them regain control.

- Gather information. Do not jump to conclusions or take sides; pose simple questions to find out the reason for the conflict so you can guide children toward a solution that meets their needs.

- Restate the problem. Summarize the conflict in simple terms and check with the children to make sure you have stated it correctly; if necessary, rephrase their hurtful statements.

- Ask for ideas for solutions and choose one together. Solicit children's ideas or offer one or two suggestions; respect their solutions and ideas of "fairness" even if they are not the ones you would suggest or choose; carry out the idea they agree on.

- Be prepared to give follow-up support. Check back in a little while to see if the solution is working. If it is working, acknowledge children's efforts; if not, repeat the six conflict-resolution steps.

Help children reflect on problem-solving strategies apart from actual conflict situations.

- Revisit a conflict after a crisis has passed; for example, during snacktime or as you dig alongside children at outside time.

Teaching Strategies (cont.)

- Read books and share songs and tales about people coping with similar social conflicts.

- Create a "social story" based on a classroom problem, making a book stating the problem and solutions suggested by children, and add the book to the book area.

- Encourage children to role-play problems and solutions using puppets, dolls, or other props.

- Draw pictures and make "feeling dolls" to represent and explore the feelings aroused in social conflicts.

- Pose simple and familiar "what if" situations, based on real events, for small-group discussion; suggest situations you know the children will find unacceptable or absurd (humorous) in order to elicit their ideas on how to solve the problem.

One day a group of children are playing with toys in the block area. They leave to go to the art area, and another group of children begins playing with the toys in the block area. The children in the first group come back and say, "Those are our toys. You can't play with them." The children work out a solution, but this had been a common enough problem that the teachers decide to do a "social story" about it.

The next day, at greeting circle, the teachers post several large sheets of paper that tell the story of the previous day's events with stick figures and captions. They title the story **When Children Leave** *and pose the question "What can we do to solve this problem?" The children offer various solutions that the teachers write down: They could share (divide) the toys; they could all play together; the second group should give the toys back; the first group has to wait their turn. The class assembles the pages into a book, which is added to the book area. Whenever a similar problem arises, the children look at the book and either use one of their solutions or add another one.*

Other typical problems that can be addressed with social stories include children saying "I don't want to play with you" or spending a long time using toys or equipment that only a limited number of children can use at one time (e.g., computer, rocking boat).

Social stories can also be used to help individual children deal with interpersonal situations or problems. For example, one boy had trouble entering play with his peers. He would attempt to be included by taking a toy or telling the others what to do, and they would inevitably tell him to go away. Sitting with him at work time, his teacher made up a storybook titled, "I Want to Play With You," and they discussed strategies he could use to be accepted in a play situation (watch from the side and wait to be invited; ask if he could be a kitty, too; offer to help fetch materials). This was his book, it told his story, and it was something the boy could refer to on his own or with the teacher's encouragement. Sometimes just holding the book helped him to use effective strategies. (See pp. 122–123 for another example of a social story; see Chapter 8, "Engaging in Cooperative Play," for other strategies to help aggressive or withdrawn children join their peers in play.)

Children can also be engaged in conflict resolution when they role-play scenarios with puppets, dolls, or other props. For example, "I don't want to sit next to you" was a frequent comment heard in one classroom. At the beginning of large-group time one day, one teacher sat down and a second teacher sat next to her. The first teacher huffed, "I don't want you next to me!" and left the group. When children reacted (with emotions ranging from surprise to anger), it provided an opportunity to discuss questions such as the following: Does this happen

Using Social Stories to Help Resolve Common Conflicts

Talking about common conflicts in moments of calm — when they are not happening — can make it easier for children to think about the problem and offer solutions. "Social stories" are an effective way to bring up typical classroom problems, discuss children's ideas for solving them, and turn them into "storybooks" the children can refer to when these conflicts occur again. Here is an example of a social story in which a child talks about joining others safely in play.

Children make a plan and start to play

I Want to Play!

At school children play

Sometimes children are playing and I want to play too.

I want them to see me and to know that I want to play.

Using Social Stories to Help Resolve Common Conflicts *(cont.)*

I could say...

I could ask a teacher to help me play with children.

Sometimes I get really excited. Things break and children get hurt.

It is okay to get excited, but when I hurt children and toys, children get upset

I will keep things and children safe.
I will not throw, hit, or break things.

It's fun to play with children when we are all safe.

the end

in our classroom? How do you feel when it happens to you? How can we deal with this problem? Children offered various ideas, such as leaving more space between the people sitting together; saying the other person could sit next to him or her later or tomorrow; and picking someone they both liked to have sit in the middle. This "social story" was recalled whenever a comparable situation occurred later that year, and children were able to choose from solutions they had generated themselves.

Here are some other ways you can help children reflect on problem-solving techniques:

- *Draw pictures and make "feeling dolls."* This is a nonthreatening way for children to represent and explore the feelings that are aroused in social conflicts.

- *Pose simple and familiar "what if" situations, based on real events, for small-group discussion.* Suggest situations you know the children will find unacceptable in order to elicit their ideas on how to solve the problem. For example, if children have been arguing over using the paint pumps, say, "What if I decided only teachers could mix paints?" Take advantage of the fact that preschoolers are beginning to develop a sense of humor. They can understand the absurdity of what you are proposing, but the light-hearted mood can also make it easier for them to join safely and comfortably in the discussion.

In Conclusion

Preschoolers' emerging emotional and social abilities in other domains — dealing with feelings, empathy, community, cooperation, tolerance, and morality — also prepare them to resolve interpersonal conflicts. The role of the teacher is to guide, rather than control, the problem-solving process. Because the potential for conflict is normal and pervasive in the early childhood classroom, it is not surprising that many of the strategies used to prevent and handle these conflict situations also reflect general best practices. These factors include establishing a consistent daily routine, arranging and equipping the learning environment with interesting and plentiful materials, limiting the number and length of transitions, and setting clear behavioral expectations for children.

There are also specific techniques that teachers can use to mediate conflicts, notably a multistep approach that helps children cope with their feelings and arrive at mutually determined solutions. Establishing a classroom where conflicts are treated as educational opportunities and are peacefully resolved not only builds important social skills but creates a safe and supportive learning environment for all children.

Creating and Following Rules

Justin, Zachary, and Trevor are playing the board game Candyland. They discuss the rules:

Justin: *You go the number that's on here (points to the die).*

Zachary: *If you get a little number you can throw it again.*

Justin: *No. That's not the law.*

Zachary: *Just one more time.*

Justin: *Okay. Only one.*

Trevor: *(Throws the die) What number is that?*

Zachary: *Two. You go two squares.*

Trevor: *(Moves four squares)*

Justin: *No, to here (Moves Trevor's piece back two places). I'm next and Zachary is last 'cause he's biggest.*

Definition

A rule is an authoritative statement or direction that governs people's behavior. Rules — also called norms — tell us how to act and may also include sanctions for when rules are violated. All educational settings and child care programs have norms or rules with specific expectations that teachers establish for individual and group behavior.

Three kinds of norms. Based on interviews with teachers in a multiage early childhood program, DeVries and Zan (2003) identified three kinds of norms or rules in their classrooms: safety and health norms, moral norms, and discretionary norms.

- **Safety and health norms** ensure children's well-being and are often established to meet the standards set forth in licensing requirements. Early childhood settings

Rules

A *rule* is an authoritative statement or direction that governs people's behavior. Rules — also called norms — tell us how to act and may also include sanctions for when rules are violated. All educational settings and child care programs have norms or rules with specific expectations that teachers establish for individual and group behavior. Teachers in multiage early childhood programs have identified three kinds of norms in their classrooms: Safety and health norms, which ensure children's well-being; moral norms, which pertain to respect for people and morals; and discretionary norms, which help classrooms run smoothly and include rules created for games invented by children (DeVries and Zan, 2003).

adhere to regulations governing health, safety, adult-child ratios, and other operational issues. Examples that apply directly to children's behavior include "No walking in the hallways alone" and "Keep shoes on at outside time." These rules are nonnegotiable, and children are generally quick to pick up and follow them, sometimes taking on the role of enforcer:

At work time in the house area, Jonetta is pretending to cook at the play stove. "Don't touch the stove, it's hot!" she tells her teacher.

At small-group time, Natasha covers her mouth with her hand when she coughs.

At breakfast, Danielle says to two boys at her table who are pouring juice on their muffins, "Stop! You're making me mad."

At lunch, Madison watches Zachary gargle his milk and tells him, "Watch, Zachary, I will show you how to drink milk." Madison picks up her cup, takes a sip, and swallows. "See? Like this," she says.

- **Moral norms** pertain to respect for people and animals. They often relate to fair treatment ("Take turns") or doing no harm ("No hurting animals"). Moral norms remain stable across situations. Preschool children are beginning to understand and evaluate their behavior and that of others in terms of these norms or principles (see Chapter 10, "Developing a Framework for Moral Behavior"). In the following pair of anecdotes, for example, preschoolers have moved beyond the toddler's "It's mine" or "I want it!" to invoke the moral principle of "I had it (or I was there) first."

  At work time in the block area, Anthony and another child are having a disagreement over a truck. Anthony says, "I had it first."

  At greeting time, after Mikayla gets a book, there is another girl in her beanbag chair. Mikayla says, "That's my spot! I was there first."

- **Discretionary norms** are routines and procedures that make classrooms run smoothly and facilitate learning. They also include societal norms for politeness and individual responsibility and may translate moral norms into specific behaviors: "Wait until everyone is seated before beginning lunch" (fairness) and "It's okay to call teachers by their first names but the bus driver likes to be called 'Miss Johnson'" (respect). Preschoolers are able to understand the concept of politeness, as illustrated in the following anecdote:

  Madison is talking to the teacher at the table and another child interrupts. Madison says, "When someone is talking, you have to say

'Excuse me. I want to talk to you.' If you don't say that, it is very rude. Right, teacher?"

Discretionary norms also typically deal with issues about sharing responsibility or resolving conflicts, such as who will pass out snacks, feed the class pet, sit next to the teacher, choose the song for circle time, or use the computer. Discretionary norms can be changed by order or consensus; for example, if they are not working for those affected by them. Young children can participate in creating discretionary norms or rules.

Preschoolers can understand, carry out, and even create simple discretionary rules that help the classroom run smoothly, such as using a sand timer to make sure everyone gets an equal turn.

Discretionary rules may also be created for games invented by the children, such as the start and finish line in a race, what constitutes "in bounds" when tossing a bean bag, or how to prevent hurtful behavior during rough-and-tumble play. Sometimes a need arises to establish policies for preserving quiet areas, circumventing block structures built by others, or protecting "work in progress" that children want untouched until the next day. Such rules may affect just one or two individuals, but they typically affect groups of children or the whole class.

When children participate in creating these types of rules, they reflect their growing understanding of how one individual's behavior affects the well-being of others (empathy):

> *Reflecting on the day at the end of large-group time, Rosy says, "I'm so sorry that some kids got hurt today at outside time." A group discussion about the problem of swinging sticks in the air takes place:*

Gabriel: *They shouldn't have picked up the sticks.*

Rosy: *The stick was fast. It hurt Ashley's nose. She cried.*

Nicholas: *I felt sorry for her.*

Bianca: *Sticks should stay down.*

Joshua: *On the ground.*

Children also recognize how discretionary rules affect the orderly operation of the classroom (community):

> *At the end of work time (9:50), Brendan points to the minute hand on the "10" and says, "Look. It's cleanup time! Hey, everybody, start to put your stuff away!"*

Development

Most young children are not accustomed to making rules, nor are they encouraged to voice honest opinions about norms for their behavior. Children typically receive rules from parents and teachers and operate within a framework of "heteronomous morality"; that is, conforming to outside rules without questioning them. However, when children do participate in generating and following their own rules, they are exercising "autonomous morality"; that is, reflecting an internal understanding of the needs of others (see Chapter 10).

Children who are given opportunities to create and follow rules generally exhibit the developmental progression described below (DeVries & Zan, 2003).

Creating and Following Rules: Development

Children who are given opportunities to create and follow rules generally exhibit the following developmental progression (DeVries & Zan, 2003):

- Parroting adult rules
- Reinventing (elaborating on) established rules
- Inventing original rules

Children's competence in making and respecting rules continues to develop into adolescence and early adulthood. Early childhood programs can be instrumental in laying the foundation for creating and following rules by engaging preschoolers in making meaningful decisions about their classroom community.

Parroting adult rules. Children will repeat, often verbatim, the rules adults give them, such as "Never talk to strangers." This unvarying recitation happens when children are not sure if their opinions matter. They view rule-making as an exercise in figuring out the right answer or saying what they think adults want to hear. The rules children suggest do not yet reflect a real understanding of the needs of others or the functioning of the classroom community.

> *When Mrs. Mel shows her a picture of Bows standing by the street, Hailey says, "She isn't supposed to cross the street alone." When the picture shows Buttons crossing the street without asking his mom, Monica says, "He shouldn't do that."*

Reinventing (elaborating on) established rules. Although these elaborations are not truly original, they reflect the child's growing sense of autonomy, or power to create rules. By translating norms into words that make sense to them, children make rules meaningful or real. They take something abstract and define it in terms of concrete behaviors. For example, a classroom of four-year-olds, working within the norm "Don't hurt animals," generated the following rules for chicks that had recently hatched in their classroom (p. 66):

- Pick them up safely.

- Don't push them.

- Don't squeeze them.

- Don't put things in their box.

- Don't punch them.

- Don't put them on the light bulb.

- Don't drop them.

- Don't throw them.

- Don't pick them up by their wings.

- Don't color on them.

- Don't pull their heads off.

Inventing original rules. Invented rules reflect children's power to make decisions in the classroom. Often they arise from concerns voiced by the children — the children therefore have a personal stake in solving the problem.

For example, a preschool class invented a new rule in response to something one of them observed during the daily routine. In this classroom, children had a one-hour block of time for free play during which they could also eat a snack that was set up in the corner. At the end of this period, they cleaned up and went outside. One child was upset when he saw another child finishing a snack during cleanup time. He told the teacher, who raised the issue at small-group time. When she asked, "What should our rule be?" the children suggested several possibilities.

At the end of the discussion, the teacher clarified the choice between "No snack during cleanup time; throw it away" or "Finish snack before going outdoors." The children voted to throw away their unfinished snacks when cleanup time started. Although the teacher would have preferred giving children more time to finish their snack, she respected their decision as being fair and reasonable.

Moreover, because the children had created the rule themselves, no one objected to following it.

Like establishing a personal code of morality, children's competence in making and respecting rules continues to develop into adolescence and early adulthood. Merely having rules will not change preschoolers' behavior overnight; so don't expect that by making rules you will no longer have to deal with typical and recurring problems. However, early childhood programs can be instrumental in laying the foundation for creating and following rules by engaging preschoolers in making meaningful decisions about their classroom community.

Teaching Strategies

Young children need explicit information and adult guidance to understand, establish, and follow the rules governing their behavior. They also need help sorting out which rules are discretionary, or fluid (for example, participants can agree to change the rules of a game), and when they are fixed and nonnegotiable (for example, rules dealing with health or safety). You can use the following strategies to help preschoolers understand and participate in the process of creating and following rules.

Make children aware of basic health and safety rules that have everyday meaning to them. Repeat these rules often, especially at the beginning of the program year. Say them in context; that is, when the situation to which the rules apply is occurring. Post the rules at the children's eye level, using simple words and pictures. Be concrete in communicating rules — children relate to the do's and don'ts of behavior, not to abstract principles of protection or well-being. For example, don't lecture the children about proper hygiene. Instead, tape a picture of a running faucet and hands over the sink to remind them to wash after they use the bathroom. Children eventually internalize these rules (though they may need occasional reminding), and even take responsibility for making sure their classmates adhere to them as well:

At work time at the water table, Hailey notices she is getting water on her shorts. She asks her teacher, "Do I need a paint shirt?"

Children Can Make Up Rules to Govern Their Own Play

When play becomes too rough or danger-ous, adults often need to step in to set limits. However, there are times when children themselves can be involved in creating rules to guarantee their own comfort or safety. Engaging in this process is especially valu-able when the game or activity is something that the children enjoy and that has the potential to teach them something in one or more content areas. The anecdote below was recorded by a team of preschool teachers when a child-initiated wrestling game got out of hand.

A child went to a wrestling match and got several classmates interested in playing "wrestling" during choice time. They used an area rug as their mat, pushed up their sleeves, and got down to wrestle. The game went on for several weeks and became more elaborate; for example, they gave themselves wrestlers' names and developed a "scor-ing" system. In the second week, however, it became clear that a few children felt the play was too rough. The teachers also wor-ried about children getting hurt, yet they did not want to stop a game that many children clearly enjoyed and that promoted learning in many areas. At the beginning of choice time, when the wrestlers were setting up their game, a teacher gathered them and voiced her concern. She said, "What rules can we make up so children will not get hurt?" She wrote down their ideas and posted them on the wall above the mat. Here are the rules the children came up with:

1. Take off your shoes (but not your socks).
2. No hitting.
3. No punching. (The children debated whether punching was the same as hit-ting, but decided it deserved its own rule.)
4. No pinching.
5. You can't call someone a bad name.
6. No spitting.
7. No head butts.
8. ~~Only boys can play.~~ (Several girls pro-tested this rule and it was dropped.)
9. At least three people have to play so one can be the referee and make sure the fight is fair.
10. The referee has to be able to count to ten. (After a count of ten, the match is declared over.)
11. You can't wrestle if you don't have a wrestler name.
12. You can't have the same wrestler name as someone else.
13. Everyone who wants to wrestle gets a turn. The referee decides who goes next.
14. People who want to watch have to stand behind the line. (After some debate, they decided the edge of the block shelf would mark the "watching line.")

The children referred to the rules in subse-quent weeks as their interest in wrestling continued. If one of them broke a rule, the other children, rather than the teacher, were quick to point out the infraction. Later in the year, when some children wanted to "box" in the sandbox, it was their idea to set up rules for alternating use of the space with those who wanted to play in the sand and also to guarantee safety when the space was used as a boxing ring.

Creating and Following Rules: Teaching Strategies

Make children aware of basic health and safety rules that have everyday meaning to them.

- Repeat health and safety rules often, especially at the beginning of the program year; say them in context; that is, when the situation to which the rules apply is occurring.

- Post the rules at children's eye level, using simple words and pictures.

- Be concrete in communicating rules — children relate to the do's and don'ts of behavior but not to abstract principles of protection or well-being.

Discuss an issue that affects everyone, and invite children to create rules (strategies) for dealing with it.

- Create a time and place for guided group conversations to provide children and teachers with a forum for identifying and solving problems and making decisions that affect the classroom climate.

- Solve problems using strategies similar to those used for conflict resolution: allow participants to have their feelings heard and acknowledged, gather information from all perspectives, clarify the problem, discuss solutions, reach a decision by consensus or majority, and (later) evaluate whether the solution is working and, if not, repeat the problem-solving process.

- Teachers and/or children can write down and post the resulting rules or make them into a book so everyone can refer to them when appropriate.

- Group discussions about classroom issues work best before a problem emerges (prevention) or soon after it appears (before emotions escalate or behavioral patterns are firmly established).

- Establish and model a few simple guidelines for guided group discussions: Everyone has a chance to speak; we listen to each other; we treat everyone with respect.

- If some children seem hesitant or others monopolize the discussion, try using a prop, such as a talking stick passed around from child to child to signify whose turn it is to speak and to remind others to listen.

- Give children the opportunity to make up their own rules to govern their play.

Help children think through how rules apply to them.

- Engage children in anticipating how the rules will work for them and what to do if they need to be changed.

- Help children come up with simple strategies to help them remember and use rules.

Encourage children to share responsibility for taking care of the classroom.

- Help children feel a sense of ownership for the classroom by creating and following rules for such tasks as setting the table, helping to serve snacks and meals, weeding and watering the garden, and feeding the class pet.

Teaching Strategies *(cont.)*

- Involve children in keeping track of whether the classroom tasks are performed.

Make simple rules for yourself.

- Draw attention to the fact that you make and follow rules yourself to help make children aware of the importance of rules in everyone's life.

- Explain the reason for a given role in simple terms; for example, establish your own guidelines for how to decide who gets to sit in your lap at story time each day.

- Write down and share your rules with children; point out when you are following them.

When several boys are being loud and running around, Anthony says, "You're not being nice to the teacher. Mrs. Bev told us 'No running!'"

Discuss an issue that affects everyone, and invite children to create rules (strategies) for dealing with it. Guided group discussions provide teachers and children with a forum for identifying and solving problems and making decisions that affect the classroom climate. To fulfill these goals, teachers create a safe environment in which children's learning, opinions, and concerns are taken seriously, and children participate as valued and influential contributors to the classroom community. Variously known as class meetings (Vance & Weaver, 2002), group problem-solving (Evans, 2002), or social stories (see Chapter 11 "Resolving Conflicts"), these conversations can be held with the whole group (for example, at greeting time) or with a smaller group (for example, at snacktime).

The problems typically addressed are interpersonal, such as name-calling, taking someone's property without permission, excluding others from play, or bullying. They may also involve nonsocial behaviors that affect the entire class — for example, cleanup takes so long that it shortens outside time. The steps used to solve classroom problems are similar to those used for conflict resolution (see Chapter 11). They allow participants to have their feelings heard and acknowledged, gather information from all perspectives, clarify the problem, discuss solutions, reach a decision by consensus or majority, and (later) evaluate whether the solution is working and, if not, repeat the problem-solving process. The teacher and/or children can write down and post the resulting rules — or make them into a book — so everyone can refer to them when appropriate. Recording the decision(s) also makes it easier to clear up any confusion and revisit the rules during follow-up.

Education professor Dan Gartrell (2006) says discussions work best if they are held before a problem emerges (prevention) or soon after it appears (before emotions escalate or behavioral patterns are firmly established). To create a safe and secure setting, teachers should establish and model a few simple guidelines: Everyone has a chance to speak; we listen to each other; we treat everyone with respect. If you observe that some children seem hesitant or others monopolize the discussion, a prop, such as a talking stick passed around from child to child, can signify whose turn it is to speak and remind others to listen. This concrete, hand-held device may be especially helpful for preschoolers.

Educators often question whether preschoolers are developmentally capable of meeting as a group to create a set of rules and then carry them out with a sense of ownership and responsibility. However, just as researchers have found that we underestimate the young child's capacity for showing empathy or developing a moral framework, there is strong evidence that preschoolers can successfully participate in rule-making activities when given an authentic opportunity (DeVries & Zan, 1994). Consider the example in the sidebar on page 129, in which preschoolers solved a problem that threatened to disrupt a popular form of play.

Help children think through how rules apply to them. Don't stop with just involving children in creating classroom rules. Engage them in anticipating how the rules will work for them and what to do if they need to be changed. In the following example, preschoolers not only generated a rule for bike safety, they came up with a simple but creative strategy to help them remember and use it.

One bike in the preschool is taller than the others. Its center of gravity is such that it tends to tip over when accelerating down the hill from the sidewalk to the gate. Children are getting hurt, so the teachers have a problem-solving discussion with them. The children decide to make a rule that "The tall bike cannot go down the hill."

One teacher asks where to write the rule so children will remember it. The children say to write the rule on the sidewalk at the top of the hill. "How will you know which bike not to ride down the hill?" asks the other teacher. The children look thoughtful and then one of them says to paint the tall bike a different color to make it easy to tell apart from the others. After examining all the bikes, the children determine that there are no red ones. "Paint the tall bike red!" they say. So the teachers spray-paint the tall bike red. Also using paint (so it won't wash away), the teachers draw the rule at the top of the sidewalk — a line and a picture with a red bike crossed off — and there are no problems with too-tall bikes tipping over after that.

When children create and follow rules to take care of the classroom, their sense of ownership and commitment to it are increased.

Encourage children to share responsibility for taking care of the classroom. The classroom is the children's workspace and, outside their homes, the place where they are likely to spend most of the time. Children, like adults, need to feel a sense of ownership for the spaces that are important to them. When children create and follow rules to take care of that space, their sense of ownership and commitment to it are increased. Children are capable of, and enjoy, assisting with such tasks as setting the table and helping to serve snacks and meals, weeding and watering the garden, or feeding the class pet. You can establish rules and procedures with the children for carrying out these roles and involve them in keeping track of whether they are performed. Often it is the children who notice when classmates are not fulfilling their responsibilities.

Make simple rules for yourself. If we want children to be conscientious about creating and obeying rules, we should set an example ourselves. Draw attention to the fact that you are engaging in this process to help make children aware of the importance of rules in everyone's life — including adults'. Explain the reason for the rule in simple terms. For example, establish your own guidelines for how to decide who gets to sit in your lap at story time each day. Explain that the rule guarantees that you are being fair and that everyone who wants to sit in your lap will get a turn. Write down and share your rules with the children; point out when you are following them. (For more reflections and strategies on how we can act as role models in supporting children's social and emotional development, see Chapter 14, "Preparing Ourselves to Be Role Models.")

In Conclusion

"When children care about a classroom problem ... and take part in solving it, they are more likely to view the resulting rules as fair. Having *made* the rules, they are more likely to observe them. Just as important, participating in the process of rule-making supports children's growth as moral, self-regulating human beings" (DeVries & Zan, 2003, p. 64). Helping to establish the rules and procedures in their classrooms gives young children a sense of ownership toward their environment, engages them in a community-building process, and also helps to develop their skills in thinking and reasoning. These are all traits that we value in adults, and by taking advantage of preschoolers' emerging cognitive and social skills, we can start to instill them early.

Creating and Participating in a Democracy

The class has recently begun recycling paper and containers in bins provided by the city. Many families take part in the municipal recycling program at home, too. The children have been talking about why it is good to reuse things and not waste them. The following conversation takes place one day at the end of snacktime:

> **Teacher:** *Jonathan, can you please throw away the empty cereal box? (Pointing to the trash can)*
>
> **Giselle:** *We don't have to throw it away, Mrs. Conte. We could use it in the art area.*
>
> **Teacher:** *What could we do with it?*
>
> **Giselle:** *Cut it up and use it to make something or for decorations.*
>
> **Raquel:** *And this empty yogurt cup.* (It had been washed clean.) *I want to use it.*
>
> **Teacher:** *How will you use it?*
>
> **Raquel:** *To mix paint in.*
>
> **Giselle:** *I can bring in more yogurt cups from home. Raquel and I will do a project together.*

Definition

Democracy in the early childhood classroom means operating under conditions of equality and respect for the individual. Developing a sense of democracy grows out of group experiences with rule-making and problem-solving. For young children, it means learning that everyone has a voice in setting policies, even those with minority opinions. Democracy entails compromise and negotiation; it is the opposite of an authoritarian approach to establishing rules for behavior. In a democracy, the individual does not always get his or her way, but everyone has a chance to be heard and there is a process to review and revise decisions, if needed.

Thus the children in the opening anecdote feel free to raise objections to the teacher's statement, the teacher listens to and respects their contributions, and the ensuing discussion results in additional ideas that extend municipal awareness and policies about recycling into the classroom.

Democracy in the Early Childhood Classroom

Democracy entails compromise and negotiation; it is the opposite of an authoritarian approach to establishing rules for behavior. Democracy in the early childhood classroom means operating under conditions of equality and respect for the individual. In a democracy, the individual does not always get his or her way, but everyone has a chance to be heard and there's a process to review and revise decisions, if needed.

Development

Democracy in education. Enter the search terms "democracy," "education," and "preschool" in a Web browser, and John Dewey's *Democracy and Education* (1916/1966) pops up. Dewey was perhaps the first to argue that schools should be democratic communities in which students blend their individual skills and interests, participate in collaborative deliberation and decision-making, and thereby develop and become committed to common goals (Battistich, Solomon, & Watson, 1998). Like Vygotsky, Dewey viewed the mind and its formation as a communal process, an interaction between the individual and society.

For Dewey and his followers who promoted what came to be called "progressive education," the job of schools was not merely to teach facts, but to promote the development of problem-solving and critical-thinking skills. This view emphasizes that, rather than focusing on memorization, teaching methods should promote experiential learning. In this approach, students are thought to learn best by reflecting on past experiences, working through present ones, and preparing for the future. Such an educational process is itself democratic (that is, learning is not dictated by an authority figure), and participating in this form of education in turn prepares students to live in a democratic society.

Participating in a Democracy: Development

Active learning practices can provide the basis for learning about participating in a democracy when children direct their own learning, discipline themselves, and control their behavior for the benefit of the group (Krogh, 1982). Learning to participate in a democracy is related to other areas of social development, particularly developing a sense of community, valuing diversity, and creating and following rules. While balancing the desires of the group against those of the individual can be difficult for preschoolers, with appropriate adult guidance and modeling, preschoolers can contribute their ideas, learn to listen to and respect the viewpoints of others, and weigh two (and occasionally more) variables in reaching a decision.

Most writing on this subject addresses how schools and classrooms can be structured to promote democratic processes, rather than how students themselves develop an understanding of it. When educational researchers do investigate emerging concepts about democracy, they more often focus on the abstract reasoning abilities that appear in early and late adolescence. However, the part of democratic education that stresses experiential learning is certainly highly relevant to young children. Hands-on learning is the hallmark of early childhood and an essential component of the best teaching practices for this age group. While more directive teaching strategies wax and wane in popularity, research consistently shows that children learn best through planning, carrying out, and reflecting on their own actions (see Chapter 2, "An Overview of Child Development and Teaching Practices").

Maria Montessori, a pioneer in preschool education, believed young children were capable of practicing a simplified form of democracy, directing their own learning, disciplining themselves, and controlling their behavior for the benefit of the group (Krogh, 1982). She thought the learning environment should be structured so that democracy would naturally evolve. Her emphasis on multiage groupings, peer teaching, low student-teacher ratios, use of real tools (rather than toys) that promoted feelings of mastery and security, and teachers who acted as collaborators and facilitators rather than as directors, were all designed toward this end. Many of today's early childhood settings, regardless of the curriculum approach they use, incorporate these democratic features.

Creating and participating in a democracy can perhaps be seen as the culmination of socialization in our society. As such, its importance and developmental profile are very much related to the other areas of social development already addressed in this book, particularly developing a sense of community (Chapter 7), valuing diversity (Chapter 9), and creating and following rules (Chapter 12).

The group and the individual. What is unique about the practice of democracy, however, is achieving a balance between the group and the individual, weighing the desires of the majority against those of the minority. These sometimes competing considerations require a flexibility of thought that may be difficult for preschoolers, who tend to categorize people, objects, and ideas into two clearly bounded groups. The nuances of democracy are sometimes beyond them. Nevertheless, participating in basic democratic institutions is a process that young children are capable of. With appropriate adult guidance and modeling, preschoolers can contribute their ideas, learn to listen to and respect the viewpoints of others, and weigh two (and occasionally more) variables in reaching a decision. It is from this developmental perspective that early childhood practitioners can create a democratic classroom.

Teachers who act as collaborators and facilitators, rather than as directors, model democratic processes.

Teaching Strategies

The skills and policies necessary to run a democratic society are the same as those involved in running an active-learning classroom. They include "reflective problem-solving and decision making, managing one's emotions, taking a variety of perspectives, and sustaining energy and attention toward focused goals" (Elias et al., 1997, p. 8). Preschoolers are not ready for abstract civics lessons about the meaning of democracy. However, fostering appropriate concrete skills prepares them to become responsible and productive citizens who will safeguard the "life, liberty, and happiness" guaranteed in the Declaration of Independence. To bring about this understanding in ways that make sense to young children, you can use the following strategies.

Encourage children to consider alternative ways to reach a goal. Examining a problem from more than one perspective helps children build the flexibility they need to participate in a democracy. You can use this strategy in any learning context as you interact with children — at work/choice time, small-group time, outside time, and so on. As you work alongside them and comment on what they are doing, ask children, "What do you think would happen if … ?" or "Can you think of another way to do that?" Encourage them to plan more than one way to accomplish a task. Pose questions to help them anticipate consequences and reflect on outcomes. For example, you might wonder aloud, "What will you do if the children who build ramps in the block area tomorrow don't follow the rules you came up with today?"

Build perspective- and turn-taking skills. As noted in several chapters throughout this book, preschoolers are beginning to develop the capacity to see things from perspectives other than their own. Exercising their imagination is one way to support their emerging perspective-taking skills. Role playing helps them adopt other people's behaviors and viewpoints through imitation and elaboration. You can also foster this ability by modeling it yourself; practice and actively show children your own listening skills as a way to encourage them to use theirs. Give children opportunities to share what they hear others say; for example, "Terri, did you hear Aiden? He said he wants to work with the blocks, too!" Let children know they have a right to be heard.

> Rebecca says, "I'm getting upset because no one is listening." She draws a sad face and says, "Will you hang it by my cubby so tomorrow everyone will remember to listen to me and you and Ms. Jessica."

Introduce the use of a sand timer, or other concrete device, to help young children develop turn-taking skills; for example, in conflict situations where two or more children want to play with the same object. Using these strategies means children do not have to fight for a turn to speak or to lay claim to communal property. Such techniques can be especially effective in guaranteeing that shy or quiet children participate in group processes and

Preschool Democracy in Action

Here is an example in which the children helped to solve a classroom safety problem. Some experienced the satisfaction of seeing their ideas adopted, one had to deal with the disappointment of "majority rule." All ended up feeling good about contributing to the well-being and enjoyment of the group.

Many of the children enjoyed carrying water from the sink to various areas in the classroom, such as the house area when they were "cooking spaghetti." The teachers supported the idea, but were concerned by the large amounts of water being spilled on the floor. Because virtually everyone was affected by the situation, the teacher decided to bring up their concerns at a class meeting and asked the children for ideas to solve the problem. They wrote down the children's suggestions and, after the group discussed each, they took a vote on which one to adopt.

Tamika: *Make a rule that no one can carry water any more.*

Teacher: *What if someone wants to fill pots for cooking? (Several children said they liked being able to cook "just like at home.")*

Dominic: *Turn off the water. My mommy did that when we had a flood in the kitchen.*

Lisa: *We can put a towel in the house area. Whenever someone spills water, they have to go back and wipe it up.*

Leah: *We can put a towel in every area! Then we can bring water there, as long as we clean up.*

Lisa: *We can put two towels so children can wipe up together.*

Teacher: *(After reading back the list of ideas) Which idea should we try? (Dominic voted to turn off the water but all the other children were in favor of the towels.)*

Teacher: *We have five areas in the room. If we put 2 towels in each area, we'll need 10 towels. Where can we get that many towels?*

Tamika: *We can buy them at the store.*

Teacher: *We don't have enough money for that. Any other ideas? (The children could not think of another way to get towels, so the teacher offered a suggestion.) Do you suppose if we asked parents, they could bring in some old towels your family doesn't use any more?*

All the children agreed this was a good idea. The teachers posted a request on the Parent Bulletin Board, and by the following week, families had donated a dozen old towels. Water carrying (and probably some intentional spilling) actually increased for a while, because children enjoyed wiping up after themselves. They invented different wiping methods, including "skating" towels along the floor or having one child hold each end of the towel. Dominic, whose idea had been voted down, was one of the most avid spiller-wipers.

— From *The Intentional Teacher* (Epstein, 2007, p. 84)

feel their individual needs are met. And for children who have grasped the idea of turn-taking and sharing, they will often be the peer enforcers of this "democratic principle" on their own:

> *At recall time, a classmate does not want to pass the turn-taking hoop to the next child, so Bria says, "You had a turn and now it's Eliot's turn."*
>
> *Destiny says, "Tia, you need to share the cups with everyone because these are for the water table, not just for you."*

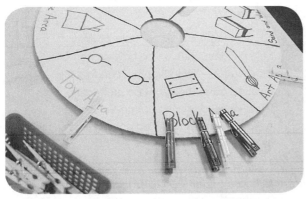

The concepts of "more" and "fewer/less" underlie "majority rule" in a democracy. Here, children voted on which area of the room to store a new material.

Create rules in partnership with children. Research shows children are more likely to follow rules they help develop (Elias et al., 1997). Express satisfaction when a group of children or the class as a whole works to solve a problem collectively, especially when everyone performs roles according to his or her interests and abilities. Observe how much more you can accomplish as a team than as one or two individuals. To draw out the lessons that explicitly help children understand how democracy works — including the idea that it involves compromise — be prepared to acknowledge and support children's needs even when they do not necessarily get their way (see the sidebar on p. 138). (For more on creating and following rules, see Chapter 12).

Introduce vocabulary words and ideas at the core of democratic principles and actions. Many of the words we use in other contexts can also be applied to ideas about democracy. For example, the concepts of "more" and "fewer/less" in mathematics are the foundation of the "majority rule" principle. Many other early mathematics ideas and activities can also be applied to understanding the democratic process. For example, ask children to indicate their preferences (for a color or food) by a show of hands. Count and record the results on chart paper, using the appropriate vocabulary words. Terms we associate with early scientific investigation can also apply to social processes — for example, words related to classification: is/is not, same/different, all/some, other/else, before/after, now/later, and when/where/with whom. When children are encouraged to apply these concepts to people and actions, as well as to concrete objects, these terms can become tools in participatory decision-making.

In general, opportunities to enhance their descriptive vocabulary help children understand and explain how people act with one another. Democracy is essentially the process of governing such human interactions. Thus, as children learn to apply relevant words and ideas to their own actions and those of their peers (e.g., it's not fair for some children to get "all" while others get "none"), they develop the rudimentary knowledge to appreciate how democracy works in society as a whole (e.g., it's better to distribute resources fairly). The more children can articulate their ideas and describe the reasons behind them, the more they can participate as active members of their community.

At election time, expand conversations and role plays children may initiate about voting. The electoral process is too abstract to be of interest or relevance to young children. However, if their families are politically aware or involved, then election talk may be a commonplace subject at home, and it will find its way into the classroom. So, if an interest in this topic emerges from the children's initiative, find ways to make it concrete. For example, if there are polling booths in the school, ask permission to visit them with children during nonvoting hours. In simple terms, explain the voting process to the children; for example, you might say, "Everyone gets to say who they want to do the job. Whoever is picked by the most people, gets to do the job." If it is meaningful to children (because they have done these things with family

Creating and Participating in a Democracy: Teaching Strategies

Encourage children to consider alternative ways to reach a goal.

- As you work alongside children and comment on what they're doing, ask "What do you think would happen if … ?" Or "Can you think of another way to do that?"

- Encourage children to plan more than one way to accomplish a task.

- Pose questions to help children anticipate consequences and reflect on outcomes (e.g., "What will you do if the children who build ramps in the block area tomorrow don't follow the rules you came up with today?").

Build perspective- and turn-taking skills.

- Encourage children to role play to help them practice adopting others' behaviors and viewpoints through imitation and elaboration.

- Practice and actively show children your own listening skills as a way to encourage them to use theirs.

- Give children opportunities to share what they hear others say.

- Introduce the use of a sand timer, or other concrete device, to help young children develop turn-taking skills; for example, in conflict situations where two or more children want to play with the same object.

Create rules in partnership with children.

- Express satisfaction when a group of children or the class as a whole works to solve a problem collectively, especially when everyone performs roles according to his or her interests and abilities.

- To draw out the lessons that explicitly help children understand how democracy works — including the idea that it involves compromise — be prepared to acknowledge and support children's needs even when they do not necessarily get their way.

Introduce vocabulary words and ideas at the core of democratic principles and actions.

- Use words from other contexts that can also be applied to ideas about democracy (e.g., the concepts of "more" and "fewer/less" in mathematics are the foundation of the "majority rule" principle).

- Use other early mathematics ideas to help children understand the democratic process (e.g., ask children to indicate their preferences for a color or food by a show of hands; record the results on chart paper using the appropriate vocabulary words).

- Apply terms from simple scientific investigation (e.g., same/different,

Teaching Strategies *(cont.)*

all/some, now/later) to social processes to help children describe the human behaviors that democracy addresses.

At election time, expand conversations and role plays children may initiate about voting.

- If an interest in an election emerges from the children's initiative, find ways to make it concrete; for example, if there are polling booths in the school, ask permission to visit them with children during nonvoting hours.

- Explain what voting means in simple terms; for example, "Everyone gets to say who they want to do the job. Whoever is picked by the most people gets to do the job."

- Provide materials children can use as props to reenact their own voting experiences.

members), provide materials they can use as props if they want to recreate activities such as going to campaign rallies or voting.

Trevor says to his teacher, "We took a vote on what color to paint the Camaro. I wanted to paint it orange, then my dad wanted to paint it orange, then my brother wanted to paint the Camaro orange. Then mom wanted to paint it pink because that's her favorite color." His teacher asks, "So what color is the Camaro?" Trevor replies, "It's pink because my mom told my dad to buy the Camaro." When his teacher asks what he thinks of the outcome, Trevor says, "That's not what's supposed to happen [when you vote]. But my dad says it's okay because my mom is happy."

In Conclusion

Democracy sounds like a high-minded abstract principle, yet young children can begin to experience it in concrete ways. Many of the issues they confront in other areas of social and emotional development can be applied to participating in the democratic process — equality, respect, diversity, problem-solving. Ideas from other domains of learning also apply to understanding the foundations upon which democracy is based: more and fewer/less, same, if/then. Language development enhances children's abilities to classify and describe group attributes, and to listen to and contribute their ideas to the classroom community. Overall cognitive growth means preschoolers are increasingly able to see things from more than one perspective, anticipate the consequences of their actions, and weigh the risks and benefits of substituting "we" for "me."

In summarizing his democratic conception of education, John Dewey (1916/1966) has this to say:

Since education is a social process, and there are many kinds of societies, a criterion for educational criticism and construction implies a particular social ideal. The two points selected by which to measure the worth of a form of social life are the extent in which the interests of a group are shared by all its members, and the fullness and freedom with which it interacts with other groups. An undesirable society, in other words, is one which internally and externally sets up barriers to free intercourse and communication of experience. A society which makes provision for participation in its good of all its members on equal terms and which secures flexible readjustment of its institutions through interaction of the different forms of associated life is in so far democratic. Such a society must have a type of education which gives individuals a personal interest in social relationships and control, and the habits of mind which secure social changes without introducing disorder. (**Chapter 7**)

Instilling an appreciation for democracy — a society in which there is a free exchange of ideas and participation by all members — is a primary goal of education. We can begin this process in our early childhood classrooms.

Part Four

BEYOND THE CLASSROOM

Preparing Ourselves to be Role Models

It's easy to just focus on anti-bias lessons for the children, but the children are watching us every minute. Without even knowing it, they pick up our attitudes and behavior and see with whom we have relationships. It's so simple to do a lesson on being fair or conduct a circle time on the subject, but the message won't get through unless adults model what they teach. Teaching children to take social action in the name of equity is one thing, but doing it ourselves is another. (Gonzalez-Mena, 2008, p. ix)

About This Chapter

The purpose of this chapter is to help you honestly evaluate and enhance the social and emotional foundations of your interactions with children and their families. The professional development strategies offered will enable you to examine your assumptions about the basic nature of children and their parents and how you treat them as a result. Looking into yourself — through activities undertaken beyond or outside the classroom — can in turn help you improve your classroom teaching practices across a variety of dimensions, ranging from how you set up the learning environment to how you establish and maintain relationships with others. First we will take a look at the importance of teachers' interactions with children, and then we will look at why our beliefs and behaviors make a difference in our interactions with children's family members. By understanding the underpinnings of these relationships, we can consciously adjust our teaching practices to "model" the personal and interpersonal ideals we espouse.

Reflecting on Our Interactions With Children

When we talk about early social-emotional development, what we have in mind is not just the behavior of young children but also the kind of people we want them to be as adults. Our ideal is a society whose citizens understand and express their feelings in healthy ways ("me"), show compassion and extend help to others ("you"), and work together toward common goals that improve life on this planet ("us"). As educators, we therefore strive to prepare preschoolers to achieve the same social and emotional objectives we aspire to in ourselves. We may even have specifically chosen to become teachers so we could play a role in shaping the adults of tomorrow. And society has clearly invested our profession with this important responsibility.

To fulfill this obligation toward children, educators must first serve as role models themselves. We accept that to teach young children reading or mathematics we need to have achieved a certain level of competence in these subjects. When children see us reading a magazine or paying for tomatoes at the farmers' market, they want to be able to do those things, too. For young children, being like their parents or teachers is a powerful motivator for learning. Motivating and helping children master the knowledge and skills necessary for healthy social and emotional development is no different from fostering academic learning. Children need to see us demonstrating these abilities, and their desire to emulate us is the opening to engage them in a journey of personal and interpersonal discovery. Thus it is legitimate, and vital, to examine our own social and emotional attitudes and behaviors before we can serve as examples and guides for young children.

Why Our Beliefs and Behaviors With Children Matter

Adult-child interactions affect development. *Eager to Learn* (National Research Council, 2000a) cites decades of research to support our intuitive belief that how we interact with children affects their development: "Social competence and school achievement are influenced by the quality of early teacher-child relationships and by the teachers' attentiveness to how the child approaches learning" (p. 7). Studies further show that children respond positively, regardless of the teaching style used, when adults are nurturing — that is, warm, sensitive to children's needs, enthusiastic about learning, and flexible in their interactions rather than working from a script.

This conclusion about the importance of adult-child interaction is further supported by a 15-nation study, the International Association for the Evaluation of Educational Achievement (IEA) Preprimary Project, which was coordinated by the HighScope Educational Research Foundation (Weikart, Olmsted, & Montie, 2003). The longitudinal investigation found that the more nurturing the program environment, the better children did as preschoolers and later as primary-grade students.

Distressingly, the incidence of nurturing behaviors observed in teachers from both developed and developing nations ranged from only 1 percent to 6 percent of all interactions; adults listened to children just 1 percent to 7 percent of the time, usually when a child was answering a specific question. In all countries, much more time was spent managing children, engaging in routine tasks, or teaching in primarily adult-centered ways (for example, asking closed-ended questions, lecturing, or demonstrating). Thus teachers, whether consciously or not, often model behavior in which listening to and caring for others, sharing ideas, and acting as equals in discovery and problem-solving, are not highly valued. If young children experience this type of behavior over 90 percent of the time, the message they get about how (or how not) to treat others is powerful — and not necessarily the one we want to communicate.

The challenge for teachers. To improve our nurturing interactions with young children, we must therefore be aware of our attitudes about learning and how these affect our teaching practices. Unfortunately, researchers and teacher-educators from the Office for Studies in Moral Development and Education at the University of Illinois at Chicago reported the following in a presentation to the American Educational Research Association:

> *In the course of training teachers in developmental discipline, we have found that many hold a view of children as self-centered, manipulative, and lazy. If one sees children this way, the logical way to prevent or respond to misbehavior is to use threat or punishment, and the logical way to get children to behave well is to use rewards. We try to help teachers see children not just as self-centered but also as prosocially oriented. If one believes children are interested in learning and want to please and to be fair and kind, then the appropriate response to misbehavior is to find out why the child was not able to do the right thing, and to provide the necessary help. The way to get children to behave well is to be sure they know what is expected, have the skills required, and can see that it is a reasonable, fair, responsible, or kind thing to do* (**Battistich, Solomon, & Watson, 1998**).

Teachers' social and emotional relationships with children affect all aspects of children's learning (Raver, Garner, & Smith-Donald, 2007). Research on the transition from preschool to kindergarten shows teacher-child closeness at both levels is positively associated with children's reading ability, increased exploration of the classroom, school liking, and self-directedness. In these settings, adults recognize that the classroom does not belong just to the teacher but to the children as well. The classroom is not only an expression of the teacher's personality; its walls are full of children's artwork and writing, and children's projects are displayed (DeVries & Zan, 1994). Put simply, children learn more in classrooms where adults establish a positive and child-oriented climate.

In contrast, dependency and conflict in the teacher-child relationship are associated with children's school avoidance and poor academic performance. Disruptive students and harsh teachers have a mutually reinforcing and negative effect. If students are disruptive, teachers act harshly, which in turn worsens students' behavior. It is hard to pinpoint where the cycle starts, but even pre-schoolers are well aware when a teacher is being "mean" (Wiltz & Klein, 2001).

Warm and nurturing relationships between teachers and children have a positive effect on all aspects of children's academic and social-emotional learning.

Implications for Professional Development

The implications of these findings on adult-child interaction are that "We as teachers need to examine what we do and how we interact with children to better address our responsibility for furthering their development," says HighScope senior early childhood specialist Shannon Lockhart (2006, p. 3). As such, many "Trainer-to-Trainer" features in the newsletter *HighScope Extensions* also offer workshop ideas to help practitioners examine their own experiences and beliefs about social-emotional development and how these translate into their interactions with young children in the classroom. (See highscope.org for information on HighScope and *Extensions*.)

Other organizations such as the Center on the Social and Emotional Foundations for Early Learning (CSEFEL; at the University of Illinois and online at www.csefel.uiuc.edu) and Educators for Social Responsibility (ESR) based in Cambridge, Massachusetts (www.esrnational.org), also provide materials to help teachers focus on children's social and emotional development. What these resources have in common is recognizing the importance of defining "school readiness" as comprising more than academic skills (Quesenberry & Doubet, 2006).

Strategies for awareness of social-emotional issues. To enhance teachers' self-awareness about social-emotional issues, and to help them become more reflective about their teaching practices, the following strategies for professional development can be implemented with the members of a teaching team and their supervisor or used as a group inservice training activity:

- *Document teachers interacting with children throughout the day.* Use videotapes and/or written vignettes that illustrate various segments of the daily routine and a range of adult-child interaction strategies.

- *Make a list of the strategies for promoting social-emotional competence listed in Chapter 2,* such as the following:

  ○ Create a program environment that is warm and nurturing. For example, offer children comfort and contact; participate in children's play; converse with children as equals; and encourage children to solve problems and turn to one another for assistance.

  ○ Use overall classroom practices conducive to healthy development. For example, organize and label the classroom; follow a consistent daily routine; and plan for and support children during transitions.

  ○ Use teaching strategies specifically found to support young children's social-emotional development. For example, promote sociodramatic play; model empathy; mediate conflicts to encourage children's independent problem solving; and allow ample opportunities to practice social and emotional skills.

- *Review the videotapes and written observations, and compare the interactions with the strategies on the list.* Identify strengths as well as areas for improvement.

- *As a teaching team or in small groups, discuss 2–3 behaviors and develop a plan to continue and enhance effective interaction strategies and improve other relationship-building practices.* For example, teachers might identify strengths (what is working) and modifiable issues (areas for improvement) in three areas dealing with children, colleagues, and parents, respectively: (a) conversing naturally with children; (b) implementing efficient and individualized daily team planning; and (c) making the program welcoming to non-English-speaking families.

- **Ask supervisors and other teachers to observe and model effective strategies in one another's classrooms.** In this strategy, sometimes called "peer teaching," colleagues visit one another's classrooms, observe and/or demonstrate on a predetermined area of focus (for example, providing children leadership opportunities at large-group time), then meet afterward to share observations of strengths and modifiable issues. They discuss ideas for supporting one another in extending their strengths and changing the modifiable issues.

- **(If done as a supervisor and teaching team): Use the interaction strategies plan developed above for subsequent observation and feedback.** Have the supervisor observe in the classroom and note which ideas are (or are not) being implemented. Acknowledge which goals are being accomplished (teacher strengths). Examples of teacher strengths might be that teachers are talking less and listening to children more; objective child anecdotes are being written and used as the basis for planning; and parent newsletters are being translated into several languages. If needed, generate additional ideas for improvement (modifiable issues). Examples of modifiable issues might be to decrease the number of questions (even open-ended ones) that teachers ask children; to maximize planning time by cleaning up more efficiently after children leave; or to post more non-English resources on the parent bulletin board. Decide how to objectively measure whether these planned improvements are being accomplished.

[*Note:* For supervisors to use observation and feedback effectively with teachers requires intensive training. To learn more about training opportunities related to this technique and other aspects of professional development, visit the HighScope Web site at www.highscope.org.]

- **(If done as a group activity): Discuss what aspects of the interaction strategies plan are working (strengths) and share ideas for enhancement and improvement** with the group as a whole (modifiable issues). Agree on strategies for documenting and measuring each of these

behaviors. At follow-up meetings, share the outcomes, acknowledge changes and accomplishments, and discuss ideas for revising and/or better implementing the plans.

- **Use individual and group implementation plans to develop additional professional development workshops.** Identify resources to help teachers carry out their plans.

Reflecting on Our Interactions With Families

Why Our Beliefs and Behaviors With Families Matter

Our observations of and interactions with young children and their families inevitably reflect our personal biases. We see their behavior through the eyes of the culture(s) we grew up with and live in today, yet we are often unaware of how our attitudes and actions are shaped by our experiences. For optimum social-emotional development, children need synchronicity or agreement — not necessarily sameness, but compatibility — between home and school. Therefore, understanding our own cultural background, and its relationship to those of our children's families, can help us address children's social-emotional needs more consistently and effectively.

Learning to dialogue with others. The best way to deal with differences in our systems and those of the colleagues and families we work with is to enhance our ability to "dialogue" with them — that is, to listen and share and discuss rather than try to convince others that we know what is best for young children (see the sidebar on p. 149). Says early childhood specialist and diversity consultant Janet Gonzalez-Mena:

> *"Let's figure this out together," should be the theme song of teachers in the face of disagreements over what children need. In the face of disagreements, the parent education approach is inadequate. A better strategy is to focus on transformative education, where two people or groups come together and everyone is changed by the encounter* (2008, p. 27).

Areas of cultural variation. Areas in which culture can affect how we interact with children and their parents,

Communicating With Others About Diversity Issues

When ideas about children and families differ, we need to dialogue with others rather than try to persuade them of the "rightness" of our own beliefs. Early childhood specialist and diversity consultant Janice Gonzalez-Mena and professor Intisar Shareef developed a process for working openly with diversity issues that they call RERUN:

R = REFLECT others' thoughts and feelings; engage in self-reflection.

E = EXPLAIN, but only after listening.

R = REASON, but don't let giving your reason overwhelm your understanding of the other's position.

U = UNDERSTAND others' perspectives and also your own history and beliefs.

N = NEGOTIATE, but only after you have achieved mutual understanding; don't rush it.

(Gonzalez-Mena, 2008, pp. 58–60). For ideas on using these steps to help staff examine their own attitudes, beliefs, and practices regarding diversity, see also Shareef & Gonzalez-Mena, 2008. For more on diversity and modeling respect for others, also see Chapter 9, "Valuing Diversity."

as well as with colleagues from different backgrounds, include the following issues:

- *Personal space* — Cultures vary on how close to sit or stand when communicating.
- *Smiling* — Others may only smile to convey happiness, but we misinterpret their lack of smiling as unfriendliness.

- *Eye contact* — Some show respect by making eye contact, and others, by looking away when you talk to them.
- *Touch* — Touch is interpreted variously as a sign of warmth and friendliness, insult, or even danger.
- *Silence* — Silence may or may not be comfortable; it may be seen as either a sign of respect or of disregard for others.
- *Time concepts* — Cultures are differentially oriented toward the present, past, or future; punctuality may (or may not) be important; getting to the point may be appreciated or may be seen as rude.
- *Gender roles* — Cultures differ on whether and what roles are assigned to men and women; parents may feel uncomfortable, or may even feel disrespected, if they are asked to assume a nontraditional role.
- *Autonomy* — Some cultures value autonomy and independence; others deemphasize the individual and focus primarily on the welfare of the group.
- *Adult authority* — Some cultures view encouraging children to question adults as intellectually and emotionally healthy; others see such challenges as disrespectful and want teachers to act as "authority" figures with children; the same attitudes may apply to staff-administration relationships (how teachers interact with supervisors).

As a result of these differences, especially as applied to early care and education, contentious areas for early childhood programs are often *eating (foods and feeding), sleeping, attachment and separation, autonomy versus independence, learning through play, choice, talking versus silence (signs of respect),* and *guidance and discipline.* We often do not become aware of how culture affects our practices in these social and emotional domains until we encounter opposition from parents or coworkers.

"We become conscious of our systems when they bump up against ones that are different, and we notice that we have a reaction. Interacting with others who are different gives you a clue about your own system" (Gonzalez-Mena, 2008, p. 3).

Therefore, the best way to make our programs welcoming to all children, regardless of their background, is to evaluate how our own cultural values affect our behavior in the classroom. We must ask ourselves, says HighScope early childhood specialist Polly Neill (2005), "How do our cultural beliefs, internal biases, and previous experiences shape our expectations of children's behavior, our interactions with the children and the other adults in the classroom, and our relationships with the children's family members?" (p. 2).

Reflecting on how culture shapes our own beliefs and behavior can help us understand the diverse viewpoints of the families in our programs.

Understanding different world views. Neill notes that the majority of the world's cultures may be categorized as either *individualistic/independent* or *collectivistic/ interdependent*. Western culture holds the first world view, while many Hispanic or Asian cultures subscribe to the second. The advantage of the individualistic approach is that "it may result in a high level of natural productivity and individual liberty. The disadvantage is the likelihood of strained relationships and social isolation" while a collectivist view "produces a strong sense of interconnectedness, sharing, and solidarity. The disadvantage lies in the possibility that individual development will be suppressed" (p. 2).

Both orientations are valuable to the development of social-emotional competence, for example, initiative and independence on the one hand, and empathy and collaboration on the other. Therefore, understanding and promoting both world views can not only help us accom-

modate different cultures in our classrooms, it allows us to support the balanced development of all children in the classroom, regardless of their background.

Implications for Professional Development

As the populations served in early childhood programs become increasingly diverse, it is essential that we as teachers become role models for effectively living with — and embracing — both our commonalities and our differences. To serve in this capacity, we must first confront our own beliefs and practices, then develop strategies for learning about and meeting the needs of the children and families in our agencies.

Understanding diversity. Early childhood consultant Chris Boisvert has conducted workshops for teachers and caregivers whose clients and colleagues comprise a wide range of linguistic and cultural backgrounds. Below are several ideas for beginning to address the complex issues surrounding diversity, adapted from her HighScope "Trainer-to-Trainer" workshop on exploring personal biases (2005).

- Discuss and compare what each of the following quotes means to members of the group personally:

* "We hold these truths to be self-evident: That all men are created equal...." (Declaration of Independence)

* "All animals are created equal, but some animals are more equal than others." (George Orwell's *Animal Farm*)

- Talk about how our own experiences with (in)equality affect our responses to these quotes.

- Distribute the handout "Aspects of Humanity" (see the sidebar on p. 151) and discuss how people are advantaged and/or disadvantaged by these characteristics.

- Individually or in small groups answer "10 Questions for Examining One's Own Cultural Viewpoint" (see the sidebar on p. 152). Share answers with the rest of the group.

- Ask participants to share examples of situations in which their personal values conflicted with those of a child's family (for example, about eating and sleeping, cleanliness, the role of play in learning, expressing feelings,

Aspects of Humanity

Aspects of Humanity	Am I advantaged by this? How?	Am I disadvantaged by this? How?
Skin color		
Ethnicity		
Gender		
Age		
Size — height, weight		
Hair color (or amount of hair)		
Religion		
Job		
Eductional level		
Income		
Marital status		
Sexual orientation		
Political views		

— From Boisvert, "Exploring Personal Biases" (2005, *High/Scope Extensions* newsletter insert)

10 Questions for Examining One's Own Cultural Viewpoint

1. Is my culture considered "individualistic" or "collectivistic?" What are three ways in which my answer to this question has implications for how I interact with children and parents in my early childhood program?

2. What do I consider to be my culture's "Top 5" values?

3. How do my personal values fit or clash with those cultural values?

4. How does my culture view being on time? What implications does that have for my work with children, families, and other classroom adults? How do I respond to those who treat time differently?

5. What are my feelings and beliefs about individual achievement versus making contributions to a group effort?

6. What are my feelings and beliefs about how elders and authority figures should be regarded?

7. What does my culture consider to be most important regarding mealtimes? What mealtime traditions are important in my own family? Do they fit with cultural expectations?

8. How does my culture view art and creative work? Do I agree with those views?

9. How do people learn "life lessons" in my culture? How does that affect the way I teach and learn?

10. How does my culture expect people to set and achieve goals? How does this affect my expectations of myself and others?

— From Boisvert, "Exploring Personal Biases" (2005, *High/Scope Extensions* newsletter insert)

and so on). How did they deal with the situation? Based on the lessons learned in the workshop, why was their interaction with the family effective (or not effective)? What would they repeat (or change) next time?

- Ask participants to list the kinds of information they think are important to gather about the families of the children in their program. At a follow-up workshop, share and discuss the information they gathered and how it influenced their subsequent interactions with children and family members.

For more information on how to help families, regardless of background, and support their young children's social-emotional development at home, see Chapter 15.

In Conclusion

For young children, social-emotional development requires more than discourse and a supportive environment: "Even when children are in a caring environment and want to treat others fairly and considerately, they are likely to fail on numerous occasions [because] of their inability to see how humane values apply in a particular situation, or because they haven't yet developed the skills needed to apply those values" (Battistich et al., 1998). Teachers must therefore take an active role by serving as examples and providing guidance as children acquire the skills needed to act in ways consistent with their emerging values. When adults encourage children to respect themselves and others, they help them become the kind of adults they and we admire and aspire to be.

To journey with children along this road, teachers must first evaluate how their own cultural values affect their teaching practices and interactions with family members. Through self-examination, professional development, and reflection, we educators can better understand our motivations and adjust our behavior accordingly. Although the process is not always comfortable, looking at and changing ourselves can help us become the role models we strive to be in making our programs welcoming to all children.

Social–Emotional Learning at Home

Research has shown that children are more accepted by peers when their parents are warm, responsive, and in tune with their children. In contrast, children tend to have more difficulty getting along with peers when parental interactions are hostile and controlling. In other words, an adult-child relationship that involves listening to one another, cooperating, and displaying mutual enjoyment provides a model for interacting with others. (Riley, San Juan, Klinkner, & Ramminger, 2008, p. 54)

About This Chapter

This chapter explores the areas of early social and emotional development that most concern parents and in which they can play a significant role. The importance of each topic is briefly summarized, followed by practical suggestions that you can share with families about supporting their young children's emotional learning and social competence at home. Much of the material was adapted from two sets of publications published by the HighScope Educational Research Foundation (2001a and 2001b, respectively). *All About High/Scope* was written to introduce readers to all the components of the preschool curriculum and features sections on how to apply classroom practices in the home. *You and Your Child* was specifically developed for parents and addresses their role in supporting their children's early development in many different areas. In this chapter, the relevant portions of these publications are updated with new information about the impact of the home environment on early social and emotional development.

Another useful HighScope publication for working with parents is *The Essential Parent Workshop Resource* by early childhood specialist and program director Michelle Graves (2000). This book offers concrete ideas for conducting 30 parent workshops across a wide range of early-learning topics. The sidebar on page 154 lists the workshops that deal specifically with social-emotional development. (Other chapters in this book also address issues that concern working with parents, most notably Chapter 14, "Preparing Ourselves to be Role Models.")

Working With Families

As the foregoing chapters show, young children develop social and emotional skills through their independent explorations and their interactions with others. Through these experiences, they learn who they are, what they can do, how to express their feelings and ideas, and how to care about and get along with others. Social and emotional learning therefore comes about indirectly for the most part — through adult-guided experiences with objects, people, events, and ideas — rather than through direct instruction about how to think, feel, or behave.

The value of "indirect but guided learning" is an important message for educators to share with families. In their eagerness to raise emotionally secure and socially competent children, parents may think they have to directly teach or instill a prescribed set of values or behaviors. Instead, their goals for their children can best be achieved by creating a home environment that is rich in opportunities to learn through personal exploration and positive interpersonal experiences. In addition to providing appropriate materials and varied activities for their young children, parents also serve as primary models of the kinds of adults they want their children to become.

Parent Workshops on Early Social and Emotional Development

The Essential Parent Workshop Resource by early childhood specialist and program director Michelle Graves (2000) provides all the information needed to conduct parent workshops on a wide variety of topics that typically concern families. Each of the 30 workshops presents the learning goals, a list of workshop materials (including handouts), how to introduce the workshop, an opening activity, the central ideas to discuss and share with participants, reflections and ideas for applying the lessons learned at home, and follow-up ideas.

Below is a list of the workshop topics that are particularly relevant to helping parents understand how to support their young child's social and emotional development at home.

- The Importance of Consistent Routines

- Transitions — Smooth Sailing or Daily Struggle?

- Understanding Children's Responsibilities Around the House

- Power Struggles at Home

- Understanding and Dealing Effectively With Children's Outbursts

- Solving Everyday Problems: Opportunities for Learning

- Feeling Comfortable With Children's Social Bloopers

- Helping Children Resolve Social Conflicts

- Helping Children Cope With Childhood Losses

- Rules — Set in Stone or Open to Family Discussion?

- Presenting a United Front: Parental Teamwork

- When Other Adults Criticize Your Child

Supporting Emotional Development at Home

Young Children as Competent and Confident Learners

The features in an active-learning early childhood program that support the development of confident young learners work equally well in the home. These include an organized environment, a consistent daily routine, and opportunities for children to plan and reflect on their own learning. Share with parents the following ways in which they can implement these program practices in their own households:

- *Make your home a place where learning is expected and cherished.* Parents cannot make their children learn. The desire to learn comes from within. Young children learn through their independent explorations and their interactions with others. If you establish your home as a setting where learning is supported, your children will identify themselves as able and resourceful learners.

- *Make your home a place for active learning.* Everything that children and adults do in an active learning program can be done at home. Whenever possible, encourage children to make choices; for example, about what to wear, which toys to put away first, or what books to read at bedtime. Pay attention to what your children find interesting, and provide materials and experiences that allow them to pursue these interests. Learn to feel comfortable letting your children do things for themselves, even if it takes a little longer or is not done perfectly. Have conversations with your children as you do things together. You'll be surprised to discover how actively your children are thinking about the world and how it works! Being allowed to tell you about it in their own words is a key to their intellectual and social-emotional development.

- **Help your children become aware of how your home is organized.** You may be surprised to realize that your home already has many important organizational features that reflect and support early learning. For example, your children know that different rooms in your home are used for different things. They may know which shelf in the refrigerator holds the milk or which drawer to open to find a spoon. Many other school ideas can be used at home. For example, offer different types of learning materials for your children to play with and store the materials where they can be found and easily put away. You might want to attach simple labels to toy shelves and containers to help your children sort and store things. Another idea is to tape their name, initials, or letter link in the space where they hang their coat or backpack each day. (A letter link is a nametag with a letter-linked picture of an object that starts with the same letter and sound as the child's first name; DeBruin-Parecki & Hohmann, 2003.)

- **Follow a consistent daily routine at home.** Since children as well as adults benefit from a predictable daily schedule at work or school, all members of your family will benefit from a regular routine in the home as well. Your weekend routine may differ from the weekday one, but as long as both are consistent, children will learn important concepts about time and dependability. When there is a need to go off-schedule — for example, during a vacation or an illness — explain to your children why there is a change. Tell them when you expect things to return to the normal routine, and help them keep track of when this will happen. You'll discover that when your children know when something will happen, they will feel more secure and become more able to regulate their own behavior and take responsibility for it.

- **Use the plan-do-review process at home.** Once children are in the habit of planning, carrying out, and evaluating their own activities at school, they often want to bring the process home. You can support them by designating a "your choice" time each day. Encourage your children to plan what they would like to do at these times and provide them with enough time and materials to carry out their plans. Afterwards, as you clean up or share a meal, ask your children to tell you what they did and encourage them to share their experiences with other family members.

Use the morning travel time to ask your children about their plans for the day. At the end of the day, remind them about your conversation and ask them to tell you what happened. Avoid general questions such as, "What did you do at school today?" Instead, ask specific questions and make comments that pick up on your children's plans. For instance, you might say to a child, "This morning you told me you wanted to play in the block area with Ashanti. I wondered if you did that and what the two of you did there." (Remember, however, that a plan is not a contract. Be prepared for your child's plan and activities to have changed.) With your help, the plan-do-review process will become a lifelong — and self-regulating — way for your children to think and act.

Young Children as Decision Makers

Learning how to make good decisions and choices takes lots of time and practice, but the benefits last a lifetime. People who know how to go about making and evaluating decisions not only feel confident about their own abilities, they inspire the trust and confidence of others. Offer the following suggestions to parents so they can help their young children become competent decision makers:

- **Make your home a place that offers young children the opportunity to make choices.** If you look at your home through your young child's eyes, you will find many low-cost or no-cost objects that offer them choices for play time — pots and pans, brooms, boxes of different sizes, empty plastic containers, old hats and scarves, empty paper towel rolls, junk mail and scrap paper, rocks, leaves, acorns, old tires, and blocks of wood.

In addition to these everyday household objects, offer your children a few good-quality, store-bought materials

Research shows that children whose parents are interested in and responsive to them at home develop better relationships with their teachers and peers at school.

and toys they can choose to play with — books (in addition to those you check out of the library), music CDs, crayons and pencils, plain and colored paper, a riding vehicle, a set of wooden blocks, a doll, jigsaw puzzles. Encourage family members and friends who want to give your child gifts to consider these types of toys. Store toys where children can easily retrieve and return the items they choose to work with. Then children will not only be able to make choices and set goals, but gain confidence in carrying them out on their own.

- **Show an interest in the choices your children make.** What you say carries a lot of weight with your child. When your child calls out, "Come quick! See the tower I made," stop your own activity for a moment and look at what your child is doing. Acknowledge it with a comment that describes what your child did, such as, "Jamal, you used up almost all the blocks to build that big tower!" These instantaneous displays of your

interest, even if they only last a couple of minutes, are just as important as the longer periods of "quality time" you spend with your child.

- **Give your children time to make decisions.** With all the new opportunities in the world, young children often need time to choose. For example, they may want to look at every tub in the display case before deciding what flavor ice cream to order. You may find yourself getting impatient, but it is important to encourage your children's independent decision making. If a child seems overwhelmed by too many choices, limit them to two or three. For example, before you leave for the ice cream shop, you might say, "I know you like vanilla, mint chip, and chocolate swirl. Think about which flavor you would like today." As you approach the store, you could say, "We're almost there. Have you decided which flavor you want?" As your child becomes more skillful at making choices, you can offer a wider variety.

  Children also need time to make good decisions in social situations, and the lessons may not be spontaneous. Give them time to experience the consequences so they can explore other options. For example, a friend may become angry or visit less often if your child refuses to share toys. Don't force your child to share. One day you may hear your child say, "You can play with the truck and I'll play with the car. I'll play with the truck when you are finished."

- **Encourage your children to make child-sized choices and decisions throughout the day.** Let your children help decide what to fix for dinner, where to go on a family outing, which sweater to wear, which video to rent, and so on. Clarify the range (and if necessary, limit the number) of acceptable choices beforehand. Once a child makes a choice, respect it. For example, if your child has a gift certificate to buy a toy, begin by limiting the choices to those that are affordable and safe. If your child chooses one you think is fragile, you can suggest something sturdier, but in the end it is your child's choice. If the toy does break, your child will learn an important lesson. Taking responsibility for one's choices is part of becoming a good decision-maker.

Young Children as Problem Solvers

Learning to solve problems helps children develop confidence. It is not always easy for parents to watch their children struggle to solve problems. Their natural inclination is to take over, whether to shelter the children from frustration, speed up the process, or guarantee a successful outcome. But letting children work things out on their own helps them develop the vital problem-solving skills they will need in school and in work. To help parents support their children's problem-solving skills, suggest they do the following:

- *Help your child see problems when they exist.* If your child does not recognize a problem, describe it in a calm, matter-of-fact voice. For example, say, "Jason, when you scream that loud, it is hard for me to hear the words you are saying" or "Anya, if you squeeze really hard, the mustard squirts all over the table instead of on your hot dog where you want it to go." Statements such as these help children realize their behaviors have consequences and give them the option of changing those behaviors to realize their goals.

- *Ask your child to describe the problem to you.* Being able to identify a problem is the first step in figuring out what needs to happen next. You may be surprised to learn your daughter gets hot, thirsty, and bored while watching her big sister's softball game. By describing the problem, she can discover the key to its solution — wear a hat, bring a juice box and a snack, and take a small toy to play with.

- *Acknowledge (recognize) the problem and your child's feelings.* Rather than just react to your child's feelings, acknowledge them and help your child identify the cause. For example, if your child throws his boot across the room while getting dressed in the morning, you might say, "It's hard to get boots on when your hands are still small. It makes you mad when you try really hard and it doesn't work." Think about your child's reaction to such a statement. Instead of seeing himself as someone who loses control, he learns his feelings can be explained and that you are there to support and help him solve the problem.

- *Respect your child's ideas about how a problem might be solved.* Try out your children's ideas, even if you are pretty sure they will not work. This shows you respect the children's thoughts and efforts; it also allows them to observe the consequences of their ideas and self-correct their thinking. And if the plan does work, your children have the satisfaction of having solved the problem and received your acknowledgment.

- *Remind your child of other times that she or he solved similar problems.* A simple statement such as "Opening the lid on this tube reminds me of how you twisted the lid off the marker this morning," helps a child see that the solution to one problem can be applied to another situation. It also reminds the child that he or she is a capable problem solver. Having succeeded before, the child can feel confident about succeeding again.

- *Watch for signs that your child is becoming discouraged or frustrated.* If you see that your child is ready to give up or is becoming angry, offer help in a way that allows your child to remain engaged with the task and continue to pursue a solution. For example, you might say, "Sometimes when I have trouble attaching things with the stapler, I use a paper clip instead." Use your judgment about those times when direct help on your part will allow your child to achieve a more important goal. For example, close the zipper on your child's jacket if going outside to play ball with you is the main objective.

- *Whenever possible, plan ahead for the extra time it will take your child to solve a problem.* For example, head to the car five minutes early so your child can practice fastening the seat belt. To keep yourself from becoming impatient, use the time in a way you find helpful — listen to the news, check the day's schedule, or just relax before facing a busy day. Take a few minutes to enjoy your child's emerging abilities and share pride in his or her accomplishments. Offer your child encouragement; for example, "You got the strap over your shoulder. You're halfway there. Now you're looking for the slot to snap the buckle in."

Teachers can help parents see how allowing children to solve problems on their own helps them become confident learners.

Young Children as Challengers

Children's challenging behaviors can be frustrating and embarrassing for parents, especially when it takes place in front of others. It helps parents to know that children's tantrums, refusals, and angry words directed at them are a normal part of growing up. Children act this way because they are focused on their own needs and desires, not because they want to be bad. They are impatient because they do not have a good concept of time. Children also assert themselves because they are testing the limits of their competence and independence. These are all valuable goals. The role of adults is to understand the feelings and desires behind the challenging behavior and help children express them appropriately. To deal with their children's challenging behaviors, parents can do the following:

- *Anticipate and try to avoid situations that trigger challenging behavior.* Children who are rested and well fed are less likely to be disruptive or negative. It also helps if they are engaged with something that interests them. So, if they are accompanying you on errands, bring along snacks and toys. When possible, involve them in the activity. For example, make an "I spy" game finding packages of a certain color on supermarket shelves. Play their favorite CD and sing along in the car. Tell children beforehand, in simple and concrete words, the purpose of the errand and how long it will take. Say, for example, "We have to drive Suzie to gymnastics, but we'll be home in time for your play date with Ryan."

- *When children do challenge you, stay calm and be patient.* Remember that children are not trying to embarrass adults; they are simply frustrated trying to follow through on their own intentions. You do not need to give in to their desires, but understanding that their behavior is normal can help you be sympathetic and not overreact. Remember, too, that most people witnessing a tantrum have been on the receiving end of such outbursts. They will not judge you on your child's behavior but on how you respond to it. If you remain calm but firm, others will see you are in control and will go about their own business.

- *Let children know you understand and accept their feelings, even when you do not accept their behavior.* Children can scare themselves when they lose control. They may fear losing your love. Reassure them that you understand that they do not mean to be bad, and that you love them. Emphasize it is the behavior, not them or their feelings, that is the problem. Say something like "I understand you want that candy bar, but we are going home for lunch now. It's okay to feel hungry and unhappy, but it's not okay to kick the cart."

- *Do your best to stick with your chosen course of action.* Just as you respect their plans and choices, it is important for children to see you following through on yours. Do your best to satisfy their needs in a way that does not interfere with your goals. Offer them feasible choices; for example, you might say to a child, "Should we buy cereal or fruit first?" Your primary resource in challenging situations is your own calm and resolve. If you carry on, it will be easier for your children to settle down and go along.

Supporting Social Development at Home

Young Children as Family Members

The home environment is the first community to which young children belong. How their parents and siblings interact with them will set the stage for how they in turn interact with teachers and peers when they enter group care and education settings. By treating children as respected and valued members of their families, parents can help them make the transition to other communities. Here are some strategies to share with parents:

- *Share control with children.* Sharing control does not mean giving up control. Adults still need to set limits that guarantee everyone's physical and psychological health and safety and that allow for the overall smooth functioning of the family. However, in a household with shared control, parents can achieve a reasonable balance between meeting adults' needs and children's desires. One way to share control with children is to focus on what they can do, rather than on their limitations. Allow them to make their own decisions whenever possible and to act as "leaders" in a family game or outing. By encouraging children to contribute to the family in the ways they are capable, children will feel like valued members of the home community.

- *Listen and talk to your children.* Any time you are together is a good time to talk. Children have a lot to share, if only we take the time to listen to them. Along with naturally occurring times, set aside a special time to talk with your children each day. Your full attention shows you think their thoughts are important. Whenever you talk to children, make the conversation natural. Rather than asking them to recite what you know they already know (children learn nothing new from this line of questioning), ask genuine questions to learn about their feelings, ideas, and thought processes. Observe and play alongside them, describe and comment on what they do, imitate them, and ask for their ideas on how to use materials or carry out an idea. Natural dialogue and interactions between children and adults establishes children as equal family members.

- *Reflect on what you have accomplished as a parent.* Let your children know how rewarding and valuable it is to you to be their parent. Share with other family members your memories of experiences with your children — the time you have spent together talking, playing, doing chores, reading books, going to interesting places, and helping others. From your example, children will learn what it means to be a parent and to nurture others. They will see that time and effort spent on family relationships can be an important source of satisfaction in life.

Young Children and Resolving Conflicts

- *Use the conflict resolution process at home.* As your children learn the steps to resolving conflicts in their program (see Chapter 11, "Resolving Conflicts"), you may see them using these techniques with siblings and playmates at home. As you help and support them in this process, you may also find yourself using similar steps to resolve your own conflicts with family members and friends, as well as to settle disagreements with your children. Don't be discouraged if success — yours and the children's — is not instant. These steps take practice but they can be learned by everyone.

Young Children and Dramatic Play

Pretending helps young children make sense of their world and gain control over the events that touch their lives. Children are often very active and talkative during dramatic play, whether they are doing it alone or with others. Playing provides many opportunities to cooperate and solve problems with materials and people. Young children gain information and skills via imitation, exchanging and elaborating on others' play ideas, explaining their own ideas, and having their reasoning challenged. They also expand their communication skills. To help parents support and guide children's natural interest in dramatic play, suggest the following ideas to them:

- *Provide materials that support pretend play.* Provide children with old clothes and accessories to play dress-up (shirts, dresses, jackets, shoes, handbags, hats, scarves, costume jewelry, wallets). Encourage them to make props with everyday household objects (buckets, sheets and blankets, brooms, towels, safe kitchen utensils and carpentry tools). Provide materials they can use to create props (paper, crayons and markers, scissors, string, tape, staplers, glue, old carpet and wallpaper samples, rocks and shells they collect outside). Save materials you would otherwise recycle or throw away (empty and clean food containers, supermarket circulars, ticket stubs, old calendars, grocery bags, empty appliance cartons, expired charge cards, take-out menus). You will be amazed at children's creative transformations: A paper towel tube becomes a magic wand, a child wearing a tool belt becomes a master electrician, and pebbles become a restaurant's daily couscous special. (*Note*: Make it clear to parents that they do not need to supply all these items at home. Rather, they can choose a few materials that are readily accessible and of interest to their children. These materials can be rotated as their availability and the children's interests change.)

Encourage parents to join in pretend play to foster their children's imagination, vocabulary, social skills, and cognitive growth.

- *Join in children's pretend play.* If children haven't invited you to play, observe from the sidelines until you understand the theme of their play. Slip unobtrusively into the action; for example, say "May I please have a menu? I'm very hungry." If children do invite you to play, follow their lead. Let them choose the roles and the characters' actions. Don't take over and direct the play, even if you think they would like your idea. If you want to try expanding their play, offer a suggestion within the established play theme. For example,

if they are playing "driving to grandma's house," you can try saying "I think we took a wrong turn and now we're lost." Drop your idea if they don't pick up on it. Remember that you are a guest in their pretend world.

- *Extend your child's pretend play interests with other activities.* When you observe what your children find interesting, provide them with materials and experiences that will enrich their play. For example, if your children enjoy making artwork, provide art supplies and tools in a variety of media. Go to a museum or gallery that welcomes children (check with the docent or owner beforehand), or arrange to visit an artist in his or her studio. Take photos, provide props, and find related books that encourage your children to recreate or build on this experience. Share and discuss reproductions (postcards, brochures) of artwork with your children. (Again, make it clear that parents need not do all of these extending activities. These are ideas they can choose among.)

- *Accept that your child's pretend play will sometimes be disturbing.* Children act out experiences that affect and interest them, including the things they see and hear but do not fully understand. For example, if they overhear an argument in the supermarket or at home, they may act out a scene with angry voices. Illness, the death of a family member or pet, a friend moving away, car accidents, natural disasters, and other upsetting themes may recur in their pretend play. When you observe this type of play, remain calm and be available to reassure children and answer their questions. Provide resources to help them; for example, a storybook about a child whose parents are getting divorced or whose grandparent died. The more practice children have with pretend play, the more they can differentiate it from reality. Acting out "What if … " lets them try different scenarios while taking comfort in the fact that the imaginary situation is not real. Children control their own responses during play, so if a disturbing situation does occur in reality, their "pretend practice" can help them feel less vulnerable.

In Conclusion

Children's healthy social and emotional development is fostered when they have good relationships at home, positive interactions at school, and consistency and collaboration between home and school. It is important for schools to acknowledge that parents are the first and most important teachers that young children have. They set the stage for how children think of themselves and others, how they feel about learning and the role they play in their own education, and whether they can exert control over the world and be a contributing member of the community. Teachers can support and extend this learning when children come to school. Working together and learning from one another, teachers and parents can help young children grow into emotionally and socially mature adults who value themselves and are valued by others.

16

Reaching Out to Our Communities

The school is part of the community in which it is located and should be connected to the rest of the community in meaningful and helpful ways. It is widely acknowledged that community involvement in, and support for, SEL [social-emotional learning] programs is essential for these programs to be maximally successful. The actions of the school are enhanced when it engages the wider community in its work of educating and developing the community's children. (Elias et al., 1997, p. 89)

About This Chapter

This chapter takes a look at how education professionals can work with both the community inside their agency and the outside community to promote children's social-emotional learning. For each of these areas, the chapter examines how these communities are structured and provides practical strategies for fostering relationships within and between them.

Working Within Communities

Just as young children become part of their classroom community (see Chapter 7, "Developing a Sense of Community"), so, too, do classrooms function within a larger community context. One level up, the classroom is nested within an agency, which provides an administrative structure. There may be one or more layers of supervision, other teachers in other classrooms, and a set of policies that govern what happens within and between classrooms. We can think of the agency as forming the "inner community" within which the classroom resides. This inner community provides resources, technical assistance,

professional development, and emotional as well as logistical support to teachers so they can in turn nurture the children in their care.

Moving up another level, the agency itself is embedded in a surrounding area that encompasses its neighborhood or city, local and state government, businesses, other educational and social services agencies, and the individuals and families who live within its boundaries. The early childhood agency provides direct services to some of these community members (families with young children), and interacts with many other branches of the system (including merchants, government licensing inspectors, and other service providers). We can think of this broader group as the "outer community" within which the agency functions.

In order for the classroom community to provide nurturing and effective early learning experiences, a program must maintain positive relationships with its own inner and outer communities. Children turn to adults for material resources, information and thought-provoking ideas, rewarding social interactions, and personal warmth and encouragement. Staff members rely on agencies to provide corresponding types of support, and agencies in turn elicit assistance from, collaborate with, and draw strength from the individuals and institutions that define their community. In sum, the social and emotional learning that transpires within an early childhood setting requires an interdependent network that extends far beyond the classroom.

The Community Inside the Agency

The importance of community within an agency. When we talk about the role of "community" in early childhood

How Communities Promote Social-Emotional Learning

Just as young children become part of their classroom community, so, too, do classrooms function within a larger community context. One level up, the classroom is nested within an agency, which provides an administrative structure. We can think of the agency as forming the "inner community" within which the classroom resides. This inner community provides resources, technical assistance, professional development, and emotional as well as logistical support to teachers so they can in turn nurture the children in their care.

Moving up another level, the agency itself is embedded in a surrounding area that encompasses its neighborhood or city, local and state government, businesses, other educational and social services agencies, and the individuals and families who live within its boundaries. The early childhood agency provides direct services to some of these community members and interacts with many other branches of the system. We can think of this broader group as the "outer community" within which the agency functions.

In order for the classroom community to provide nurturing and effective early learning experiences, a program must maintain positive relationships with its own inner and outer communities. Staff members rely on agencies to provide support, and agencies in turn elicit assistance, collaborate with, and draw strength from the individuals and institutions that define their community. In sum, the social and emotional learning that transpires within an early childhood setting requires an interdependent network that extends far beyond the classroom.

programs, we typically think of the classroom community and the neighborhood community within which our organizations are located. However, there is an intermediate level; namely, the community created by the agency itself. Staff members, through a combination of intention and happenstance, form a professional and personal community. Our relationships with colleagues are a major determinant of the affective climate within which we thrive or struggle every day.

Katz and McClellan (1997) emphasize how important this community of peers is to our work with young children, particularly our ability to support their social-emotional development: "We have found that teachers who learn to work, strategize, and share deeply with others are those who find the greatest joy in their work and are able to pass on to children a deeper sense of what collaboration is about. Collaboration is not an easy process; however, teachers need each other to share insights, information, strategies, and support. They also can give one another courage to make the changes that are important to the 're-creation' of schools for young children" (p. 30).

Strategies for building community within an agency. Despite this need for community right outside the classroom, many caregivers and teachers complain of feeling isolated. Pressured to meet the needs of children and administrative demands for accountability, they have no time to interact with colleagues. Teachers and caregivers in small (one-classroom) programs, rural areas, or home-based programs are also literally isolated — that is, working on their own. To support our adult need for contact, which in turn allows us to nurture the children in our care, it is therefore imperative to establish and maintain professional communities. Strategies for creating and sustaining ties with colleagues include the following:

- *Hold staff meetings.* Schedule regular staff meetings in which colleagues learn together, share problems, brainstorm solutions, and are acknowledged for their effort and success. Keep meetings that are devoted to curriculum and teaching issues separate from discussions of administrative or "business" matters. Use meetings about curriculum and pedagogy to focus exclusively on professional development; that is, supporting and enhancing the child development knowledge and teaching skills of staff.

- *Attend conferences.* Encourage teaching teams or groups to attend conferences together. Provide release time for staff, and hire substitute teachers to cover their classes if conferences are held during regular program hours. Also, if your budget permits, allocate funds to help defray the cost of registration and travel. Most agencies cannot afford to sponsor attendance at national or regional events. However, conferences sponsored by local or state branches of early childhood organizations are often feasible for staff to attend. By having teachers go to conferences in pairs or small groups, they can continue to discuss and reflect on the conference sessions together and support one another (through classroom visits and exchanging resources) as they implement what they have learned. Those who attend conferences can collaborate on making peer presentations to the rest of their colleagues.

The agency is the "inner community" within which a program resides. Attending staff meetings and professional conferences together helps foster a sense of community among program staff.

- *Join a professional organization.* Teachers feel that their work has higher value when they see themselves as part of the wider community of early care and education. Membership in a professional organization helps to confer this status and offers practitioners many other benefits, such as networking opportunities, informative newsletters, policy updates, and free or reduced-cost conference attendance.

- *Distribute informational resources.* Provide staff with print, audiovisual, and online resources about early childhood development and effective teaching practices. Be sure to include material on social and emotional development as well as academic areas such as literacy and mathematics. Establish a resource center; for example, in the library or staff lounge, where teachers can access and discuss information together.

- *Develop a trusting atmosphere.* Create an agency environment in which teachers feel safe sharing their problems, seeking help, or just unburdening themselves from the pressures of the job. Although educating children and supporting families can be rewarding work, it can also be highly stressful. Teachers whose own needs for collegial support are not met can burn out. Stressed teachers not only endanger their own well-being but are likely to fall short of meeting the social and emotional needs of those they care for. By contrast, teachers who feel supported by administrators and colleagues have the resources and strength to nurture children.

The Community Outside the Agency

The importance of community outside the agency. As the quote that opens this chapter notes, programs to support children's social-emotional development are most successful when they are connected to the communities in which they operate. It is thus imperative that our programs reflect the skills, attitudes, and values that are priorities in the community (Elias et al., 1997).

We as early childhood educators have two responsibilities in this regard. One is taking responsibility for our own behavior by becoming knowledgeable about our local communities and their leaders and establishing relationships with other service providers to nurture the well-being of young children and their families. Our other obligation is to help shape the behavior of these leaders by acting as advocates for social-emotional learning in early childhood programs. We can and should take an active role informing the public why it is important to devote resources to affective education — as stated in *Neurons to Neighborhoods* and quoted in Chapter 1 — "on a par with those focused on literacy and numerical skills" (National Research Council, 2000b, p. 5).

As we reach out from the agency to the community, we should identify those who are in a position to advocate for high-quality and comprehensive early childhood programs. Possible advocates among individuals and organizations within the educational sector include elementary and secondary school principals and administrators, school leadership teams (often comprised of administrators, faculty, and parents), school boards, parent-teacher organizations, adult literacy and continuing education programs, and community colleges. Beyond education, outreach can extend to legislators (local, state, national), pediatricians and other physical health care providers, nutrition services, mental health professionals, financial and legal aid agencies, business leaders, religious institutions, news media (public and private), entertainment and sports figures, law-enforcement officers, and the arts community.

We can help these individuals and organizations in leadership positions become more aware not only of the academic benefits of early childhood education, which is now widely recognized, but of the particular value of promoting social-emotional development. Staff can use the knowledge gained from their own experiences, plus information provided in this book and other resources, to make the case for early childhood programs that focus on the "whole child" in fostering school readiness. (For information on making a case for comprehensive education to school administrators and other policy makers, see *A School Administrator's Guide to Early Childhood Programs* by HighScope Educational Research Foundation President Larry Schweinhart, 1988; for a comprehensive assessment tool to help schools determine if they are ready to receive young children and promote their development in all areas, see the Ready School Assessment kit developed by HighScope researchers, 2007.)

Strategies for building community outside the agency. An agency's connections with the outer world operate in two directions; that is, extending from the agency to the community and returning from the community back to the agency. Reciprocity makes these relationships true partnerships and is essential to the agency's ability to deliver high quality, valuable services. Likewise, the community's understanding of and support for the agency's

mission is vital to realizing their shared interests in shaping society's future citizens.

Program staff have many options and opportunities to *reach out to other service providers and leaders in the community* with messages about early social-emotional development. Strategies include the following:

- Establish parent-teacher organizations.

- Network with the kindergarten programs your children will be entering; serve as a liaison between the parents in your program and the staff in the elementary schools where the kindergartens are located.

- Make comments to and invite input from the school board at public hearings.

- Join a community mental health team to address ongoing and crisis issues.

- Distribute program newsletters to community members as well as parents.

- Publish newspaper articles and press releases about social-emotional program initiatives and outcomes.

- Offer to make presentations at meetings of their organizations.

- Be open to visits from community members.

- Invite community members to attend staff training on topics such as conflict resolution that they can apply in their own organizations.

In return, *community organizations can support an early childhood agency's social-emotional program initiatives* in several ways, including the following:

- Provide opportunities for children to participate in community-based projects. Even preschoolers can help with simple tasks such as picking up litter (while wearing appropriate safety gear), planting flowers in public spaces, playing with animals (screened for child-friendliness) at the local shelter, or bringing pets to visit the sick and elderly. Participating in these activities helps to develop a sense of civic responsibility.

- Contribute funds and other resources to assist programs that promote social-emotional education. Tell potential contributors what the program does and what it can accomplish. Share the outcomes with them. Acknowledge their sponsorship in your program's promotional and recruitment literature.

- Provide guest speakers. Invite community representatives to address program staff and parents at workshops and meetings. Give them background information on the audience(s) and types of information that would be helpful. Encourage them to leave materials about their agency and the services it provides.

- Volunteer in the program. Many service organizations are eager to find volunteer opportunities for their members. In addition, an increasing number of businesses, both local enterprises and major national chains, are encouraging their employees to become involved in community-service activities. Employees generally get release time and may also enjoy other benefits such as bonuses and peer recognition.

Whenever possible, bring community resources into the program. This approach has two advantages. First, children and families are more likely to use the services if they are offered onsite, in a trusted setting. Once the services and providers become familiar, families are more likely to seek them out in the community when needed. Second, while they are onsite, service providers can learn about the early childhood program firsthand, value its contribution to the community as a whole, and refer clients with young children to the agency.

Once these interagency connections are established, early childhood program staff can use them to advocate for promoting children's social-emotional development, explaining to community service providers why the importance of social-emotional learning equals that of "academic preparedness" in getting young children ready for school. The following illustrates the value of such interagency connections:

> As parents and children arrive in the morning, they are greeted by a nutritionist from the county extension office who hands out warm muffins. The parents also get a recipe card and information on nutrition programs offered by the extension office. What could be more welcoming than freshly baked muffins? This treat was

easy to arrange because the extension office was looking for ways to reach out to parents of young children. Both organizations, the early care and education program and the extension office, benefitted from working together (Riley, San Juan, Klinkner, & Ramminger, 2008, p. 115).

Another example of promising school-community partnerships particularly appropriate for early-childhood programs is intergenerational collaborations. Preschools can partner with agencies serving senior citizens such as residential facilities or volunteer organizations. These partnerships can take several forms, ranging from seniors volunteering in the early childhood center (for example, reading or cooking with the children), children visiting a senior facility to share music and movement activities, short excursions to parks and nature trails, and joint birthday parties. The social and emotional benefits accrue for both the children and the seniors in the partnership, as illustrated by this pair of anecdotes from *Let's Do Something Together: A Guidebook for Effective Intergenerational Programs* (Epstein & Boisvert, 2005):

> When the program administrator finds out that Eduardo, a gentleman in the senior program, has been a construction worker, she adds books about tools and buildings as well as related materials to the book, toy, and work areas of the intergenerational space. At the next meeting time, Lewan, a four-year-old, walks into the book area where Eduardo sits flipping through an architecture magazine. Eduardo points to the picture of a skyscraper on the front cover and says, "I wonder what it would be like to be way up there." Lewan moves closer to the book. "It would be like sitting on a cloud," Eduardo says. Lewan laughs and points to a cloud outside the window (pp. 13–14).

> When talking with a program administrator, the daughter of a senior with dementia comments, "My mother really enjoys being with Dylan and helping him at snacktime. It's something she feels comfortable with because Dylan doesn't demand anything of her. No one is focusing on her memory loss like when I talk with her or ask her

questions. She also doesn't feel pressured to finish when others do or eat a certain amount of food. Everything is more relaxed for her" (p. 20).

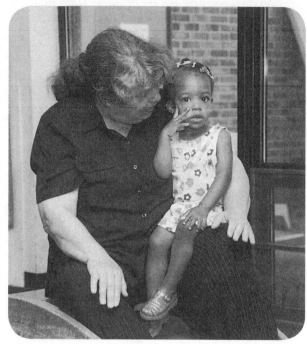

Early childhood settings and the "outside community" offer one another mutual benefits, such as the senior-youth bonds formed in intergenerational programs.

In Conclusion

Larry Schweinhart, president of the HighScope Educational Research Foundation, describes the importance of social-emotional learning as a vital component of any educational initiative for young children:

> *Early childhood education — as practiced by the nation's child care centers and homes, and in Head Start, prekindergarten, and kindergarten programs — is not merely the transmission to young minds of the concepts of numbers, letters, shapes, and colors. It is our first public statement of the values we wish to pass on to our children. We say that we value personal initiative, collaborative problem solving, and tolerance and respect for others. These, then, are the values that should be evident in every setting where young children spend their time and have the opportunity to create their own futures* (Schweinhart, 1988, p. 58).

Through self-examination and informed interactions with children, families, and communities, early childhood educators can be models and practitioners of the following key elements of social-emotional learning:

- *Positive self-identity* — Projecting that our gender, ethnicity, and other traits are to be valued

- *Feelings of competence* — Valuing the importance of the work we do

- *Emotional honesty and self-regulation* — Experiencing and expressing our feelings appropriately

- *Collaboration* — Emphasizing cooperation over competition

- *Honoring diversity* — Embracing our differences and recognizing our commonalities

- *Resolving conflicts* — Seeing disagreements as opportunities for learning and reaching accord

- *Community* — Joining with others to advocate for policies that support children and families

In the end, we all want the same things for ourselves, our loved ones, our communities, and our leaders: to be comfortable in our own skins and enjoy what we do; to accept others for who they are and value their feelings, thoughts, and actions; and to create relationships characterized by mutual respect and an abiding trust that together we will do what is right for the world. An early and sustained recognition of the importance of social-emotional development in our lives can help us achieve these individual and collective goals.

References

American Psychological Association. (2003). *Report of the Task Force on Psychology in Early Education and Care*. Washington, DC: Author.

American Sign Language Browser. (2000). Online at http://commtechlab.msu.edu/sites/aslweb/browser.htm.

Bandura, A. (1977). *Social learning theory*. Englewood Cliffs, NJ: Prentice-Hall.

Bandura, A. (1994). Self-efficacy. In V. S. Ramachaudran (Ed.), *Encyclopedia of human behavior* (Vol. 4, pp. 71–81), New York: Academic Press.

Bandura, A. (1997). *Self-efficacy: The exercise of control*. New York, Freeman.

Banks, J. (1993). Multicultural education for young children: Racial and ethnic attitudes and their modification. In B. Spodek (Ed.), *Handbook of research on the education of young children* (pp. 236–250). New York: Macmillan.

Barton, K., & Levstik, L. (1996). "Back when God was around and everything": Elementary children's understanding of historical time. *American Education Research Journal, 33,* 419–454.

Battistich, V., Solomon, D., & Watson, M. (1998, April). *Sense of community as a mediating factor in promoting children's social and ethical development*. Paper presented at the American Educational Research Association, San Diego, CA.

Baumeister, R. F., Bushman, B. J., & Campbell, W. K. (2000). Self-esteem, narcissism, and aggression: Does violence result from low self-esteem or from threatened egotism? *Current Directions in Psychological Science, 9,* 26–29.

Baumeister, R. F., Campbell, J. D., Krueger, J. L., & Vohs, K. D. (2004). Exploding the self-esteem myth. *Scientific American, 292*(1), 84–91.

Bekoff, M. (2007). *The emotional lives of animals: A leading scientist explores animal joy, sorrow, and empathy — and why they matter*. Novato, CA: New World Library.

Belsky, J. (2002). Quality counts: Amount of child care and children's social-emotional development. *Journal of Developmental and Behavioral Pediatrics, 23,* 167–170.

Bigler, R. S. (1995). The role of classification skill in moderating environmental influences on children's gender stereotyping: A study of the functional use of gender in the classroom. *Child Development, 66,* 1072–1087.

Bigler, R. S. (1997). Conceptual and methodological issues in the measurement of children's sex-typing. *Psychology of Women Quarterly, 21,* 53–69.

Boisvert, C. (2005, November/December). Exploring personal biases. *High/Scope Extensions, 20*(3), 6.

Brownell, C. A. (1990). Peer social skills in toddlers: Competences and constraints illustrated by same-age and mixed-age interaction. *Child Development, 61,* 838–848.

Buzzelli, C. A. (1996). The moral implications of teacher-child discourse in early childhood classrooms. *Early Childhood Research Quarterly, 11,* 515–534.

Center on the Social and Emotional Foundations for Early Learning (CSEFEL). (2003). *What works briefs*. Champaign, IL: University of Illinois at Urbana-Champaign. See also csefel.uiuc.edu/whatworks.html

Chafel, J. A. (1984). "Call the police, okay?" Social comparison by young children during play in preschool. *Early Child Development and Care, 14,* 201–216.

Clark, K. B., & Clark, M. P. (1947). Racial identification and preference in Negro children. In T. M. Newcomb & E. L. Hartley (Eds.), *Readings in social psychology* (pp. 169–178). New York: Holt, Rinehart, & Winston.

Clements, D. H. (1999). The effective use of computers with young children. In J. V. Copley (Ed.), *Mathematics in the early years* (pp. 119–128). Reston, VA: National Council of Teachers of Mathematics and National Association for the Education of Young Children.

Cole, D., & LaVoie, J. C. (1985). Fantasy play and related cognitive development in 2- to 6-year-olds. *Developmental Psychology, 21*(20), 233–240.

Cummings, C. (2000). *Winning strategies for classroom management.* Alexandria, VA: Association for Supervision and Curriculum Development.

Damon, W. (1990). *The moral child: Nurturing children's natural moral growth.* New York: The Free Press.

Daniels, M. (2000). *Dancing with words: Signing for hearing children's literacy.* Westport, CT: Bergin & Garvey.

DeBruin-Parecki, A., & Hohmann, M. (2003). *Letter links: Alphabet learning with children's names.* Ypsilanti, MI: HighScope Press.

Denham, S. A. (2006). The emotional basis of learning and development in early childhood education. In B. Spodek & O. N. Saracho (Eds.), *Handbook of research on the education of young children* (2nd ed.; pp. 85–104). Mahwah, NJ: Erlbaum.

Derman-Sparks, L. (1989). *Anti-bias curriculum: Tools for empowering young children.* Washington, DC: National Association for the Education of Young Children.

DeVries, R., & Zan, B. (1994). *Moral classrooms, moral children: Creating a constructivist atmosphere in early education.* New York: Teachers College Press.

DeVries, R., & Zan, B. (2003, September). When children make rules. *Educational Leadership, 61*(1), 64–67.

Dewey, J. (1916/1966). *Democracy and education.* New York: The Free Press.

Diamond, A. (2006). The early development of executive functions. In E. Bialystok & F. Craik (Eds.), *Lifespan cognition: Mechanisms of change* (pp. 70–95). New York: Oxford University Press.

Diamond, K. E., & Hestenes, L. L. (1996). Preschool children's conceptions of disabilities: The salience of disability in children's ideas about others. *Topics in Early Childhood Special Education, 16,* 458–475.

Diamond, K. E., Hestenes, L. L., Carpenter, E. S., & Innes, F. K. (1997). Relationships between enrollment in an inclusive class and preschool children's ideas about people with disabilities. *Topics in Early Childhood Special Education, 17*(4), 520–536.

Diamond, K. E., & Innes, F. K. (2001). The origins of young children's attitudes toward peers with disabilities. In M. J. Guralnik (Ed.), *Early childhood inclusion: Focus on change* (pp. 159–178). Baltimore, MD: Brooks.

Dittmar, H., & Van Duuren, M. (1993, Spring). Human nature beliefs and perceptions of the economic world. *Abhigyan 22,* 49–62.

Dixon, J. A., & Moore, C. F. (1990, October). The development of perspective taking. *Child Development, 61*(5), 1502–1513.

Douville, P., & Wood, K. D. (2001). Collaborative learning strategies in diverse classrooms. In V. J. Risko & K. Bromley (Eds.), *Collaboration for diverse learners: Viewpoints and practices* (pp. 123–151). Newark, DE: International Reading Association.

Dunlap, G., Conroy, M., Kern, L., DuPaul, G., VanBrakle, J., Strain, P., et al. (2003). *Research synthesis on effective intervention procedures: Executive summary.* Tampa, FL: University of South Florida, Center for Evidence-Based Practice: Young Children With Challenging Behavior.

Egertson, H. A. (2006, November). In praise of butterflies: Linking self-esteem and learning. *Young Children, 61*(6), 58–60.

Eisenberg, N. (1989). The development of prosocial values. In N. Eisenberg, J. Reykowski, & E. Staub (Eds.), *Social and moral values: Individual and social perspectives.* Hillsdale, NJ: Erlbaum.

Elias, M. J., Zins, J. E., Weissberg, K. S., Frey, M. T., Greenberg, N. M., Kessler, R., et al. (1997). *Promoting social and emotional learning: Guidelines for educators.* Alexandria, VA: Association for Supervision and Curriculum Development.

Emde, R. (1998). Early emotional development: New modes of thinking for research and intervention. *Pediatrics, 102*(5), 1236–1243.

Epstein, A. S. (1993). *Training for quality: Improving early childhood programs through systematic inservice training.* Ypsilanti, MI: HighScope Press.

Epstein, A. S. (2007). *Essentials of active learning in preschool: Getting to know the High/Scope Curriculum.* Ypsilanti, MI: HighScope Press.

Epstein, A. S. (2007). *The intentional teacher.* Washington, DC: National Association for the Education of Young Children.

Epstein, A. S., & Boisvert, C. (2005). *Let's do something together: A guidebook for effective intergenerational programs.* Ypsilanti, MI: HighScope Press.

Evans, B. (2008). *I know what's next: Preschool transitions without tears or turmoil.* Ypsilanti, MI: HighScope Press.

Evans, B. (2002). *You can't come to my birthday party! Conflict resolution with young children.* Ypsilanti, MI: HighScope Press.

Favazza, P., & Odom, S. L. (1997). Promoting positive attitudes of kindergarten-age children toward people with disabilities. *Exceptional Children, 63,* 405–418.

Fight Crime: Invest in Kids. (2000). *America's child care crisis: A crime prevention strategy.* Washington, DC: Author. *See also* www.fightcrime.org

Fox, L., & Lentini, R. H. (2006, November). "You got it!" Teaching social and emotional skills. *Young Children, 61*(6), 36–42.

Fromberg, D. P. (1999). A review of research on play. In C. Seefeldt (Ed.), *The early childhood curriculum: Current findings in theory and practice* (pp. 27–53). New York: Teachers College Press.

Fulghum, R. (1988). *All I really need to know I learned in kindergarten.* New York: Villard Books.

Furnham, A., & Stacey, B. (1991). *Young people's understanding of society.* New York: Routledge.

Gartrell, D. (2006, November). The beauty of class meetings. *Young Children, 61*(6), 54–55.

Geography Education Standards Project. (1994). *Geography for life: National education standards — 1994.* Washington, DC: Author.

Gilligan, C. (1982). *In a different voice: Psychological theory and women's development.* Cambridge, MA: Harvard University Press.

Ginsburg, K. R., Committee on Communications, & Committee on Psychosocial Aspects of Child and Family Health. (2007, January). The importance of play in promoting healthy child development and maintaining strong parent-child bonds (Clinical report). *American Academy of Pediatrics, 119*(1), 182–191.

Goleman, D. (1995). *Emotional intelligence.* New York: Random House.

Goleman, D. (2006). *Social intelligence: The new science of human relationships.* New York: Random House.

Goleman, D. (n.d.). Retrieved June 26, 2007, from www.danielgoleman.info

Gonzalez-Mena, J. (2008). *Diversity in early care and education: Honoring differences* (5th ed.). Washington, DC: National Association for the Education of Young Children.

Graves, M. (2000). *The essential parent workshop resource.* Ypsilanti, MI: HighScope Press.

Harrah, J., & Friedman, M. (1990). Economic socialization in children in a midwestern American community. *Journal of Economic Psychology, 11,* 495–513.

Hartup, W. (1991). *Having friends, making friends, and keeping friends: Relationships as educational contexts.* (ERIC Digest). Urbana, IL: ERIC Clearinghouse on Elementary and Early Childhood Education (ED 345-854).

Head Start Bureau (2005). *Head Start child outcomes framework: Domain 6: Social and emotional development.* Retrieved July 3, 2007, from http://www.headstartinfo.org/leaders_guideeng/domain6.htm

Hemmeter, M. L., & Ostrosky, M. (2003). Classroom preventive practices. In G. Dunlap, M. Conroy, L. Kern, G. DuPaul, J. VanBrakle, P. Strain, et al. (Eds.), *Research synthesis on effective intervention procedures* (Chapter 4). Tampa, FL: University of South Florida, Center for Evidence-Based Practice: Young Children with Challenging Behavior.

Henig, R. M. (2008, February 17). Taking play seriously. *The New York Times Magazine.* Retrieved February 17, 2008, from http://www.nytimes.com/2008/02/17/magazine/17play.html

HighScope Educational Research Foundation. (1998). *Supporting children in resolving conflicts* [VHS & DVD]. Ypsilanti, MI: HighScope Press.

HighScope Educational Research Foundation. (2001a). *All about High/Scope.* Ypsilanti, MI: HighScope Press.

HighScope Educational Research Foundation. (2001b). *You and your child.* Ypsilanti, MI: HighScope Press.

HighScope Educational Research Foundation. (2007). *Ready School Assessment* kit. Ypsilanti, MI: HighScope Press.

Hirschfeld, I. A., & Gelman, S. A. (1997). What young children think about the relationship between language variation and social difference. *Cognitive Development, 12*, 213–238.

Hoffman, M. L. (2000). *Empathy and moral development: Implications for caring and justice.* New York: Cambridge University Press.

Hohmann, M., Weikart, D. P., & Epstein, A. S. (2008). *Educating young children: Active learning practices for preschool and child care programs* (3rd ed.). Ypsilanti, MI: HighScope Press.

Howes, C. (1988). Peer interaction of young children. *Monographs of the Society for Research in Child Development* (Serial No. 217), *53*(1).

Hyson, M. (2004). *The emotional development of young children: Building an emotion-centered curriculum* (2nd ed.). Washington, DC: National Association for the Education of Young Children.

Jantz, R. K., & Seefeldt, C. (1999). Early childhood social studies. In C. Seefeldt (Ed.), *The early childhood curriculum: Current findings in theory and practice* (pp. 159–178). New York: Teachers College Press.

Joseph, G. E., & Strain, P. (2003). Comprehensive evidence-based social-emotional curricula for young children. In G. Dunlap, M. Conroy, L. Kern, G. DuPaul, J. VanBrakle, P. Strain, et al. (Eds.), *Research synthesis on effective intervention procedures* (Chapter 5). Tampa, FL: University of South Florida, Center for Evidence-Based Practice: Young Children With Challenging Behavior.

Kagan, S. L., Moore, E., & Bredekamp, S. (Eds.). (1995, June). *Reconsidering children's early development and learning: Toward common views and vocabulary.* (Goal 1 Technical Planning Group Report 95-03.) Washington, DC: National Education Goals Panel.

Katz, L., (1993). *Self-esteem and narcissism: Implications for practice.* Urbana, IL: ERIC Clearinghouse on Elementary and Early Childhood Education. (ED358973). Online: www.ericdigests.org/1993/esteem.htm

Katz, L., & McClellan, D. (1997). *Fostering children's social competence: The teacher's role.* Washington, DC: National Association for the Education of Young Children.

Kauffman Foundation. (2002, Summer). Set for success: Building a strong foundation for school readiness based on the social-emotional development of young children. *The Kauffman Early Education Exchange, 1*(1). Kansas City, MO: Author.

Kavanaugh, R. D. (2006). Pretend play. In B. Spodek & O. N. Saracho (Eds.), *Handbook of research on the education of young children* (2nd ed.; pp. 269–278). Mahwah, NJ: Erlbaum.

Kline, S. (1993). *Out of the garden: Toys and children's culture in the age of TV marketing.* London, UK: Verso.

Kohn, A. (1993/1999). *The trouble with gold stars, incentive plans, A's, praise, and other bribes.* Boston: Houghton Mifflin.

Kreidler, W. J., & Whittall, S. T. (1999). *Early childhood adventures in peacemaking.* Cambridge, MA: Educators for Social Responsibility.

Krogh, S. L. (1982, November). *Preschool democracy: Ideas from Montessori.* Paper presented at the Annual Meeting of the National Association for the Education of Young Children, Washington, DC. ERIC document ED224610.

Ladd, G. W., Herald, S. L., & Andrews, R. K. (2006). Young children's peer relations and social competence. In B. Spodek & O. N. Saracho (Eds.), *Handbook of research on the education of young children* (2nd ed.; pp. 23–54). Mahwah, NJ: Erlbaum.

Lamm, S., Groulx, J. G., Hansen, C., Patton, M. M., & Slaton, A. J. (2006, November). Creating environments for peaceful problem solving. *Young Children, 61*(6), 22–28.

Legerstee, M. (2005). *Infants' sense of people: Precursors to a theory of mind.* New York: Cambridge University Press.

Levin, D. E. (2003). *Teaching young children in violent times: Building a peaceable classroom* (2nd ed.). Washington, DC: Educators for Social Responsibility and National Association for the Education of Young Children.

Liben, L. S., & Bigler, R. S. (2002). The developmental course of gender differentiation: Conceptualizing, measuring, and evaluating constructs and pathways. *Monographs of the Society for Research in Child Development, 67*(2, Serial No. 269).

Liben, L. S., & Downs, R. M. (1993). Understanding person-space-map relations: Cartographic and developmental perspectives. *Developmental Psychology, 29*(4), 739–752.

Liben, L. S., & Yekel, C. A. (1996). Preschoolers' understanding of plan and oblique maps: The role of geometric and representational correspondence. *Child Development, 67,* 780–796.

Lockhart, S. (2006, January/February). Teacher-child relationships: Do adults' behaviors really matter? *High/Scope Extensions, 20*(4), 1–4 & 8.

Lucier, R., & Gainsley, S. (2005). Amazing days: Celebrating with children and families. In N. A. Brickman, H. Barton, & J. Burd (Eds.), *Supporting young learners 4: Ideas for child care providers and teachers* (pp. 433–441). Ypsilanti, MI: HighScope Press.

MacNaughton, G. (2000). *Rethinking gender in early childhood education.* Thousand Oaks, CA: Sage Publications.

Marcon, R. (2002, Spring). Moving up the grades: Relationship between preschool model and later school success. *Early Childhood Research and Practice, 4*(2). Retrieved June 10, 2002, from http://ecrp.uiuc.edu/v4n1/marcon.html

Martin, S. (2007, October 29). In the bird cage: Finding out what funny is. *The New Yorker, 83*(33), 48–55.

Marvin, R. S., Greenberg, M. T., & Mossler, D. G. (1976). The early development of conceptual perspective taking: Distinguishing among multiple perspectives. *Child development, 47*(2), 511–514.

Meece, J. L. (1997). *Child and adolescent development for educators.* New York: McGraw-Hill.

Meltzoff, Nancy. (1994, Fall-Winter). Relationship, the fourth "R": The development of a classroom community. *School Community Journal, 4*(2), 13–26.

Mosenthal, P. B., & Kirsch, S. (1990). Understanding general reference maps. *Journal of Reading, 34*(1), 60–63.

National Association for the Education of Young Children. (n.d.). *Standard 2: NAEYC accreditation criteria for curriculum: 2.B: Area of development: Social-emotional development.* Retrieved July 3, 2007, from http://www.naeyc.org/academy/standards/standard2/standard2B.asp

National Center for Clinical Infant Programs. (1992). *Head start: The emotional foundations of school readiness.* Arlington, VA: Author.

National Council for Social Studies. (1994). *Expectations of excellence: Curriculum standards for the social studies.* Washington, DC: Author.

National Education Goals Panel. (1997). *Special early childhood report.* Washington, DC: Author.

National Institute for Early Education Research. (2007a, November-December). Rx for behavior problems in pre-k. *Preschool Matters, 5*(5), 4–5.

National Institute for Early Education Research. (2007b, November-December). Tools that address social development. *Preschool Matters, 5*(5), 2.

National Institute of Child Health and Human Development (NICHD). (2006, January). *The NICHD study of early care and youth development: Findings for children up to age 4½ years* (NIH Publication No. 05-4318). Washington, DC: U.S. Department of Health and Human Services, National Institutes of Health, National Institute of Child Health and Human Development.

National Research Council. (2000a). *Eager to learn: Educating our preschoolers.* Washington, DC: The National Academies Press.

National Research Council. (2000b). *Neurons to neighborhoods: The science of early childhood development.* Washington, DC: The National Academies Press.

Neill, P. (2005, November/December). The world at your door: Working with culturally diverse children. *High/Scope Extensions, 20*(3), 1–4 & 8.

Office for Studies in Moral Development and Education. (2007). *Studies in moral development and education: An overview.* Chicago, IL: University of Illinois at Chicago, College of Education: Author. Retrieved November 8, 2007, from http://tigger.uic.edu/~lnucci/MoralEd/index.html

Orellana, M. F. (1994). Appropriating the voice of the superheroes: Three preschoolers' bilingual language uses in play. *Early Childhood Research Quarterly, 9,* 171–193.

Panksepp, J. (1998). *Affective neuroscience: The foundations of human and animal emotions.* New York, NY: Oxford University Press.

Pellis, S. M., Hastings, E., Shimizu, T., Kamitakahara, H., Komorowska, J., Forgie, M. L., & Kolb, B. (2006, February). The effects of orbital frontal cortex damage on the modulation of defensive responses by rats in playful and nonplayful social contexts. *Behavioral Neuroscience, 120*(1), 72–84.

Perrett, B. (1996). Group times: What makes them work? In N. A. Brickman (Ed.), *Supporting young learners 2: Ideas for child care providers and teachers* (pp. 71–76). Ypsilanti, MI: HighScope Press.

Perry, B. D. (1994). Neurobiological sequelae of childhood trauma: PTSD in children. In M. M. Murburg (Ed.), *Catecholamine function in post-traumatic stress disorders: Emerging concepts* (pp. 253–276). Washington, DC: American Psychiatric Press.

Piaget, J. (1932/1965). *The moral judgment of the child.* New York: The Free Press.

Piaget, J. (1950). *The psychology of intelligence.* London: Routledge.

Pianta, R. C., Cox, M. J., & Snow, K. L. (2007). (Eds.), *School readiness and the transition to kindergarten in the era of accountability.* Baltimore, MD: Brookes.

Pinker, Stephen. (2008, January 13). The moral instinct. *The New York Times Magazine,* 32–37, 55–56, & 59.

Power, F. C., Higgins, A., & Kohlberg, L. (1989). *Lawrence Kohlberg's approach to moral education.* New York: Columbia University Press.

Power, F. C., & Makogon, T. A. (1995, July). The just community approach to care. *Journal for a Just and Caring Education, 2,* 9–24.

Quesenberry, A., & Doubet, S. (2006, November). A framework for professional development focused on social and emotional competencies. *Young Children, 61*(6), 30–32.

Quintana, S. M. (1998). Children's developmental understanding of ethnicity and race. *Applied and Preventive Psychology, 7,* 27–45.

Ramsey, P. G. (1991). The salience of race in young children's growing up in an all-White community. *Journal of Educational Psychology, 83,* 28–34.

Ramsey, P. G. (2006). Early childhood multicultural education. In B. Spodek & O. N. Saracho (Eds.), *Handbook of research on the education of young children* (2nd ed.; pp. 279–302). Mahwah, NJ: Erlbaum.

Randolph, J., & Gee, P. Center for Education, Rice University School Literacy and Culture Project. (n.d.). *Building community in the classroom.* Retrieved November 8, 2007, from http://centerforeducation.rice.edu/SLC/Randolph011406.pdf

Raver, C. C., Garner, P. W., & Smith-Donald, R. (2007). The roles of emotion regulation and emotion knowledge for children's academic readiness. In R. C. Pianta, M. J. Cox, & K. L. Snow (Eds.), *School readiness and the transition to kindergarten in the era of accountability* (pp. 121–147). Baltimore, MD: Brookes.

Raver, C. C., Izard, C., & Kopp, C. B. (2002). Emotions matter: Making the case for the role of young children's emotional development for early school readiness. *Society for Research in Child Development Social Policy Report, 16*(3), 1–19.

Reynolds, A. J., Temple, J. A., Robertson, D. L., & Mann, E. A. (2001). Long-term effects of an early childhood intervention on educational achievement and juvenile arrest: A 15-year follow-up of low-income children in public schools. *Journal of the American Medical Association, 285*(18), 2339–2346.

Riley, D., San Juan, R. R., Klinkner, J., & Ramminger, A. (2008). *Social and emotional development: Connecting science and practice in early childhood settings.* St. Paul, MN: Redleaf Press; and Washington, DC: National Association for the Education of Young Children.

Rodgers, R., & Hammerstein, O. (1949). *You've got to be carefully taught.* New York: Williamson Music Co.

Rosten, L. (1968). *The joys of Yiddish.* New York: Pocket Books.

Schweinhart, L. J. (1988). *A school administrator's guide to early childhood programs.* Ypsilanti, MI: HighScope Press.

Schweinhart, L. J., Montie, J., Xiang, Z., Barnett, W. S., Belfield, C. R., & Nores, M. (2005). *Lifetime effects: The High/Scope Perry Preschool study through age 40.* Ypsilanti, MI: HighScope Press.

Schunk, D. H., & Hanson, A. R. (1985). Peer models: Influence on children's self-efficacy and achievement. *Journal of Educational Psychology, 77,* 313–322.

Schunk, D. H., & Pajares, F. (2001). The development of academic self-efficacy. In A. Wigfield & J. Eccles (Eds.), *Development of achievement motivation* (pp. 16–32). San Diego: Academic Press.

Sendak, M. (1963). *Where the wild things are.* New York: Harper & Row.

Shareef, I., & Gonzalez–Mena, J. (2008). *Practice in building bridges.* Washington, DC: National Association for the Education of Young Children.

Shore, R. (2002). *What kids need: Today's best ideas for nurturing, teaching, and protecting young children.* Boston: Beacon.

Singer, D., & Singer, J. (1990). *The house of make-believe: Children's play and the developing imagination.* Cambridge, MA: Harvard University Press.

Smetana, J. G. (2006). Social domain theory: Consistencies and variations in children's moral and social judgments. In M. Killen & J. G. Smetana (Eds.), *Handbook of Moral Development* (pp. 119–154). Mahwah, NJ: Erlbaum.

Snow, K. (2007). Integrative views of the domains of child function. In R. C. Pianta, M. J. Cox, & K. L. Snow (Eds.), *School readiness and the transition to kindergarten in the era of accountability* (pp. 197–216). Baltimore, MD: Brookes.

Soto, L. D. (1999). The multicultural worlds of childhood in postmodern America. In C. Seefeldt (Ed.), *The early childhood curriculum: Current findings in theory and practice* (pp. 218–242). New York: Teachers College Press.

Sowden, S. (1996). Mapping abilities of four-year-old children in York, England. *Journal of Geography, 95.* 107–111.

Spiegel, A. (2008, March 17). Old-fashioned play builds serious skills. *Morning Edition,* National Public Radio. Retrieved March 17, 2008, from http://www.npr.org/templates/story/story.php?storyId=19212514

Stipek, D., & Tannatt, L. (1984). Children's judgments of their own and their peers' academic competence. *Journal of Educational Psychology, 6*, 75–84.

Takanishi, R., & Traylor, F. (2007). Foreword. In R. C. Pianta, M. J. Cox, & K. L. Snow. (Eds.), *School readiness and the transition to kindergarten in the era of accountability* (pp. xvii–xviii). Baltimore, MD: Brookes.

Thomas, A., & Chess, S. (1977). *Temperament and development.* New York: Brunner/Mazel.

Turiel, E. (1983). *The development of social knowledge: Morality and convention.* New York: Cambridge University Press.

Turiel, E. (2002). *The culture of morality: Social development, content, and conflict.* New York: Cambridge University Press.

Vance, E., & Weaver, P. J. (2002). *Class meetings: Young children solving problems together.* Washington, DC: National Association for the Education of Young Children.

Viadero, D. (2007, December 19). Social-skills program found to yield gains in academic subjects. *Education Week, 27*(16), 1 & 15.

Vygotsky, L. (1934–1978). *Mind and society: The development of psychological processes.* Cambridge, MA: Harvard University Press.

Warneken, F., & Tomasello, M. (2006). Altruistic helping in human infants and young chimpanzees. *Science, 311,* 1301–1303.

Weikart, D. P., Olmsted, P. P., & Montie, J. (2003). *A world of preschool experience: Observations in 15 countries.* Ypsilanti, MI: HighScope Press.

Weissberg, R. P., & O'Brien, M. U. (2004). What works in school-based social and emotional learning programs for positive youth development. *Annals of the American Academy for Political and Social Science, 591*(1), 86–97.

Wiltz, N. W., & Klein, E. K. (2001). "What do you do in child care?" Children's perceptions of high- and low-quality classrooms. *Early Childhood Research Quarterly, 16,* 209–236.

Yoskikawa, H. (1995). Long-term effects of early childhood programs on social outcomes and delinquency. *The Future of Children, 5*(3), 51–75.

Zahn-Waxler, C., Radke-Yarrow, M., Wagner, E., & Chapman, M. (1992). Development of concern for others. *Developmental Psychology, 28*(1), 126–136.

Zeiger, J. (2007, February 25). *Developing a community of learners.* Suite101.com. Retrieved November 8, 2007, from http://classroom-management-tips .suite101.com/article.cfm/ developing_a _community_of_learners

Index

A

Academic success, 8, 10–11, 47–48

Accountability for social-emotional learning, 6–7, 9

Acknowledging
   in community building, 74
   competence skills, 51, 52–53
   in conflict resolution, 116–17, 119
   cooperative play, 87
   diversity, 94–95
   emotions, 60–66, 105, 116–17, 157, 158
   moral behavior, 106–7
   in problem solving, 157

Active learning, 51, 136, 154–55

Adult-child interactions. *See also* Modeling
   attention, need for, 29–30
   and competence, sense of, 46–49
   in conflict resolution, 18, 63, 113–14, 116–19
   cultural variations in, 149
   documenting, 147
   effective, 17
   empathy in, 37–38
   evaluating, 145–52
   at home, 159
   individualizing, 37
   in problem solving, 157
   professional development and, 147–48
   role models, 145–52, 153
   rules for adults, 132

Advocates, community, 166

Agency and community, 165–68

Aggression, 83, 86, 111

All About High/Scope, 153

All I Really Need to Know I Learned in Kindergarten, 6

Amazing Days: Celebrating With Children and Families, 96–97

American Academy of Pediatrics, 7

American Psychological Association, 8

Anger management. *See* Conflict resolution

Anti-Bias Curriculum, 91

APA Task Force on Psychology in Early Education and Care, 8

Apologies, 103

Art, 42–43, 65–66, 99, 124

Asian culture, 150

"Aspects of Humanity," 150–51

Assessing and assessments, 9, 19, 166

At-risk children, 8, 10, 59

Attentive responsiveness, 69

Attitudes, social, 92. *See also* Diversity

Attitudes, teacher, 145–46

Attributes, defined, 91

Authority, cultural variations in, 149

Autonomous morality, 127

Autonomy, 70, 149

B

Bandura, Albert, 45

Banks, James, 92

Barnett, W. Steven, 6–7

Behavior management. *See* Conflict resolution

Behavior problems. *See also* Conflict resolution
   parents and, 158
   prevention, 10, 74–75
   and reading skills, 11
   and rules, 128

Bekoff, Marc, 15

Belonging, 70

Berk, Laura, 7

Bias, 91, 92, 150–52. *See also* Diversity

Bodrova, Elena, 7

Boisvert, Chris, 150

Brain functioning, 10–11

Brown, Stuart, 7

Burnout, 165

Buzzelli, Cary, 109

C

Caretaking behavior, 40

"Caring community," 70

About the Author

Dr. Ann S. Epstein is the Senior Director of Curriculum Development at the HighScope Educational Research Foundation in Ypsilanti, Michigan, where she has worked since 1975. She collaborates with a team of early childhood specialists to develop curriculum and staff training materials; develops program and child assessment tools; and evaluates federal, state, and local educational programs. Dr. Epstein has published numerous books and articles for professional and practitioner audiences, including *The Intentional Teacher* and *Essentials of Active Learning in Preschool* and is coauthor of *Educating Young Children*, *Supporting Young Artists*, and *Small-Group Times to Scaffold Early Learning*. Dr. Epstein is also the principle developer of the Numbers Plus Preschool Mathematics Curriculum. She has a PhD in developmental psychology from the University of Michigan and also holds an MFA degree from Eastern Michigan University.